The Big Book of
Texas
Ghost Stories

Alan Brown

STACKPOLE
BOOKS

Copyright ©2012 by Stackpole Books

Published by
STACKPOLE BOOKS
5067 Ritter Road
Mechanicsburg, PA 17055
www.stackpolebooks.com

Printed in the United States of America

10 9 8 7 6 5 4 3 2 1

FIRST EDITION

Library of Congress Cataloging-in-Publication Data

Brown, Alan, 1950 Jan. 12-
  The big book of Texas ghost stories / Alan Brown. — 1st ed.
      p. cm.
  Includes bibliographical references (p.   ).
  ISBN 978-0-8117-0859-3 (hardcover)
  1. Ghosts—Texas. 2. Haunted places—Texas. I. Title.
  BF1472.U6B738 2013
  133.109764—dc23
                              2012014386

Contents

Austin

Central Texas

Dallas

Fort Worth

Galveston and Houston

North Texas

Northeast Texas

San Antonio

South Texas

Introduction

*W*hy is there a need for *The Big Book of Texas Ghost Stories*? The most obvious reason is the immense size of the state of Texas, which covers 268,820 square miles. The largest state in the contiguous United States, Texas is 10 percent larger than France. Size alone, however, does not account for the vast number of tales of ghosts found in the Lone Star State. As a rule, it seems that the oldest inhabited areas in the world are also the most haunted. Long before Spanish explorers visited Texas in the sixteenth century, Indians were living in the region between the Rio Grande and Red River. But the ghost lore of Texas reflects the influence of not only its earliest Native American inhabitants, but also the Europeans and African Americans who came later. The state's turbulent history may be most responsible for the plethora of Texas ghost tales. Outbreaks of violence between various groups of residents, from the Indians and the European setters to the events at the Alamo to more recent incidents between whites and African Americans, have produced an impressive body of yarns that still send shivers up the spine. The men and women who died on the plains, in railroad hotels, in Victorian mansions, and on college campuses will never be forgotten because they all played a role in Texas's statehood, and many are believed to haunt the Lone Star State to this day.

The immense state of Texas may seems like a country in itself, but it is also a microcosm of the entire United States. Like the New Englanders of the eighteenth century, Texans had to fight for their independence from a despotic country. The Texans of folklore are tough, resilient, and determined. The cowboy, with his restless spirit and fierce independence, has come to embody the very soul of Texans and, in the eyes of the rest of the world, to represent all Americans. In the larger-than-life figures that populate the supernatural yarns in this book, we may catch a reflection of ourselves.

Austin

Metz Elementary School

Originally built in East Austin in 1915, Metz Elementary School became so dilapidated over the years that the school district eventually declared it unsafe for students. During the old building's demolition in 1990, it seemed that at least one odd incident occurred every day. Bulldozers stopped working as soon as they rumbled near the old brick building. Tools disappeared. Workmen fell off ladders and complained that something had started shaking the ladders once they were halfway up. *Ghost Stories of Texas*, by Jo-Anne Christenson, includes an account by Joe Torres, the owner of the trucking and excavation company working at the site. Torres said that he and his workmen heard the sounds of childish laughter in bathroom stalls and fingernails scratching on blackboards in supposedly empty classrooms. Most of the men refused to enter the crumbling old building by themselves. Equipment mysteriously stopped working, and a truck carrying replacement parts broke down en route to the old school. The demolition process was so plagued with bizarre occurrences that Torres had trouble keeping his workers from quitting.

The workmen soon concluded that something otherworldly was impeding their progress. Torres responded to their concerns by bringing in a Catholic lay evangelist named Elias Limon to conduct an exorcism inside the school. The priest walked through the old building, sprinkling holy water and blessing the rooms of the building. But any hopes the workers might have had that things would settle down after the priest left were extinguished just a few days later when a wall collapsed, killing one of the construction company workers. By the time the old building was completely demolished, six months behind schedule, approximately half of Torres's workers had quit.

The new Metz Elementary School was completed in 1992. However, teachers and students still report seeing and hearing child ghosts at the new school. Joe Torres has his own postscript to the story of the haunted elementary school. After he transplanted a small tree from the property where the old school once stood to the front yard of his daughter's home, many people have since claimed they heard the voices of children coming from the tree.

Mount Bonnell

Located in Covert Park, Mount Bonnell has been one of Austin's favorite tourist spots since 1850. At 785 feet, it is the highest point within the city's limits. People still enjoy hiking and picnicking here, just as they have been doing for more than a century and a half. After climbing the stone steps, visitors can rest inside the pavilion and take in the panoramic views of the lakes, hills, and city. A plaque in the parking lot relates the history of Mount Bonnell, but one must turn to oral history to get the full story.

The site's romantic aura has spawned at least two legends about forlorn lovers. It is said that a young Spanish woman named Antoinette, who was engaged to be married, was taken captive by a Comanche chief. The chief fell in love with her, but Antoinette's fiancé sneaked into the Comanche camp along the Colorado River and made off with his beloved. The couple fled to the top of the mountain, but the Indians caught up with them and killed Antoinette's fiancé. As his body lay riddled with arrows on the mountaintop, Antoinette kissed his forehead and then leaped to her death. Her tragic story gave the mountain one of its nicknames, "Antoinette's Leap." In a variant of the tale, a woman named Golden Nell and her husband, Beau, both jumped to their death from the peak just before they were apprehended by a band of Indians.

Another legend has it that a young man had a secret love affair with an Indian girl. When her father, a Comanche chief, learned of his daughter's affair with a white man, he tracked the pair to their rendezvous point on top of the mountain. In a fit of rage, he murdered his daughter before she had a chance to plead for her life. Sensing that the end was near, her lover plunged to his death from a cliff. A variant of this tale seems to have been influenced by Shakespeare's *Romeo and Juliet*. In this version, a young brave and an Indian maiden from warring tribes were ordered by their parents to end their romance. Unable to face the prospect of life without each other, the couple climbed the mountain, walked over to a rock outcropping, held hands, and jumped.

Not surprisingly, as with other "lovers' leaps" across the country, the legends have led to claims of otherworldly sightings. For years, people who were atop Mount Bonnell at dusk have reported seeing misty shapes standing along the cliffs.

The Eanes–Marshall Ranch

What today is known as the Eanes-Marshall Ranch was originally built in 1857 by Alexander Eanes. He eventually sold it to his brother, Robert, who built the ranch house and a log cabin to house the local school. In 1883, Robert turned the ranch over to his son-in-law, Hudson Boatner Marshall, who dismantled the ranch house and relocated it next to nearby Barton Creek. Eventually the surrounding community was named after the Eanes family. Today the ranch's neighbors include housing developments, a shopping center, and a school. But even though the Eanes-Marshall Ranch is no longer situated in a wild, isolated region, it still retains elements of its ghostly past.

The best-known ghost story connected with the property concerns a teamster who was driving his wagon down a lonely road late one night not far from the ranch house in the late nineteenth century. He had gone to town and delivered a load of hay to a livery stable. He then loaded his wagon with dry goods he had just purchased from Berryman's Grocery and Provisions and started on his return trip. The wagon was within a few yards of the Eanes Ranch when the man noticed a large rock in the middle of the road. Sensing that something was wrong, he removed his shotgun from the back of the wagon and looked around. He heard nothing out of the ordinary, so he climbed down from the wagon and removed the rock. Just as he was about to climb back into his wagon, he heard the crack of a tree branch. He turned around and raised his shotgun, but the man was gunned down before he could pull the trigger. The gunfire panicked the horses, which raced down the road with the driverless wagon. Three bandits emerged from their hiding place and walked toward the lifeless body lying in the middle of the road. Angry because the wagon was gone, the bandits contented themselves with removing their victim's wallet and returned to town. Alerted by the shotgun blast, the Eanes family awoke from their slumber and walked down the road, where they found the driver's corpse. Mr. Eanes buried the man in an unmarked grave and returned home. Because the man's wallet had been stolen, no one was ever able to identify him. According to Jeanine Plumber in *Haunted Austin*, the murder was considered to be just a legend until 1991, when Westlake police searching for the remains of slaughtered deer left behind by poachers found what appeared to be a sunken grave. They began digging and were surprised to find the bones of a man killed around one hundred years before.

After the property was abandoned, teenagers from Austin would drive out to the Eanes-Marshall Ranch in the hope of catching sight of a phantom wagon. People have reported hearing the rumbling of the wagon and pounding of the horses' hooves. Descendants of the Marshall family returned to the ranch in the 1960s. They built a new house and restored the old ranch house. One night in the late 1960s, the Marshalls' teenage son and several of his friends decided to spend the night by the Eanes Road where the teamster had been murdered. They had just unrolled their sleeping bags when they heard the creaking of a wagon and the snorting of horses. The ghostly wagon seemed to be heading in their direction. Terrified, the boys ran back to the Marshalls' home.

Other ghosts have been sighted on the old Eanes Road as well. An old man walking down the road with a hound dog has made a number of appearances. He is usually seen wearing a worn cowboy hat and has been sighted both in the afternoon and at night. A few people say they have seen a woman's ghost walking down the road. It has been speculated that she is the wife of the murdered man.

In 1966, a group of five parapsychologists visited the Eanes-Marshall Ranch in an effort to uncover the identity of the murdered man. One member of the group was a psychic, who channeled the spirit of the murder victim during a séance. Using automatic writing, he penned the name "Burns." That same year, a newspaper reporter looking through microfilm newspaper articles in the local library found an article from 1871 chronicling the murder of a man named

Barnes. Whoever the man is, he apparently has become a restless spirit who likely will continue haunting the old road until his murderers are brought to justice.

Buffalo Billiards

Across the street from the Driskill Hotel at 201 E. Sixth Street is one of Austin's most colorful nightspots. Built in 1861 by the Ziller family and originally called the Missouri House, the building was Austin's first boardinghouse. It was also said to have housed a brothel, where many a cowboy "whooped it up" after spending weeks on the dusty trail herding cattle. In 1999, it became Buffalo Billiards and was named the nation's best new pool hall by *Billiards Digest.*

According to Austin Ghost Tours, Buffalo Billiards is haunted by a ghost the employees call Fred. Fred seems to favor the Lodge, the bar area's second floor. The mischievous spirit makes his presence known by wobbling a bar stool. People have stopped the stool from shaking, only to find that one of the other bar stools has started wobbling. Occasionally a glass of beer that belongs to no one—at least, to no visible patron—appears on the bar. One bartender was in the habit of pouring a glass of beer at the beginning of his shift and leaving it on the bar to make Fred happy. Like many playful ghosts, Fred seems to enjoy moving objects around. One manager who arrives early in the morning often finds pool cues lying on the bar and pool balls sitting on tables.

The full-bodied apparition of a female has also been sighted inside Buffalo Billiards. One night, a barmaid and her coworker were walking up the back stairway to the second floor. When they turned around, both of them clearly saw the image of a woman in a white dress standing against a window. She appeared to be glaring at them. The two were so frightened that they ran down the stairs. As they were walking to their cars, they noticed the same woman staring out the window, watching them leave.

Buffalo Billiards is advertised as one of the last places in Austin where the spirit of the "Wild West" is still alive and well. Customers may find that the spirits of some of the building's former occupants also are alive and well at Buffalo Billiards.

The Inn at Pearl Street

The Inn at Pearl Street is located in Austin's Judges Hill neighborhood, which includes a number of historic buildings. Many of those buildings were once the homes of judges and lawyers. Today the inn consists of four buildings, one of which is a Greek Revival home built in 1896. In 1914, it became the private home of Judge Charles A. Wilcox and his family. Charles Wilcox was held in such high esteem in Austin that after he died, official buildings closed in his honor.

By the early 1980s, the old house had fallen into disrepair. In 1993, Jill Bickford, a contractor, purchased the run-down historic home with the intention of transforming it into a bed-and-breakfast. Jill and her father restored the house to its turn-of-the-century appearance, and in 1995, she opened it up as a B&B. Period antiques and collectibles afford guests a window to a more genteel era in Austin's history. The occasional appearance of a female spirit also makes the past come alive.

The first claims that the Inn at Pearl Street might be haunted were made by a carpenter who helped Jill bring the old house back to life in 1993. While he was working in the hallway, he said, he glimpsed a woman carry a small child from one room to the next. A few days later, he walked into a room and saw a woman in a rocking chair holding a child in her lap.

Jill also had her own encounter with the ghost that haunts the inn. During the restoration process, she arrived at the house one day and was surprised to see a light in one of the upper windows. Not only was the house supposed to be empty, but the electricity was not turned on. Jill walked around the back of the house, but by the time she reached the backdoor, the light in the window was gone.

One of the employees at the inn was a seventeen-year-old high school student named Jessica, whose mother worked there as a maid According to Jessica, one day her mother was working in the sitting room by the breakfast bar area on the first floor when she heard music coming from one of the upstairs rooms. As she walked up the stairs, she heard someone moving around on the second floor. She thought that Jill was working up there, so she said, "Jill, do you need anything?" She had no sooner finished talking than the music stopped and she realized she was all alone.

In 2011, a couple of Jessica's male friends were staying in the French Room on the second floor. The next morning, they asked her how many guests were staying in the inn the night before. "You were the only ones here last night," Jessica told them. One of the young men said, "Seriously, how many people were here last night?" Jessica responded, "No one. You were all alone. What made you think there were other people here?" In the middle of the night, her friend said, they had heard what sounded like a lot of partying going on in the sitting room, with people talking and laughing. They could also hear people go up the stairs, get some ice from the container at the top, and walk back down.

Although the old Wilcox home has been brought into the twenty-first century with cable television and other modern amenities, the intermittent paranormal activity is a shocking reminder that in some old buildings, it seems that the past refuses to stay dead.

The Driskill Hotel

During the Civil War, Col. Jesse Driskill accrued a fortune selling cattle to the Confederate army. By the 1880s, the cattle baron began making plans to build his dream hotel and purchased a large plot of land at the corner of Sixth and Brazos Streets in downtown Austin. Construction of a sixty-room Romanesque luxury hotel was completed in 1886 at a cost of $400,000. Two weeks after its grand opening, the hotel hosted an inaugural ball for Gov. Sul Ross. However, the cost of spending a night was so high that few people could afford to stay there, and Driskill was forced to close the hotel after losing much of his staff to another hotel. Legend has it that Driskill eventually lost the hotel in a card game.

By 1895, the Driskill Hotel had had five different owners. Throughout the twentieth century, the old hotel became the hub of Austin's social scene. Election watch gatherings, inaugural balls, and an untold number of weddings were held here. President Lyndon Baines Johnson reportedly had his first date with his future bride, Lady Bird, in the Driskill's dining room in 1934. Decades later, in November 1960, he and John F. Kennedy awaited the election results at the hotel. Again in 1964, he was at the Driskill the night of the presidential election. The

Driskill had become run-down though. By the end of that decade it faced demolition, but a community effort raised enough money to save the hotel. It has remained open ever since. In the 1990s, a new owner restored the old hotel to its former grandeur.

Austin is a city with a lively nightlife, and according to local lore, even some of the long-departed guests and employees of the Driskill Hotel find it difficult to lie still all night long. The first reported paranormal activity at the Driskill was that of the playful spirit of a four-year-old girl. As the story goes, one day in 1887, a senator's little daughter was chasing a ball inside the hotel when she fell down the grand staircase. A week after her death, guests and hotel staff heard her giggling spirit bouncing a ball in the first-floor lobby, the second-floor ladies' restroom, and the staircase leading to the mezzanine. Cold spots have also been reported on the staircase. In the late 2000s, a woman walking through the mezzanine noticed that one of the six rocking chairs lining the wall was rocking on its own. No breeze was blowing through the hotel at the time.

One of the most active ghosts in the old hotel is thought to be the spirit of Jesse Driskill, the hotel's original owner, whose portrait still hangs in the grand lobby. People usually know when he is around when they detect the scent of cigar smoke in unoccupied rooms. His mischievous spirit has been blamed for turning lights off and on in the guest rooms. And some say that death has not snuffed out his passion for the ladies. In March 1991, the alternative rock band Concrete Blonde was staying at the hotel while acting as the backup group for Sting. The band's lead singer, Johnette Napolitano, said she was taking a shower when she saw a disembodied face staring at her. That night, she was awakened by all the lights in her room turning on and off. In desperation, she unplugged all the lamps, but a few minutes later the closet door opened and the light inside came on. Johnette sat up in bed and addressed the spirit directly: "I know you're here, but I know that you're not going to hurt me, so I'm going to sleep now." She went back to sleep and was not disturbed for the remainder of the night. A few months later, she wrote about her ghostly experience in a song titled "Ghost of a Texas Ladies' Man." Unbeknownst to Johnette, a female member of Sting's band who was also staying at the Driskill felt something tickle her toes while she was trying to sleep.

When she turned on the lights, she saw a shadowy figure dart under the bed.

Another singer who reported having a paranormal experience at the hotel was Annie Lennox of the Eurythmics. In the early 1980s, while staying at the Driskill, she laid two dresses on the bed in her room shortly before she was scheduled to perform and went to take a shower. When she emerged from the bathroom, she was shocked to find only one of the two dresses lying on the bed. The other had been neatly hung up in her closet. Chills crept up her spine when she realized that she was the only one with a key to the room.

Another apparently "overly dedicated" person who worked at the hotel was a desk clerk known only as Miss Bridges, employed here during the early 1900s. She did not die at the hotel, but her deep attachment to the Driskill seems to have brought her back. Her specter, wearing a Victorian-era dress, is usually sighted at night around where the front desk used to stand. She apparently is in the process of arranging the flowers on the spectral desk, as guests and staff have reported detecting the strong odor of flowers when she appeared.

My wife, Marilyn, and I had our own paranormal experience at the hotel not long ago. On August 10, 2011, we were present when the spirit of one of the early employees of the hotel may have made an appearance. We had just finished a ghost tour, on which a guide told us about the spirits believed to be haunting the Driskill Hotel. Several of those who had taken the tour with us were photographing the Driskill's ornate lobby. One lady, named Sunshine, and a friend of hers were looking at the pictures on Sunshine's camera when they noticed something highly unusual. Their excitement prompted the rest of us to gather around. In the background of a picture Sunshine had taken of her friend and the woman's young son, we could see the semi-transparent figure of a woman dressed in a dark brown, nineteenth-century maid's dress. No living person had been standing behind the woman and her son when the photograph was taken.

Several rooms are said to be ideal places to encounter ghosts in the hotel. One is Room 29, where a woman now known as the "Houston Bride" once stayed. As the story goes, in 1989, a socialite who had been jilted by her fiancé on her wedding day stole his car and credit cards and drove from Houston to Austin. She checked into Room 427 of the Driskill and went on a shopping spree in some of Austin's finest stores. She returned to her room laden with shopping bags, one of which contained a pistol she had just purchased. The last time anyone saw her alive, she was standing in front of the door, trying to hold her bags and open the door at the same time. When she finally got the door open, she set down the bags, removed the pistol, and loaded it. She then grabbed a pillow and lay down in the bathtub. She placed the pillow on her stomach, pressed the barrel of the pistol against the pillow, and shot herself. The pillow muffled the report of the gun, and her body was not discovered for three days. Ever since that fateful day, people have reported seeing her ghost walking the hallways, wearing a wedding gown and carrying a gun in her hand. Sometimes people have seen her apparition out of the corner of the eye, but when they turned their heads for a better look, no one was there. Staff have also heard weeping and the sound of a woman talking on the fourth floor.

In 1999, ten years after the suicide of the "Houston Bride," two women checked into the 1930s section of the hotel. At 1 A.M., they decided to take a stroll through one of the old sections of the hotel that was being renovated at the time. They were headed south on the fourth floor when they saw a woman holding several shopping bags struggling with her room key. One of them asked her if she minded all the construction noise. The woman gave the pair a cold, piercing stare and replied, "No." The next morning, they told the manager about their strange encounter. He said that no one was staying there and escorted them up the stairs to the room where they had seen the woman. When he unlocked the door, the women saw that the room had no toilet and no bed. They left convinced that they had had a brush with the "other side" the night before.

People have also had bizarre experiences in the Maximilian Room, which was named after the emperor of Mexico, even though he never stayed at the hotel. The room's name is derived from the eight ornate mirrors hanging from the walls: Maximilian ordered the mirrors from Austria as gifts for his wife, Carlotta. After her death in 1927, the mirrors ended up in a warehouse in New Orleans, where they were discovered in the 1930s. The Driskill bought the mirrors and hung them in the former men's smoking room, which was converted into a dining room and named for the late emperor. Guests have reported looking into the mirrors and seeing the figure of a woman standing where their reflection should have appeared. In addition, some people have felt a hand touching their shoulder.

Room 419 is said to be haunted by the spirit of Peter J. Lawless, who lived in the Driskill Hotel from 1886 to 1916. Lawless made his living selling tickets for the railroad and stayed at the Driskill even during periods when it was closed. Housecleaning staff have vacuumed the floor of this room, only to find fresh footprints on the carpeting just before they leave the room. Guests who have checked into the room have found dresser drawers open and bedcovers ruffled. The ghost of Peter Lawless has been sighted standing near the elevators on the fifth floor. Witnesses claim that when the elevator doors open, he checks his pocket watch before vanishing completely.

The area of the Driskill Hotel with the most paranormal activity is believed to be Room 525, which is said to be haunted by the ghosts of the "suicide brides." One of these brides was scheduled to be married at the Driskill Hotel, but her fiancé called off the wedding the night before. The despondent young woman hanged herself in the bathroom in Room 525. Her specter is often sighted by guests at weddings or bachelorette parties. As a rule, her appearance is considered to be a good omen. Twenty years after the first suicide, another bride killed herself in the bathroom of this same room. Soon after her death, the hotel staff blocked off the bathroom area, and eventually the entire room was closed off. When the Driskill was renovated in 1998, Room 525 was reopened.

Today the Driskill Hotel is the pride of Austin. Its level of luxury and service ensures that every guest's stay is a memorable one. Occasionally, the ghosts that float along the hallways and nestle in its guest rooms and suites also do their part to make a guest's stay there unforgettable.

The Omni Austin Hotel

The Omni Austin Hotel is known for its amenities and its luxurious furnishings. Guests whose interests lie within the realm of the paranormal will find the hotel's signature ghost story to be another plus.

The hotel is said to be haunted by the ghost of a guest known only as "Jack," who jumped off the balcony and landed on the concrete pavement below. Guests and employees of the hotel have reported seeing the apparition of the despondent man on the anniversary of his death, usually in the room where he spent the last night of his life. People have heard strange noises and the sound of someone walking around in the room when no one is staying there.

The Omni Austin Hotel prides itself on its close proximity to some of the city's most popular tourist attractions. It is within walking distance from the Governor's Mansion, the Austin Public Library, the Paramount Theatre, the Sixth Street entertainment district, and the Texas State Capitol. Some guests and staff believe that staying at the hotel brings one closer to the "other side" as well.

The Texas Governor's Mansion

The Texas Governor's Mansion is the oldest governors' home in continuous use west of the Mississippi. It is also thought to be one of the most haunted. Although Texas acquired statehood in 1845, the governor did not have an official residence until 1856, when a beautiful Greek Revival structure was built. The first occupants were the fifth governor of Texas, Elisha Marshall Pease, and his family. Over the years, the mansion was remodeled several times by the resident governors and their wives, including George W. Bush.

Several spirits are believed to haunt the Governor's Mansion, including that of Sam Houston, whose ghost has been seen in the bedroom he occupied while he was governor. The mahogany four-poster bed that Houston slept in while governor is still in the room. Not long after his death, visitors claimed to have seen the former governor's ghost in the bedroom. As a rule, he vanished when they attempted to talk to him. Houston's shadow has been seen hovering around a specific corner of the room. In the mid-1980s, Glenda Gale White, the wife of Gov. Mark White, said she saw Sam Houston's apparition in his bedroom. She said that one night, she turned off the light above Houston's portrait and went to bed. When she awoke the next morning, she was shocked to discover that the door to the bedroom was open and the light above the portrait had been turned off.

The best-known ghost story associated with the Governor's Mansion dates back to the administration of Gov. Pendleton Murrah, the last Confederate governor of Texas. The story goes that in 1864, the governor's nineteen-year-old nephew began courting Mrs. Murrah's niece at the mansion. One evening, the young lady informed her suitor that she did not want to see him anymore. The heartbroken young man returned to the north guest bedroom where he was staying and shot himself in the head. Not long thereafter, the room acquired a haunted reputation. Servants refused to clean the blood spatter from the walls, saying that when they were in the room, they could hear someone crying and moaning. Guests refused to spend the entire night in the room because they were awakened by the sound of someone banging on the wall. They also said that certain parts of the room became unbearably cold. The complaints of supernatural activity within the room escalated to the point that the next governor, Andrew Hamilton, closed it off. After the room was unsealed in the twentieth century, the noises were heard once again, especially on Sundays, the day when the jilted suitor supposedly killed himself.

Two other spirits are said to haunt the Governor's Mansion. One is the ghost of an unmarried maid who was fired after she became pregnant. Her specter has been seen standing outside the house, apparently waiting for someone to invite her back in. The other is the ghost of Governor Murrah, whose spirit has been sighted both inside the house and on the grounds.

Many of those who have resided or stayed in the Texas Governor's Mansion are as legendary as the building itself. This is the place where Gov. James Hogg's children slid down the banister, President William McKinley and Will Rogers paid a visit, and Gov. John Connally recovered from the gunshots inflicted by Lee Harvey Oswald. However, the most enduring legends seem to be the mansion's ghost stories, which have been passed down for more than a century and a half.

The Paramount Theatre

The Majestic Theatre, which later came to be known as the Paramount Theatre, opened its doors to the general public in 1915. The theater was originally designed by John Eberson of Chicago as a venue for vaudeville performers, like Harry Houdini. In 1930, the theater was extensively remodeled, with carpeting, an upgraded sound system, and upholstered seats. The newly remodeled Art Deco building was renamed the Paramount. Besides showing movies, the Paramount also hosted performances by local dance schools and theater groups. During the early 1940s, it supported the war effort by running recruiting and training films and selling war bonds.

The theater's gradual decline began in the 1950s and 1960s, when the advent of television reduced the size of the movie audience. By the 1970s, the dilapidated theater was operating as a B-movie house. The Paramount was spared the sad fate of so many other old movie palaces, however, when new management took over and began hosting live performances and showing classic movies. It was renamed the Paramount Theatre for the Performing Arts, and the building was added to the National Register of Historic Places. In the 1980s and 1990s, the Paramount was once again one of the city's premier theaters, hosting live performances such as *A Chorus Line* and *Evita*, as well as Hollywood movie premieres. In 2000, it merged with the State Theatre to form the Austin Theatre Alliance, which today offers audiences a wide variety of drama, comedy, and music performances—as well as unscheduled appearances of its ghost.

Longtime employees of the Paramount claim the theater is haunted by the ghost of a projectionist named Walter Norris, who they say died during a showing of the movie *Casablanca* in 2000. Employees occasionally leave candy bars or chocolate donuts for Walter to ensure that the equipment does not malfunction. Actress Shirley MacLaine, whose affinity for the paranormal is well documented, visited the Paramount and informed executive director Ken Stein that the theater was haunted but that he probably would not have an encounter because he was not "ready." A custodian named Johnson claims to have heard disembodied voices in the projectionist's bathroom. One night, Johnson heard ghostly footsteps behind him as he was sitting in the auditorium. Two weeks later, he was sitting in the same place in the auditorium when he heard someone rise up out of a seat directly behind him. Another time, he saw the stage lights begin flashing when they were not plugged in.

In many cases, people who work in historically haunted buildings become accustomed to strange noises and unexplained occurrences. This is certainly not the case with the theater's employees. Stein refuses to enter the projectionist's booth, and Johnson only works at night. It would be an understatement to say that Norris does not get along with his fellow employees.

The Austin Pizza Garden

Customers and employees alike have had strange supernatural encounters in the Austin Pizza Garden. The building was originally the Old Rock Store, constructed in 1898 and operated by James Andrew Patton, who had a colorful career as a Texas Ranger, civic leader, merchant, and postmaster. At one point in its history, the Woodmen of the World lodge hall was housed on the second floor of the building. In 1970, the building was named a Texas Historic Landmark. The Austin Pizza Garden opened up inside the historic building in 1994, and before long, its staff and customers alike discovered that the secret dough recipe is not the only thing responsible for its mysterious aura.

Much of the paranormal activity that has been occurring with some regularity since 1993 seems to be the work of a poltergeist. In the early 2000s, an employee working alone in the kitchen was shocked to see a pizza cutter spinning by itself on the table. Jayne Ganza, the weekend manager, said that several times she has heard footsteps on the second floor. Other employees have heard someone calling their names in a low whisper. They can usually tell when they are in the presence of something otherworldly by the chill bumps and tingling sensations that creep over their bodies. Most of the cold spots have shown up in the kitchen. One employee was really shaken up when she reentered a room where she had just placed a tub of knives and forks and discovered that the silverware had been scattered all over the room. That same morning, the opening manager unlocked the door, just as she always did when the restaurant opened. A few minutes later, the hostess banged on the door, yelling that it was locked. After the manager unlocked the door, the first customer of the day also complained that the door was locked. A few minutes later, the door locked itself a third time. Jayne believes she has caught a glimpse of the mischievous spirit that has been causing mayhem inside the Austin Pizza Garden. One night, she saw the image of a white figure reflected off a laminated menu hanging on the wall.

Customers have had otherworldly experiences as well. One night, a woman and her granddaughter were having dinner together. During their meal, the grandmother went to the restroom. Later, she told one of the staff members that she had a conversation with a lady in the restroom who disappeared after a few seconds. She returned to the table but did not tell her granddaughter what had happened. A few minutes later, the granddaughter went to the restroom and spoke to the same apparition.

On September 27, 2008, eight members of Texas Spirit Seekers conducted a formal investigation of the Austin Pizza Garden. The investigation had just begun when three members of the team were afflicted with bouts of nausea. Brandon Stephens was setting up a tripod in the same spot where the investigators had become ill when an invisible force scratched his back. Two hours later, a member was monitoring the equipment upstairs when he caught sight of a shadowy figure. At 1 A.M., one of the female members of the group was sitting at the bar, gazing down the corridor, when she saw the specter of a man wearing a blue shirt and blue jeans walking toward the soda machine. She was all alone at the time. Later that night, she went to the bar to get a glass of soda when she heard a loud noise behind her, as if someone were stomping his foot on the floor. The restaurant had high EMF (electromagnetic field) levels that interfered with the team's EMF detectors, so most of the evidence collected that night took the form of personal experiences.

Not everyone who works at the Austin Pizza Garden feels the same way about working in a haunted restaurant. Some of the employees think it's cool to share the building with a ghost, while others prefer not to talk about the ghostly activity in the building. Line cook Matthew Millner became a believer in the paranormal after spending a short time in the restaurant. "I'm not uncomfortable here," Millner says. "I think there's something strange afoot at the Austin Pizza Garden, but unless something ridiculous happens, I plan to continue working here."

The Clay Pit

The Clay Pit is an Indian restaurant that is said to be haunted by at least one of the building's former residents. Constructed in 1853, the building originally served as a trading post, where white settlers from Austin and American Indian tribes that were camped where the University of Texas now stands traded goods. After O. R. Bertram purchased the building in 1872, he converted the former trading post into a family residence. Bertram lived with his wife and children in the former trading post for eight years, before he opened a general store and saloon on the first floor. After this, the family lived on the second floor. Other families continued running a general store in the old building for the next thirty-four years. In the 1880s, the State Treasury was housed in the double-arched wine cellar. Legend has it that local businessmen paid for the privilege of using a tunnel leading from the grocery store to a brothel in order to escape detection. The building stood vacant between 1920 and 1939. Since the 1940s, a series of restaurants have been operating out of the historic building, including the Old Madrid Café, the Old Seville, the Old Toro, and the Red Tomato. In 1996, the Clay Pit opened its doors in the former trading post and remains there to this day.

Staff and customers of the various restaurants housed in the old trading post have been reporting unearthly occurrences for decades. Some employees have heard the sounds of a raucous party from the second-floor banquet room on nights when nobody—living, that is—was up there. Not long thereafter, a cook fell asleep in the banquet room, only to be startled awake when he felt someone strangling him. He was all alone at the time. Some people have also seen the full-body apparition of a little boy. Local historians believe that he could be the spirit of Bertram's five-year-old son, who contracted typhoid fever in the 1880s. The child was quarantined to his upstairs bedroom until he passed away after a few days.

The building in which the Clay Pit is housed is a classic example of Texas limestone architecture. Lovers of Indian cuisine flock to the old restaurant, where they can treat their western palates to an exotic meal. The Clay Pit's clientele also includes fans of the paranormal, who go there in the hope of seeing the tragic spirit of the little boy who apparently is reluctant—or unable—to leave the family home.

The Tavern

The Tavern is a sports bar located in yet another former store that's thought to be haunted. Some say that its popularity owes as much to its ghosts as it does to the dozens of TVs it provides for its patrons to watch sporting events. In 1916, the Enfield Grocery Store was constructed at 922 West Twelfth Street, designed after a German public house. The store was housed in the building until 1929, when it was moved next door so that a steak house could open in the original building. It seems that one could purchase more than just steak at the restaurant—a speakeasy and brothel were rumored to have operated on the upper floors. In 1933, following the repeal of Prohibition, the former grocery store was changed into a bar known simply as the Tavern. It was on the verge of being razed in 2002 because it did not conform to city code, but three Austin businessmen took it over and transformed the old watering hole into a trendy sports bar.

According to bartender Reuben Guerra, the Tavern is haunted by the spirit of a prostitute named Emily, who was murdered when a brawl broke out in the bordello in the 1940s. Some longtime employees believe that the apparition is the ghost of the daughter of a prostitute who worked there. The discovery of a little girl's shoe during the renovation of the Tavern lent credence to this story. A man who was working across the street claimed he saw a ghostly female staring out of an upstairs windows in the Tavern late at night. He was surprised to find that no one was inside the Tavern at the time of his sighting. Employees at the Tavern have had their own bizarre encounters inside the bar. In 2001, a worker had just turned off all the lights at closing time and was on his way out the door when he discovered that the neon sign had turned back on. Other employees have heard

phantom footsteps upstairs where the speakeasy and brothel operated. Sometimes the television channels change on their own or
glasses fly off the shelves. On one occasion, an unseen hand broke a
rack of pool balls.

The Tavern has established itself as a place where busy Austinites
can grab a bite for lunch, dinner, or a late-night snack. The ghostly
activity, it seems, comes at no extra charge.

The Speakeasy

The Speakeasy is a popular night spot that consists of three levels. On
the main level, guests sitting at candlelit tables can take in the music
of local bands. On the mezzanine, they can watch television or play
pool. The third level, called Terrace 59, offers customers a full-service
bar and contemporary music underneath beautiful palm trees. Additional entertainment is provided on all three levels by the ghosts that
haunt the old building.

The building that houses the Speakeasy dates back to 1889. Its first
owners, Mr. and Mrs. Kreisle, operated a furniture store and a funeral
parlor. At this time, many furniture stores also served as funeral
homes because of their ability to make coffins. Ten years later, the
Southwestern Telephone and Telegraph Company took over the
building. On July 26, 1916, a devastating fire raced through the building. Two women were trapped in the elevator, and several firemen
were making their way up the stairs to rescue them when the staircase
collapsed. Five firemen were severely burned; one, named James
Glass, died of his injuries a few days later.

The spirit of James Glass is thought to haunt the building to this
day. He is described by employees as a playful ghost. He seems to be
particularly fond of tormenting new employees when they enter a
small closet that the staff members call the "ghost closet." When a
newly hired employee begins working at the Speakeasy, the other
employees send him or her to the closet to change a lightbulb. After
spending several minutes attempting to complete what should be a
very simple task, the employee discovers that only a red lightbulb
will work in the closet. Some staff members believe that the ghost

prefers the red lightbulb because it reminds him of firemen or the firehouse.

The general manager, Chet Butler, says that the ghost of a woman frightens people in the elevator. In the early 2000s, a member of the band Dysfunction Junction was in the process of breaking down the equipment after closing time when he saw the spectral woman standing in the elevator. Some people have heard a woman's shriek from the back room. The ghost, who some believe is the spirit of Mrs. Kreisle, has also been sighted by a maid.

The apparition of a man, possibly also James Glass, has been seen in the bar area of the main level. One night, the bar manager had just turned off the lights when he saw a man staring at him in the darkness. After just a few seconds, the man vanished. The sound of heavy footsteps running up the stairs has also sent shivers up the spines of employees.

Like many haunted nightclubs, the Speakeasy does not hide its haunted past. After all, these days, ghosts are very good for business.

The Dream of Josiah Wilbarger

One of the state's most oft-repeated legends is that of Josiah Wilbarger, who was scalped alive by Indians but managed to survive and lived for eleven more years, despite the hideous wound he had received in the horrifying incident. Born in Kentucky in 1801, Josiah was recruited by one of Stephen Austin's agents in 1823 to help establish a colony on the upper Colorado River in Texas. A few years later, he married Margaret Baker and began teaching school. His desire for a more exciting life led him to become a scout whose job was to survey upriver for the planning of new colonies. In 1830, Josiah built a stockade along a bend in the Colorado River near present-day Bastrop and brought his wife and son, John, to the remote area. Two years later, Reuben and Sarah Hornsby built a double-log cabin on Hornsby's Bend.

In August 1833, Josiah traveled to Hornsby's Bend, where he joined a survey party assigned to scout for headrights to the northwest. After spending the night at Reuben and Sarah Hornsby's cabin, the men rode their horses on a path along Walnut Creek about six miles from present-day Austin. They were clearly taking a risk traveling so far beyond the settlement line. At 10 A.M., the men had just rounded a bend in the river when they spotted a lone Comanche Indian twenty-five yards away. The Indian, who was on foot, immediately took off. Josiah ordered the men to give chase. They pursued the Indian up Walnut Creek but lost him in the brush. While the exhausted men stopped for lunch in a shady grove near Pecan Springs, the group was suddenly attacked by a large band of Comanches. Two surveyors were killed and two others were wounded. Josiah, who had been hit by both a bullet and an arrow, attempted to drag a wounded comrade to safety behind a large rock. He had not gotten very far when a bullet entered the back of his neck and exited through his chin. Two members of Wilbarger's party jumped on their horses and rode off.

While the Comanches were busy scalping the two dead men, Josiah, who was temporarily paralyzed from his neck wound, lay perfectly still while the Indians stripped him and the other two men of their clothing. Before leaving, one of the braves walked over to Josiah's prostrate body and cut seven pieces of scalp from his head. The pain was so severe that Josiah mercifully passed out.

By the time Josiah regained consciousness, blowflies were already laying eggs on his exposed skull. He could even feel the maggots crawling around the top of his head. Summing up all of his remaining strength, he managed to drag his body three hundred yards to a spring, where he immersed his still-bleeding body into the water and cleaned his wounds. As the sun began sinking below the horizon, Josiah caught and ate a few snakes he found on the bank, took one last gulp of water, and began crawling toward a nearby cabin, which he knew lay six miles away. He had only gone half a mile when he ran out of energy. Josiah propped himself up against a large oak tree and passed out.

Around midnight, Josiah was awakened by the intense cold that had settled over the area. He turned his head and saw his sister, Margaret Clifton, standing only two feet away from him. In a calm, soothing voice, Margaret told him not to panic because help was on the way.

Meanwhile, Sarah Hornsby awoke from a disturbing dream. She woke up Reuben and one of the surveyors. The man had fled from the Indians and made it safely to the cabin, where he was sleeping in the next room. She told them that while she was asleep, she saw a man, soaked in blood, lying naked near a creek. The men assured her that all the men left behind at the creek were probably dead and she might as well go back to sleep. At 3 A.M., she had another dream about the bloody man. This time, she could tell that he was Josiah Wilbarger. Sarah woke up all the men in the house, including her seven sons, and told them that they had to go look for Josiah. Reuben told her that they probably would not be able to find him in the dark. He promised that they would search for Josiah in the morning, so she went back to sleep.

The next morning, while Sarah was making breakfast, a few more men arrived. When breakfast was over, the rescue party set out in search of the missing men. After a couple hours, the men heard someone call out to them in a trembling voice. They found Josiah Wilbarger—still alive—lying against a tree. Reuben and his friends buried the two dead men, then wrapped up Josiah in a sheet, placed him on a sled, and dragged him back to the Hornsby cabin.

Josiah lived for more than a decade after the attack, but his body never fully recovered. The skin never grew entirely over his head wound, so a portion of his skull was exposed. His wife made skullcaps for Josiah, which he removed only at night before going to bed. He wore fur caps over the skullcaps when he went outside in cold weather. Despite his wounds, Josiah tried to live a normal life. He began farming in 1836 and even built one of the first gristmills in Bastrop County. All the while, his head wound was getting worse. Eventually, the scalp area became infected, his skull was diseased, and his brain was exposed. One day, Josiah bumped his head on a low door frame in his cotton-gin house and ruptured the wound. Before he passed away on his deathbed a few days later, Josiah said, "This is as far as I can go." He died on April 11, 1845.

This incredible story has an even more amazing footnote: Six weeks after Josiah saw his sister Margaret standing near him while he was lying against the tree, he received a letter informing him that she was dead. She had passed away the day before his survey party was attacked at Pecan Springs.

The Confederate Woman's Home

The Confederate Woman's Home opened its doors in 1908 as a residence for the indigent widows and wives of honorably discharged Confederate soldiers. All the women admitted to the home had to be at least sixty years old and have no visible means of support. Initially only three women lived in the two-story, fifteen-bedroom home, but by the second year there were sixteen. The home was run by the United Daughters of the Confederacy with donations from the general public until 1911, when a constitutional amendment turned over its operation to the state. It was expanded in 1913 with a two-story, twenty-four bedroom addition and again three years later with a brick hospital to meet the increasing medical needs of the aging residents. It reached its peak in the 1920s and 1930s, with as many as 110 residents, but the number of admissions subsequently declined.

The Board of Texas State Hospitals and Special Schools took over the home in 1949, and in the late 1950s, the nine remaining women were relocated to the hospital wing. The home was finally closed in 1963 after the last three women were moved to local nursing homes. In 1975, the original building became a home for twenty-four blind and deaf children. The children were moved to the School for the Blind in 1982, and the facility stood abandoned for the next four years until it was purchased by the Austin Groups for the Elderly. Today the former Confederate Woman's Home houses twenty nonprofit services—and, some claim, the ghosts of former residents.

Staff of the Austin Groups for the Elderly have been telling stories of the ghostly tenants of the former Confederate Woman's Home for many years. Nurses have reported a strange-looking woman outside the break room. They have followed her down the hallway, but before they reached her, she disappeared. In *Haunted Austin*, Jeanine Plummer relates the experiences of a number of employees who have had ghostly encounters inside the old building. One woman said she was working in the ElderHaven Adult Center when she saw an elderly lady wearing a white suit and gloves walk out of a storage closet. Another staff member said that one night she was working late in her office on the second floor when she heard a group of women talking just outside her door. She became alarmed because she was certain she was the only person in the building at the time. When she opened the door, no one was there. Several employees have noticed that the photocopier has a tendency to turn itself off sometimes during the day.

A large number of the widows who resided in the Confederate Woman's Home now lie buried next to their husbands in the Texas State Cemetery. However, it is believed that the spirits of many of these women live on in the old Confederate Woman's Home. Their reluctance to leave, even after death, may be a testament to the high level of care they received there.

Moore's Crossing Bridge

The history of Moore's Crossing Bridge is outlined on a Texas historical marker placed at the south end of the bridge. The marker does not, however, tell the story of the ghosts that are said to haunt the bridge.

Today Moore's Crossing Bridge, which is located on Burleson Road, extends over Richard Moyer Park. However, when it was constructed in 1884, the 910-foot, six-span bridge originally crossed the Colorado River on Congress Avenue and was operated as a toll bridge. Because a wider bridge was needed for the increasing flow of traffic, the bridge was dismantled in 1910 and placed in storage. In 1915, three of its spans were moved to a low-water crossing on Onion Creek, but the three spans were washed away when more than eighteen inches of rain fell on Austin during the Great Thrall/Taylor Storm of 1921. The remaining three spans of the original bridge were then placed over Onion Creek, and this time the support piers were elevated to ten feet to make it "flood-proof." Now known as the Moore's Crossing Bridge, it has been open only to pedestrian traffic since the 1990s. Handrails and new decking were installed for the benefit of people walking across the bridge.

Some say that it is not just the living who are using the bridge, however. According to local storytellers, a white man was lynched from the crossbeams of the original bridge in the early 1900s for committing the then-unforgivable crime of having sexual relations with a black woman. For almost a century, witnesses have claimed to have seen the corpse of a man dangling from the middle of the bridge. Another specter has been seen by a number of people crossing the bridge, who say they saw the misty figure of a woman standing below, with her gaze directed upward toward the middle of the bridge. People wearing old-fashioned clothing also have been seen strolling along the old bridge. On one occasion in the 1980s, one of these apparitions waved to a man and woman as they were driving across. The ghost dissipated after the couple backed up their vehicle to get a better look.

So far, two groups of paranormal investigators, Central Texas Ghost Trackers and Ghost Hunters of Texas, have conducted formal investigations at the Moore's Crossing Bridge. Neither group collected any proof that the bridge is haunted. However, for those people who have seen the apparitions, no other proof is necessary.

The Neill-Cochran House

Not only is the Neill-Cochran House listed on the National Register of Historic Places, but it is also on ghost hunters' lists of the most haunted places in Austin. This stately Greek Revival mansion at 2310 San Gabriel Street was designed by architect Abner Cook as a suburban mansion for a young surveyor named Washington Hill. Unfortunately, Hill ran low on funds just as the mansion was completed in 1855. He tried to raise funds by selling three slaves, but he still did not have enough money to make his house payments. Consequently, he and his family were never able to live in their new home. In 1856, Hill leased the house to the state of Texas, which used it to temporarily house the Texas Asylum for the Blind until Cook, who was also a contractor, completed building a permanent campus for the school. The house was then leased to Lt. Gov. Fletcher Stockdale.

After the Civil War, the U.S. government converted the mansion into a hospital for federal troops. During this time, Gen. George Armstrong Custer visited the house while he was stationed in Austin. The hospital closed after two years. In 1876, a Confederate veteran named Col. Andrew Neill purchased the home. After his death in 1891, his wife, Jennie Chapman Neill, continued living in the house for two more years, then moved into town and rented the house to Judge

Thomas Beauford Cochran and his wife, Bessie. Two years later, the Cochrans bought the house, and it remained in the Cochran family for more than sixty years. In 1958, ownership of the house passed to the National Society of the Colonial Dames of America in the State of Texas, which today runs it as a historic house museum.

A number of the mansion's former occupants are said to haunt the Neill-Cochran House. One of these spirits is that of Col. Andrew Neill, who has been seen riding his horse around the mansion. His apparition has also been sighted having tea with Gen. Robert E. Lee on the front porch. The ghosts of soldiers who died of yellow fever in the house between 1865 and 1867, when it served as a hospital, might also be responsible for some of the recorded paranormal activity. For years, heavy footsteps have echoed through the house at night when only one person is present.

The Neill-Cochran House is said to be one of Austin's most important historic homes. Its furnishings, spanning from the late eighteenth through the early twentieth centuries, give visitors a taste of the lifestyles of the city's most prominent families in bygone days. And some say that its ghosts also give visitors a glimpse into the home's Civil War past.

Shoal Creek

Centuries ago, Shoal Creek, located about one mile west of Austin, was the lifeblood for local Indian tribes. Not only did they use the creek as a source of drinking water, but they also dug flint and limestone along its banks. They buried their dead in sites like a seven-foot-tall mound that was discovered near Old McCall Spring in the vicinity of the creek. The Indians' spiritual connection to the creek has been felt by other people as well, who have sensed the presence of ghosts in the area.

The earliest ghost stories centered around Shoal Creek are legends of treasure that is reputed to be buried along the creek. In *The Ghosts of Austin*, Fiona Broome says that in 1770, a gold mine at Diggers Hollow near Austin was hurriedly closed for fear of an Indian attack. The miners loaded seventy-five burros with gold ingots and buried the gold in a nearby cave. They then loaded eight more burros with gold and headed toward Mexico. Realizing that they were being followed, the miners buried this second load of gold in a hole along nearby Barton Springs. Minutes after they completed their task, the Indians who had been pursuing them attacked and killed every one of them except for a small boy. Not long thereafter, settlers living nearby discovered the corpses of the miners along Shoal Creek, not far from the Colorado River. One of the families adopted the little boy. For more than a century, people have reported seeing the ghosts of the dead miners walking around Barton Springs, apparently in search of the gold they buried there.

The second ghostly treasure tale was told to famed short-story writer William Sydney Porter, also known as O. Henry, who said that he heard the story from a shepherd. According to O. Henry, in 1836, one of Santa Anna's paymasters and one of his generals conspired to steal the Mexican Army's payroll and bury it in an isolated area that was rarely frequented by white men. However, the two officials did not realize that two soldiers were planning to kill the paymaster and steal the gold for themselves. One night, while standing guard, the soldiers slit the throat of the paymaster and caught his blood in a bottle. The soldiers planned to pour the paymaster's blood over the gold just before they buried it in order to conjure up a ghostly guardian for their ill-gotten gains. Walking up a creek that emptied into the Colorado, they dug a hole at the base of a live oak tree, placed the gold in the hole, and poured the blood over it. After the pair had covered up the loot, one of the soldiers killed his partner so that he could keep all the gold for himself. A few days later, Santa Anna's army was soundly defeated at the battle of San Jacinto. Fearing for his life, the soldier never returned the place where he buried the gold along Shoal Creek. C. F. Eckhardt reports that O. Henry followed up on the lead given him by the shepherd and attempted to find the paymaster's gold, but he was unsuccessful. Broome says that there have been many reports of the ghost of the paymaster walking along Shoal Creek with his lantern, the light of which has been seen bobbing along the creek-bank on dark nights.

Also according to Broome, some of the treasure hunters have become ghosts. It is said that one of these restless ghosts is the spirit of the Travis County treasurer, who stole $4,500 from county funds to buy a map pinpointing one of the sites where treasure is reputed to have been buried. He never received the map and was unable to find the gold. When the time came for a state audit, the felonious treasurer killed himself. He still wanders the banks of Shoal Creek so that he can find the gold and replace the funds that he absconded with.

Other ghost stories surrounding Shoal Creek date back to the Civil War. Late in the war, Austin was reeling from an outbreak of cholera and yellow fever. The epidemic took a heavy toll on the Confederate troops, who were camped along Shoal Creek, and many were hastily buried there. In the early 1900s, a heavy rain caused a nearby dam to burst, and a large number of bones were washed up out of their graves along the creek and into the Colorado River. The ghosts of many of these soldiers may have joined the parade of treasure-hunting ghosts who file up and down the banks of Shoal Creek.

The O. Henry House

William Sydney Porter, whose pen name was O. Henry, came to Austin in 1884. In addition to working as a pharmacist, musician, and draftsman during this time, he also worked at the state's General Land Office, a castlelike structure at the southeast corner of the capitol grounds. To make extra money, Porter wrote stories for various Austin and regional newspaper Sunday supplements. In 1902, he moved to New York, and the 381 stories he wrote while living in the Big Apple won him international fame. During his stay in Austin, he lived in a modest-looking little cottage at 409 East Fifth Street with his wife, Alhol, and their daughter in the 1890s. In 1934, the O. Henry House was turned into a museum. Docents say that it is still occupied by the ghosts of a mother and son who lived there in the early 1900s after Porter and his family moved out.

The story goes that during one of Austin's flu epidemics, a little boy who was living in the house contracted the disease. For several days, his mother sat by the child's bedside in the front room, holding his hand. When her son finally died, she refused to release his dead hand for two days, until family members finally wrenched the boy's corpse away from her. For weeks afterward the grieving woman continued lying on the bed where her son passed away.

Docents at the O. Henry House claim that the mournful mother has never really abandoned her lonely vigil by her son's bedside. Staff members have made up the bed before leaving for the day, only to find the impression of an adult's body on the mattress when they return the next morning. Love, it seems, has the power to transcend even the bonds of death itself.

The Moonlight Restaurant

The Moonlight Restaurant is nestled in what used to be Austin's German section, in an old stone building that was originally a grocery and dry goods store built in the mid-1800s for a German immigrant named Henry Hofheintz. It served as a grocery store, called the Hofheintz Store, for nearly a century. A one-story addition, which was used as a saloon and a private residence, was added years later. Henry Hofheintz's eldest daughter, Catherine Reissig, inherited the store after her father's death, and the property remained in the Reissig family until 1966. Locals say that the Moonlight Restaurant is the place to go in Austin for good food, fine wines—and paranormal activity.

The most haunted part of the Moonlight Restaurant is the little wooden addition, which is historically significant because it is the last remaining "Sunday House" in Austin. In the nineteenth century, families who traveled to Austin on Saturdays to do their trading often spent the night at places like this so that they could go to church on Sunday morning. After the Moonlight Restaurant opened on this site, a waitress who had been working late decided to spend the night in the old Sunday House. She set her phone alarm to wake her up and fell asleep. Just before the alarm went off, she heard the voice of an elderly woman say, "Isn't it about time you woke up?" The startled waitress sat up quickly and looked around. After determining that she was indeed alone in the house, she walked back into the restaurant and asked if anyone else had been staying in the Sunday House. They assured her that she was the only one there all night long.

The Moonlight Restaurant is also thought to be haunted by the ghost of a little boy. He could be the spirit of one of the children who were washed away when flooding caused by a series of thunderstorms in 1925 wiped out entire families in Austin. Staff members say that usually he is a very helpful little spirit. One day, a waitress who had a loaded tray in her hands and was struggling to open the door was pleasantly surprised—and shocked—when the door opened by itself. While some of the denizens of the Moonlight Restaurant may be dead, it seems that chivalry is not.

The Susanna Dickinson House

Susanna Dickinson was born in rural Tennessee in 1815. She eloped when she was fifteen, marrying a soldier named Almeron Dickinson. Two years later, Susanna and her husband emigrated to the Mexican province of Texas and settled near the town of Gonzales. In 1835, Almeron volunteered his services as an artilleryman in the revolution. His wife joined him after Texas volunteers raided her home. After the Texas volunteers took San Antonio on December 3, Almeron was placed in command of artillery batteries at the Alamo. Susanna was quartered in the home of Ramon Musquiz, along with the families of other volunteers. When Santa Anna attacked the Alamo on February 23, 1836, Almeron jumped on his horse and rode to the home of Musquiz, where he picked up his wife and infant daughter and took them inside the Alamo. On the day of the final assault on the Alamo, Susanna and the other women took refuge in an anteroom of the chapel. Almeron had just enough time to stick his head inside the door and tell his wife that he hoped she and their baby would survive. He then returned to the battle that raged outside the chapel and was killed.

After the siege had ended and all the defenders of the Alamo were dead, Santa Anna singled out Susanna and gave her a message to carry to Gen. Sam Houston, informing him that everyone who resisted him and his army would meet the same fate as that of the soldiers at the Alamo. Susanna, who was illiterate, did not know what the letter she delivered to General Houston said. As she handed him the letter, she said, "Santa Anna killed my husband. Now go get 'im." She asked the Congress of the Republic of Texas for financial relief but was refused. She then entered into a series of marriages in order to make ends meet. After divorcing her second husband, an abusive drunk, she received a land bounty from the republic and worked as a laundress and boardinghouse keeper. She married a third time but was soon widowed. Her fourth husband divorced Susanna after she had already left him. She ran a boardinghouse in Lockhart for a few years before marrying her fifth husband, a German immigrant named Joseph William Hannig, in 1857.

She and Hannig moved to Austin, where he opened a furniture store. In 1869, Hannig used Susanna's savings and her relief money from the Alamo to build a house on Fifth Street about a hundred feet from where the house now stands. Susanna and Joseph became wealthy as the result of wise real estate investments, and they moved into a mansion on Deval Street. By the time Susanna died in 1883, she had achieved fame as the "Messenger of the Alamo" and the only Anglo female survivor of the siege. Her larger-than-life persona made an indelible impression on the history of Austin—and, apparently, on the little house at Fifth Street, where her ghostly presence can still be felt.

A number of different people owned the Susanna Dickinson House in the twentieth century. In the 1990s, it was converted into a popular barbecue joint called the Pit. George W. Bush is reputed to have been one of the restaurant's best customers when he was governor. In early 2000, plans were made to build a Hilton hotel on the site of Susanna's home. The rumor soon spread that the old house would be dismantled and reopened in the lobby, where it would be transformed into a taco bar. The public outcry was so great that the house was moved to its present location a hundred feet away from the hotel and deeded to the city in 2003. Seven years later, it opened as a museum.

According to local legend, Susanna Dickinson's forceful personality has not been totally suppressed by the passing of time. Many people claim to have seen the image of a large, heavyset woman wearing a nineteenth-century dress walking around the outside of the house. Some people have seen the curtains move when nobody was inside the house. It seems that Susanna's ghost is not totally satisfied with the new location of her house, however. For years, Hilton employees say, water has seeped into the hotel in the exact spot where her house once stood, although geologists have been unable to find any underground springs beneath the hotel.

The UT Tower

In 1881, the state legislature passed an act establishing the University of Texas in Austin, and architect Abner Cook was hired to design the first building. In September 1883, the university started holding classes in the temporary state capitol building, and on January 1, 1884, students began attending classes in the new Main Building on College Hill. Before long, "Old Main" acquired a reputation for being haunted. Some say that spirits took over the building because the mud from which the bricks were fired was taken from Shoal Creek, which locals have always claimed is cursed. Others say the building became haunted after ivy taken from the grave of English poet Thomas Grey was planted outside the walls. Old Main was razed in the early 1930s, and in 1937, a 307-foot, twenty-seven-floor tower was erected in its place.

Today this tower has a grim legacy, which some people blame on the fact that some of Old Main's bricks were used in its construction. During its first three decades, four people lost their lives after plummeting from the tower. One was a construction worker who slipped and fell to his death. The other three were suicides who jumped off the tower in 1945, 1949, and 1961. The tower was also the site of one of the darkest episodes in Austin's history.

On August 1, 1966, a university student and former marine named Charles Whitman climbed to the twenty-eighth-floor observation deck of the tower and began shooting at people with a high-powered rifle. By the time the Austin police and DPS officers had killed Whitman and ended his hour-and-a-half shooting spree, the troubled student had killed sixteen people and wounded thirty-two others. Although no one knows why Whitman snapped, some people believe that the impending divorce of his parents might have been a factor.

The tower was closed off right after the shootings and did not reopen until two years later. Almost immediately, students began committing suicide by jumping from the tower (a total of nine students have jumped to their deaths since the tower's opening in 1937), so the administration closed it once again. After the tower was opened again in 1999, students reported seeing the ghosts of the suicide victims walking around the bottom of the tower. The ghost of the construction worker could also be walking around the infamous tower.

In *The Ghosts of Austin*, Fiona Broome reports that the tower is also haunted by the ghost of Charles Whitman. Witnesses have described his spirit as a man in workman's clothes and as a fleeting, shadowy form. Security guards blame Whitman's ghosts for turning on the lights while they are making their rounds. In fact, some of the guards tell Charles, "Stop it!" when the lights flicker on and off.

Today the observation deck is open for tours. One wonders how many people climb the tower because of the beautiful view it offers of the campus and how many do so because they are fascinated by the story of the troubled man who took so many innocent lives from this spot on August 1, 1966.

Central Texas

Jake's Bridge

Hutto

Stories of haunted bridges are some of the most common ghost tales in southern folklore. Many of these structures are called "crybaby bridges" because, according to local legends, a distraught woman tossed her baby from the bridge before killing herself. It is said that the cries of the infant can still be heard on the anniversary of its death. Other bridges are known as "hanging bridges" because outlaws or African Americans were lynched from them by angry mobs. In Williamson County, the best-known haunted bridge is called Jake's Bridge.

The legend of Jake's Bridge is set during the Great Depression. At that time, cotton was the primary cash crop in the area. Before the stock market crash of 1929, cotton fetched 16.9 cents per pound. In the early 1930s, however, it was worth only 5 cents per pound. Understandably, many farmers who were accustomed to making their living raising cotton fell into despair. Some of them left the country for the city in search of a better life. A few took their own lives.

One of these unfortunate men is remembered today only by his first name, Jake. Unable to provide for himself or his family, Jake killed his wife and two children. Even though he had viewed the murders as the only way to spare his family the agony of starvation, Jake was wracked by guilt. He made his way to a wooden bridge near the Williamson-Travis County line. Jake then tied one end of a rope around one of the trusses and the other end around his neck.

In a variant of the legend, Jake murdered his parents, placed their bodies in their car, and pushed it over the bridge. He then died mysteriously in a house fire. In both versions of the tale, the old wooden bridge has since been replaced with the modern-day concrete structure. And in both versions, the tragic end is really only the beginning.

Locals who have parked their cars on the bridge and left them in neutral have reported feeling their cars move, ever so slowly, as if someone were pushing them. Afterward, people whose cars were dusty at the time found handprints on the trunk. In the early 2000s, disc jockeys from Austin news station KXAN tested the validity of this phenomenon by parking their car on the bridge and shifting it into neutral. Reportedly, the car moved across the bridge all by itself.

An abandoned house that is reputed to have been the home where Jake murdered his family is also said to be haunted. Passersby have claimed to have heard disembodied footsteps and the screams of children coming from inside the old house. The voice of a man stating, "I'm coming for you," has also been heard from inside the house.

Jake's ghost even seems to have been transported to the cemetery in Hutto, where he is said to have been buried. For years, reports of a glowing tombstone have attracted curiosity seekers from miles around. It is important to note, however, that no tombstones in the cemetery— including the one that reportedly glows—bear the name of "Jake."

The Hairy Man

Round Rock

Although its name might conjure up images of a Bigfoot-like creature, the Hairy Man of Round Rock is thought by most to be a ghost. The legend of the Hairy Man begins in the early nineteenth century. In one version of the tale, a pioneer family was traveling along a deeply rutted road in rural Texas. When one of the wagon wheels encountered a particularly deep pothole, the couple's young son was bounced out of the wagon. The family had traveled miles down the road before noticing that the little boy was gone. In another version of the tale, a raging flood separated the child from his parents.

One way or another, the boy was left on his own in the unsettled wilderness along Brushy Creek, and he would have perished if he had not been adopted by animals. Others say that the boy was old enough to pick up survival skills on his own, completely cut off from civilization, and became a feral hermit who was completely covered by hair.

He enjoyed jumping out of the bushes and trees and frightening people as they passed by in their wagons or on horseback, until one day, he jumped out of a tree and fell right in front of a speeding stagecoach. The Hairy Man was crushed under the horses' hooves.

For more than a century, people living in the area have reported seeing the ghost of the Hairy Man roaming around the road where he died. Many people have seen a shadowy figure standing on the bluffs along Brushy Creek. A strange howling noise that is occasionally heard around Brushy Creek and Round Rock has led some people to suggest that the Hairy Man is not a ghost, but actually a Bigfoot type of creature.

Round Rock has become one of a growing number of towns that have capitalized on their identification with a mythical creature. In 1994, Round Rock held the first of its annual Hairy Man festivals. Hundreds of people flock to the festival each October to enjoy the crafts, food, music, and children's activities. The high point of the festival is the Hairy Man Contest, in which the contestant judged to be the hairiest takes home a cash prize. Each year, the money raised by the festival helps support the town's food pantries and charities. Thus in an ironic twist of events, something good has come out of the tragic tale of the Hairy Man.

St. Olaf's Kirke and Cemetery

Cranfill's Gap

St. Olaf's Kirke, also known as the Red Rock Church, is located four miles east of Cranfills Gap on County Road 1445. It was originally planned as an extension of Our Savior's Lutheran Church, just a few miles east. St. Olaf's was designed and built in 1886 by Andrew Michelson on land that the small Norwegian community had purchased for $25. Michelson was assisted by his brothers, Christian and Ole, as well as a number of local farmers who provided limestone from the nearby hills. In the beginning, the congregation sat on handmade pews made of boards and wooden pegs. The pews rested on a dirt floor. St. Olaf's severed its connection to Our Savior's Lutheran Church in 1902, thereby becoming an independent place of worship.

All services were held in Norwegian. The original St. Olaf's was used for Sunday services until it was replaced by a new St. Olaf's Lutheran Church in 1917.

St. Olaf's Cemetery was established a year before the old church was built. One of the first burials was that of Bersven Swenson's wife, Siri, who contracted pneumonia and passed away shortly after the birth of her seventh child in 1885. When a member of the congregation died, the departed's friends and relatives slaughtered a calf or pig to feed all the people who attended the wake afterward. As time passed, the cemetery was expanded in all directions. Today, as many as six and seven generations of the church's founding families have been interred in St. Olaf's Cemetery.

Over time, St. Olaf's Kirke and Cemetery have acquired a reputation for being haunted. Shadowy figures have been seen walking through the church at night from time to time, but the most commonly reported paranormal occurrence is voices. People have often heard disembodied voices while music is being played. Most of the voices seem to originate inside the church, but some people claim to have heard them coming from the cemetery. More often than not, the voices seem angry.

In *Ghosts in the Graveyard: Texas Cemetery Tales*, Olyve Hallmark Abbott interviewed Mark Angle, who heard the voices while touring the old church with his father, photographer Lee Angle. Ed Syers, author of *Ghost Stories of Texas*, had invited Mark and Lee to accompany him to St. Olaf's in the late 1970s. Mark said that when he walked into the old building, the first thing that caught his attention was the piano near the altar. He sat down and began playing Beethoven's "Clair de Lune." Immediately, Mark and his father began hearing mumbling voices. The men could not tell if the voices were singing or merely talking. Lee said the voices were coming from the back of the sanctuary. Thinking that the voices were responding to the piano accompaniment, Lee took his son's place at the piano while Mark walked up to the balcony. Mark still heard the voices very clearly but could not tell where they were coming from. Both Mark and his father recalled the voices as sounding very sweet, not angry.

In 1983, the old St. Olaf's Kirke was listed on the National Register of Historic Places. Regular church services are no longer held here, but the old church does host a few special events each year, such as weddings and funerals. Although the original founders of St. Olaf's are dead and gone, some believe their spirits are temporarily revived when music is played in the old building.

The Orviss Family Vault

Calvert

D. A. Orviss belonged to an intrepid breed of entrepreneurs who migrated to the Brazos River bottom region after the Civil War. A former Mississippi river boat captain, Orviss moved to Texas during the Reconstruction period to sell dry goods to the influx of settlers who were moving to Texas in the hope of building small fortunes for themselves on the frontier. Today Orviss would probably be a totally forgotten figure, a minor footnote in Texas history, were it not for his marble and granite mausoleum—and the reports of ghost sightings and other paranormal phenomena surrounding it.

The Orviss family vault is located in a small burial plot in a wooded area just outside Calvert. The tomb, which cost the then-significant sum of $20,000 to build in the 1890s, contains the coffins of Orviss; his wife, Louisa; and their two children. Unfortunately, the old tomb has suffered from neglect and vandalism over the years. Locals say that grave robbers opened the coffins and removed jewelry and bones. They also say that in the 1980s, a child's metal coffin was placed on the ground in the woods. One of the windows has been broken. Not surprisingly, the spooky-looking tomb has become a hot spot for ghost hunters throughout Texas because of the high levels of paranormal activity reported there. Paranormal researchers walking around the iron fence surrounding the tomb have claimed that the temperature inside the fence is cooler than outside. People standing outside the tomb at night have heard footsteps walking through the leaves. High EMF readings have been recorded around the tomb. Shadow people are said to roam among the graves.

In November 2004, three members of The Final Crossing (TFC) Paranormal Research Team investigated the stories they had heard about the Orviss family vault. The most intriguing piece of evidence collected that night was an example of electronic voice phenomena, or EVP. Lead investigator Casey Unger, who attended school in Calvert, walked a few feet from the iron fence and conducted an impromptu session. With her tape recorder running, she said, "I'm speaking to the spirits of the children who are here. I'm speaking to the spirits of the children whose graves were desecrated here." Later on, when the members reviewed the tape, they heard the voice of a child say, "The children left."

Four years later, the TFC paranormal group and the Aggieland Ghost Hunters conducted a joint investigation of the vault. The TFC members had already gotten some high readings on their EMF detectors before the Aggieland Ghost Hunters arrived at 9 P.M. The second group did not experience any EMF spikes that night, but they did record a number of startling EVPs, including the laughter of a baby; a disembodied voice asking, "What does that mean?"; and another disembodied voice saying, "Hi." An Aggieland investigator was looking through one of the windows in the mausoleum when he heard someone whisper in his ear. After the TFC members went home, one of the Aggieland investigators was simultaneously taking photographs with his digital camera and recording EVPs when the battery power of both devices was totally drained.

Many folklorists believe that there is a price to be paid when the dead are not paid the respect due them. In the case of the Orviss burial vault, the disrespect reflected in the vandalism is amplified by the fact that D. A. Orviss was one of Calvert's most prominent citizens in the nineteenth century. Perhaps Orviss and his family are expressing their displeasure through the eerie feelings and strange occurrences that so many people experience when they visit the burial vault.

The Falls Hotel

Marlin

Marlin was founded in the nineteenth century and became known for the supposedly curative powers of its mineral springs. It was one of a number of health resorts that attracted thousands of people annually from all over the country. Even as late as the 1930s, Marlin was attracting more than eighty thousand visitors a year, who came to the little town looking for a cure for "what ailed them." The town's mineral springs continued drawing people to Marlin up through the 1960s, primarily because doctors had transformed the tradition of bathing into a tool for physical therapy.

In 1929, Conrad Hilton built the eighth of his hotels in Marlin to take advantage of the city's popularity with tourists. He named the 110-room hotel for Falls County, in which Marlin is located. A tunnel connected the hotel to the Marlin Sanitarium Bath House across the street. Guests dressed in their bathrobes walked from their hotel rooms to the bathhouse to partake of the springs' medicinal waters.

Today the upper floors of the Falls Hotel are vacant—with the exception, perhaps, of a few ghostly inhabitants. A few shops and a restaurant occupy the first floor, and dances are held in the hotel's lavish ballroom. The tunnel was closed after it was destroyed by a fire, and the Marlin Sanitarium Bath House was razed and replaced by a gazebo park and a post office.

According to past and present employees of the Falls Hotel, however, vestiges of the Marlin hotel's heyday can be still be detected. For years, caretakers living on the upper floors have heard weird noises and disembodied voices. One of the most recent caretakers was so shaken by the bizarre sounds and apparitions that he quit his job and returned to Mexico.

A formal investigation conducted by the TFC Paranormal Research Team confirmed many of these reports of paranormal activity inside the Falls Hotel. During the night, one of the members said that while he was listening to the radio, the station changed by itself. Not long thereafter, the radio slid off the stage all by itself. Another member claimed to have been pushed by an unseen force. If the entity prefers to be left alone, one would think it would not have chosen to haunt a hotel.

Dead Man's Hole

Located south of Marble Falls, Dead Man's Hole is a 155-foot-deep limestone fissure that has long been considered to be haunted by the spirits of those who were thrown into its depths. The first person recorded to have seen this natural oddity was the German naturalist Ferdinand Lueders, who discovered it in 1821 while searching for new species of insects. The hole remained hidden until two decades later, when homesteaders rediscovered it. During the Civil War, Texans who opposed secession, known as Unionists, ran the risk of being thrown down Dead Man's Hole if they expressed their opinions too loudly. A few federal officials accused of being carpetbaggers and scalawags during Reconstruction met the same fate. Some of these men are said to have been hanged from an oak tree that once stood over the hole before their bodies were thrown into the fissure. So many men were hanged from the tree, in fact, that one of its overhanging limbs was said to have rope marks.

Historians believe that a total of seventeen men were thrown into Dead Man's Hole, including a settler named Adolph Hoppe, pro-Union judge John R. Scott, and Ben McKeever, who murdered a local freedman because the ex-slave's dog bit his horse. Five of the black man's friends caught up with McKeever and ambushed him, killing him in a hail of shotgun blasts and then tossing his body down the hole. McKeever's body was retrieved from the hole a few days later. Three of the men received life sentences, one received a two-year prison term, and the fifth was found not guilty.

After Reconstruction, Dead Man's Hole was seldom used as a tomb anymore, but the mysteries surrounding the fissure continued to deepen. The presence of toxic gases made a scientific investigation of Dead Man's Hole impossible until 1951, when explorers, using breathing equipment, entered the hole for the first time. In 1968, the Texas Speleological Society mapped the fissure and measured its dimensions. Landowner Lou Roper deeded Dead Man's Hole and 6.5 acres of land to Burnet County for use as a park. Today the opening to the fissure is sealed with an iron grate.

In the mid-2000s, the Austin Paranormal Society investigated the ghost stories that people had been telling about Dead Man's Hole for many years. Mike Cox reports that during the investigation, the members recorded a number of startling EVPs, including "It's starting to rain" and "Daddy, you said you would take me to Dairy Queen." They also recorded a female voice that said, "Let's get back in the car before we get soaked." Because neither cars nor Dairy Queen existed during the period when the seventeen men died in the hole, one can safely assume that the voices recorded that night were not their spirits speaking.

The Texas Grill

Ballinger

Ballinger was named after Judge William Pitt Ballinger, a railroad lawyer, statesman, and veteran of the Mexican War. During the Civil War, he helped arrange for the defense of Galveston. One of the town's most popular attractions is the Texas Grill, as famous for its ghostly activity as it is for its fine food and ambience. Constructed around 1901, the building served as a saloon, brothel, and department store during its first fifty years of existence. It first became a restaurant in 1954. In 1991, Joyce and Larry Sikes opened up the Texas Grill in the old building.

In 1993, a psychic told the couple that their restaurant was haunted by a cowboy named Norton, who was shot and killed by Texas Rangers. Norton seems to be a playful spirit who makes his presence known by moving small objects from one location to another, opening refrigerator doors, and making bumping and rapping noises. Employees say they can tell when he is around by the sweet smell of his cologne. Occasionally, waiters and waitresses run into cold spots in the restaurant. Many people have seen the figure of a male out of the corner of the eye in the kitchen and dining areas. People working upstairs have heard footsteps late at night.

Because Norton seems to favor the kitchen and dining areas, he has made the acquaintance of cooks over the years. One of the cooks said he had to stay late one night to finish baking bread for the next day. On the way home afterward, he had a nagging feeling that he had forgotten to turn off the oven. When he returned to the hotel the next day, the bread was sitting on the stove and the oven was turned off. The cook assumed that someone else—possibly one of the owners— had come in during the night and finished up. Later that day, while he was on his way to fetch some supplies, he noticed a cowboy standing on the stairs. The cowboy told him that he was the one who had turned off the stove and set out the bread. Then he vanished.

Another cook seems to have angered Norton for some reason. While he was standing outside, a loose brick from atop the building fell off and landed at his feet. The cook thought that he must have offended Norton, but he could not think of a reason why.

People other than employees have also had encounters with Norton's ghost. A customer was enjoying his meal one morning when suddenly the knives and forks flew out of a glass right in front of him. On another occasion, a policeman was patrolling the street when he noticed that one of the doors was standing wide open. He walked upstairs and distinctly heard the sounds of someone moving around. He checked in all the rooms, but no one was there. At the end of a Christmas party that was held in the restaurant several years ago, a group photo was taken. When the film was developed, the photographer was shocked to see a cowboy wearing a hat and mustache.

In September 2006, a group of paranormal investigators named Central Texas Ghost Search conducted an all-night investigation of the Texas Grill. The digital thermometers carried by two of the members indicated a ten-degree drop in temperature in the front room and kitchen. When one of the members was in the kitchen area, he took two photographs in rapid succession. In the first photo, an orb was clearly visible. Even though the members did not collect a lot of evidence that night, what they did collect convinced them that the Texas Grill is one of the most haunted places in Ballinger.

Faust Hotel

New Braunfels

The Spanish Revival-style Travelers Hotel, built by businessman Walter Faust Sr., opened its doors on October 12, 1929—just two weeks before the Wall Street crash. The ensuing economic downturn as well as a boll weevil infestation that plagued cotton-growing areas across the country during this same period took a heavy toll and caused a number of stores in New Braunfels to close, but the Travelers Hotel remained open, due in large part to the resilience of Mr. Faust. In 1936, toward the end of the Great Depression, the hotel was renamed the Faust Hotel. During World War II, the hotel gained the reputation of being the "honeymoon capital of Texas" because soldiers from the nearby military base spent their first night of wedded bliss here before being shipped out.

After the war, the Faust Hotel had a number of different owners. In 1985, it was listed on the National Register of Historic Places and designated a Texas Historic Landmark. Two and a half decades later, the most recent owners began installing modern amenities while furnishing every room with antiques to preserve the hotel's 1930s ambience. By early 2011, many of the guest rooms had been completely refurnished, and a 1929 Model A Ford sat in the front lobby. Additional vestiges of the past apparently include the spirits of some of the hotel's previous guests.

Although several ghosts have appeared to guests and visitors over the years, the most commonly reported apparition inside the hotel is the ghost of Walter Faust Sr., who lived in the hotel. Ever since Walter's death in 1932, people have seen a well-dressed man waving to them inside the lobby. His ghost has also been seen standing at the foot of the bed in his former suite, only to disappear into thin air a few seconds later. Walter, who had the reputation of being a prankster when alive, seems to still enjoy playing pranks on guests and employees. He has been blamed for resetting fans too high, opening doors for guests, rearranging bottles in the bar, and rearranging furniture on the fourth floor. Rick Moran, in a story for *Real Travel Adventures* magazine, tells the story of an incident that occurred one "dark and stormy night." After a power outage, when a manager went to the basement to reset the circuit breakers, she noticed that although the rest of the hotel was dark, the bulb illuminating an alcove containing a portrait of Mr. Faust was on. She also heard the unnerving sound of spectral giggling. After she reset the circuit breakers, she noticed that the light over the portrait was now off. The next morning, the manager asked the maintenance man to replace the bulb. She was shocked when he replied that the wiring had not been connected for many years.

Another hotel ghost is the spirit of a little girl. According to Olyve Hallmark Abbott in *A Ghost in the Guest Room*, a maid was cleaning a guest room on the second floor when she saw a little girl standing in the hallway. She asked the girl her name, but the child ran down the hall and into a solid wall. A few days later, when the maid was walking down the hallway on the third floor, she was surprised to see the face of the little girl in a portrait of Christine Faust hanging on the wall. Christine, who was born in the 1830s, was the daughter of James and Sarah Faust, Walter's ancestors, who had lived in a house on the land where the hotel was erected.

Another ghost that frequents the second floor is the spirit of an adult male dressed in early-twentieth-century clothes. He is usually seen from the side and back. However, an employee who got a particularly good look at his face noticed that he resembled a man in a photograph of a couple that hangs on the second floor. The identity of the couple is unknown.

Sometimes the ghosts of the Faust Hotel announce their presence before materializing. Cold spots have been encountered throughout the hotel. In addition, the decades-old elevator has been known to descend to the lobby without any passengers. Apparently the ghosts as well as living guests feel right at home in the renovated hotel.

Enchanted Rock

Llano

Enchanted Rock is a huge rock formation composed primarily of pink granite that lies between Fredericksburg and Llano. This weathered granite dome covers approximately 640 acres and is one of the largest batholiths, the term for underground rock formations uncovered by erosion, in the United States. Archaeologists have found evidence of human visitation of the site, including Indian arrowheads, dating back eleven thousand to twelve thousand years. In 1970, it was declared a national natural landmark, and in 1984, the area was placed on the National Register of Historic Places. It is now the focal point of Enchanted Rock State Natural Area, which covers 1,644 acres. It is also surrounded by a number of ghost stories.

Enchanted Rock's connection to the spirit world dates back to the Tonkawa, Comanche, and Apache tribes, who believed that ghost fires could be seen flickering on the top of the rock. The Tonkawa Indians believed that the rock was imbued with magical and spiritual powers. They also claimed to have heard groaning and creaking sounds emanating from the giant rock. Some historians believe that the Tonkawa Indians revered the rock so much that they offered sacrifices on its summit. According to one legend, a band of Indians was driven to Enchanted Rock by a hostile tribe. Eventually the hostile tribe prevailed, killing all the defenders of the rock. Their ghosts are said to remain on the rock to this day. In another legend, a Tonkawa princess leaped from the top of the rock after her tribe was massacred by enemy Indians, and her ghost haunts the rock. Some locals say that the footlike indentations on the rock are the footprints of an Indian chief who was doomed to wander around on the rock forever after sacrificing his daughter. His endless pacing is said to have created the strange divots in the rock.

Another story is that a Spanish conquistador or priest who was captured by the Indians escaped by slipping into a cave, where he encountered a number of spirits. Years later, it is said, a white woman escaped her Indian captors by taking refuge on Enchanted Rock. Her screams still pierce the night air. In 1841, Capt. John C. Hays climbed to the top of the rock after being cut off from his company of Texas Rangers. He single-handedly shot so many Indians from his vantage point at the rock's summit that native tribes believed he must have been assisted by the malevolent spirits that inhabited the rock.

Today Enchanted Rock State Natural Area draws hikers, campers, hikers, rock climbers, bird-watchers, and stargazers. The park also attracts scientists, who flock here to study the area's abundance of flora and fauna. In recent years, it has also become popular with folklorists and paranormal investigators, who are eager to discover how the geological oddity got its name and hope to see some of its ghosts.

Dallas

Millermore Mansion

Millermore Mansion is thought to be the most haunted building in Dallas Heritage Village, a collection of thirty-eight historic buildings in Old City Park, just south of downtown Dallas. The buildings represent the city between 1840 and 1910. Millermore Mansion is a two-story Greek Revival home once owned by Dallas pioneer and wealthy cotton planter William Brown Miller. Using slave labor, Miller began construction of his dream house in 1855. When laying out the plans for his mansion, Miller used the North Star to guide him so that his home faced directly north. The house was finally completed six years later. Members of the Millermore family continued living in the old mansion until 1966, by which time the house was so badly deteriorated that it was on the verge of being razed. But the Dallas County Historical Society stepped in and saved the old mansion, having it completely dismantled and then reassembled in Old City Park, where it was restored to its former glory. Subsequently, the historical society moved additional historic structures to what became known as Dallas Heritage Village.

The most commonly sighted ghost in Millermore Mansion is believed to be the spirit of Minerva Miller, William's second wife, who died in 1856. People driving by have seen her silhouette in the middle pane of glass in the window in the upstairs bedroom. Witnesses report that she walks from the master bedroom to the nursery. It is said that birds smash into the pane of glass where the ghost has been seen. Many visitors and staff members have felt a female presence in the master bedroom and nursery, but only a few people have actually reported seeing her. In November 2000, a young woman who claims to have psychic abilities was following a tour guide to the bottom of the staircase when she sensed something paranormal. She glanced over at the backdoor and saw a transparent female figure sitting on a bench. In just a few seconds, the apparition was gone. The young woman was not surprised when the docent informed her after the tour that many people had seen the woman's ghost in a window in the master bedroom as they drove by.

Other spirits are said to be active entities in the house as well. Security guards have observed balls of light floating through the upper floors. One witness reported that a luminous orb was hovering just inside the same window where the ghostly female has been seen. An employee was in the building alone when she heard footsteps tromping up the back stairs. Four adults once recorded the sound of children laughing late at night. One morning, an employee who was cleaning the house placed her sunglasses on the hall tree downstairs. When she was finished a couple hours later, she was shocked to find that someone had moved her sunglasses to a different spot on the hall tree and left incriminating fingerprints on the lenses. In 2007, a local ghost-hunting group called Credible Paranormal recorded the laughter of a young woman here.

Dallas Heritage Village is a unique museum where visitors can sample living history. Tourists can witness costumed characters portraying gunfighters on Main Street and farm wives working in their garden. First-person interpreters explain what life was like in the second half of the nineteenth century for Hispanic and African American families. At the Millermore Mansion, however, the historical figures that visitors occasionally encounter may have not been alive for quite a while.

The Sons of Hermann Hall

In 1840, a small group of German immigrants formed a fraternal benefit society called the Order of the Sons of Hermann. They named their order after an early folk hero named Hermann, also known as Arminius, who was captured by the Romans and pressed into service in their army. When the Romans were ordered to persecute Hermann's people, however, he defected and organized the Germanic tribesmen into a formidable fighting machine that defeated three Roman legions in the battle of Teutoburg Forest in 9 AD. The Romans retaliated by abducting his pregnant wife, who bore a son in slavery.

Hermann, who never saw his family again, died twelve years after his victory against the Romans.

Today the Sons of Hermann is the nation's oldest fraternal benefit society. The Sons of Hermann Hall in Dallas opened its doors in April 1911. The hall was voted by the *Dallas Observer* as the Best Place to Take a Non-Texan. Longtime members also claim that it is the best place to find a ghost.

Much of the paranormal activity reported inside the lodge takes the form of unusual noises. Staff said they heard the laughter of children, disembodied footsteps, doors opening and closing, chains clanking, the scraping of furniture being moved across the ballroom floor, and the sound of a phantom bowler in the empty bowling alley. Some people claim to have heard the voice of a former caretaker, Louie Bernardt, ordering children to stop fooling around. In *A Texas Guide to Haunted Restaurants, Taverns, and Inns*, Robert and Anne Powell Wlodarski say that in the 1990s, extras from the television show *Walker, Texas Ranger* were sharing a drink in the bar when they saw a man and woman dressed in turn-of-the-century clothing walk down a hallway and into a corridor, where they vanished.

In the late 1990s, two women were doing some bookkeeping late at night. They were all alone in the building—or at least, they thought they were. Not long after they started looking at the books, one of the women exclaimed, "Someone just walked past the door!" Afterward, one of the women, Jo Nicodemus, said she was certain that she and her friend had encountered a ghost, because a photograph taken months before during a performance in the ballroom showed a skeletal woman with blonde hair sitting next to a band member.

Today the Sons of Hermann Hall is one of the most popular live music venues in the entire city. For years, favorite local bands have given audiences a sampling of genuine Texas music in the lodge. The former bowling alley now hosts private parties and local theater productions. Swing dance lessons in the upstairs ballroom attract hundreds of aspiring dancers every year. People interested simply in relaxing enjoy kicking back at the downstairs and upstairs bars. And these days, people fascinated by the paranormal flock to the old lodge in the hope of capturing a few orb photos and EVPs.

The Majestic Theatre

The original Majestic Theatre was built in 1905 on the corner of St. Paul and Commerce Streets. It was later rebuilt in two different locations, the most recent being 1925 Elm Street, where patrons can find entertainment—and perhaps ghosts—today. In its early days, the Majestic Theatre featured vaudeville acts and entertainers such as Houdini, Red Skelton, and Cab Calloway. By the 1930s, it had become one of the most famous movie palaces in the United States. The Majestic Theatre did good business during the Great Depression, offering patrons an escape from their troubles at a very reasonable price. During the 1930s and 1940s, a number of A-list actors and actresses, including John Wayne, Joan Crawford, Bob Hope, and Bing Crosby, appeared at the theater to promote their movies. The Majestic closed in 1973 and was turned over to the city of Dallas three years later; it was reopened in 1983 after extensive renovations. Today the Majestic Theatre offers patrons a variety of entertainment, including national pageants, plays, and concerts. And like many old theaters, it is rumored to be haunted.

Employees at the Majestic Theatre believe that it is haunted by the spirit of an early benefactor, Karl Hoblitzelle. Apparently he can't resist "helping out" when plays are presented in the theater. Stage crews report that backdrops move on their own, and telephone lines that have not been activated light up mysteriously. Strange smells are said to waft through the theater on occasion. Mr. Hoblitzelle, it seems, is finding it difficult to leave the theater that was so much a part of his life.

The Adolphus Hotel

Adolphus Busch is best known as the cofounder of the Anheuser-Busch beer company. However, the German immigrant also enjoyed building and running hotels. In 1892, Busch built the Oriental Hotel at the corner of Commerce and Akard Streets. The hotel was so successful that Busch and the Dallas city leaders decided that the growing city could support another luxury hotel. After the old City Hall was razed in 1910, Busch hired a St. Louis architectural firm to construct a new hotel. When the twenty-one-story Adolphus Hotel opened its doors two years later, it was the tallest building in the state. Busch stayed at the hotel whenever he could until his death the following year. His heirs retained ownership of the Adolphus Hotel until 1949, when it was sold to Leo Corrigan. Noble House Hotels and Resorts acquired the old hotel in 1980, restoring it the following year. Today the Adolphus Hotel is known far and wide for its lavish décor, its comfortable rooms, its five-diamond restaurant—and its ghosts.

Like most haunted hotels, the Adolphus is said to be haunted by the spirits of former guests who died there or are so fond of the hotel that they never left. Guests and employees claim to have heard footsteps and the unmistakable sound of doors opening and closing on their own. The disembodied conversations of ghostly guests are said to echo through the halls. The spectral strains of orchestral music have been said to emanate from the Palm Garden, the hotel's grand ballroom. Many people, including sixteen-year-old employee Louis Ford, have felt as if someone were watching them in deserted rooms or hallways. Longtime bartender Dale Rust has claimed that a mischievous spirit enjoys rearranging the beer bottles. Several maids reported feeling an invisible finger tapping them on the shoulder while they were cleaning the restaurant.

Staff members at the hotel have identified two of the spirits that make working at the Adolphus Hotel interesting, to say the least. One is the ghost of a woman who was a regular customer at the hotel's bistro. Just a few weeks after her death, employees swore that they saw her walk into the restaurant and sit down at her favorite seat. The hotel's best-known specter is the ghost of a young woman who was to be married in the Palm Garden in the early 1930s. When her fiancé failed to show up on her wedding day, the jilted bride hanged herself. The apparition of a woman in white has been sighted in the hallway of the nineteenth floor. Legend has it that the forlorn spirit is still searching for the man who broke her heart. For years, desk clerks have received phone calls from a guest staying in one of the suites on the nineteenth floor, complaining about the loud music in the room next door. When the clerks went up to the nineteenth floor to talk to the people making all the noise, they were surprised to find that the room was empty.

The guest book at the Adolphus Hotel bears the signatures of some of the biggest names in politics and show business: Rudolph Valentino, Queen Elizabeth II, Tommy Dorsey, Bill Cosby, and Nicolas Cage have all spent the night at the Adolphus. Today, however, its best-known guests are the spirits who are said to make occasional appearances in the hallways and rooms.

The DeGolyer Estate

Everett Lee DeGolyer was a geophysicist known for his contributions to the Texas oil industry, especially his pioneering methods of discovering major oilfields. Along with his wife, Nell, he also was heavily involved in philanthropic activities in Dallas. The man called "the father of American geophysics" and his wife have long since passed away, but their memory still lives on in their Dallas home. Built in 1940 on the shores of White Rock Lake, the huge, Spanish-style DeGolyer Home today is listed on the National Register of Historic Places. Nell was particularly fond of her garden, which later became the Dallas Arboretum and Botanical Garden. The estate and its gardens now attract tens of thousands of visitors annually.

Although Everett and Nell DeGolyer are no longer among the living, some believe that their spirits stroll the house and its grounds. Could it be that the couple's attachment to their beautiful hacienda-style home has transcended death itself? Employees and docents have reported feeling as if they are being watched by an invisible entity when they enter certain rooms. The estate's café is said to be haunted by a vigilant spirit whose presence is so strong that people sometimes feel as if they are intruding.

In *Ghosts of North Texas*, Mitchel Whitington recounts a story that first appeared in the *Fort Worth Star-Telegram* in 2000. The reporter interviewed a docent who told him that one evening, she had locked the doors of the estate and was walking to her car when she realized she had left her keys inside. The young woman informed a security guard of her predicament, and he opened the door so she could retrieve her keys. She was searching through the papers on the desk where she thought she had laid her keys when she heard a strange noise coming from somewhere in the house. Sensing that something was not right, the docent crossed the hall and walked into the living room. When she turned on the lamp, she was surprised to find that the lid to the piano had been opened and DeGolyer's photograph, which usually sat on top of the piano, had been moved a few feet away to a table in front of a window. She thought about closing the piano lid and moving the photograph back to its proper place, but she was filled with a sense of dread, so she returned to her office, quickly located her keys under the stack of papers, and ran out the front door. The next morning, the young woman walked into the piano room and was surprised to find the lid shut and the photograph sitting on top of it.

The DeGolyers' beautiful home was the couple's retreat from the world that expected so much from them. It is small wonder that the protective spirits of Lee and Nell DeGolyer might be somewhat curious regarding the visitors who attend the weddings, corporate parties, and other special events held at the place they once called home.

Snuffer's Restaurant

When Pat Snuffer opened his restaurant in 1978, the little café at 3526 Greenville Avenue consisted of one room, a service bar, and enough space to seat fifty-five diners. The first customers dined on hamburgers, sandwiches, and french fries. Because of the restaurant's popularity with students from Southern Methodist University, Pat expanded his restaurant considerably over the years, doubling his seating capacity by adding a back room and later opening Snuffer's Patio. These days, folks come by to sample some of Snuffer's cheese fries—and, with luck, see some of its ghosts.

The remodeling that has taken place over the years seems to have stimulated the spirit activity inside the restaurant. Customers and employees have seen the green hanging lamps in the old dining room swing in unison. A waiter claimed that one of the two lights in the attic tended to come back on after he had turned it off, although an electrician who examined the light found nothing wrong with it. One day a waitress saw a woman sitting on top of a cigarette machine in the old bar. She left to tell the manager, but by the time they returned, the woman was gone. The apparition of a woman dressed in black has been seen even more frequently in the hallway connecting the old building with the new one, and cold spots have been detected in the same hall near the old doorway. The manager has seen a misty black shape in the kitchen.

Two stories are told that might explain the identity of the ghosts. One has it that back in the 1980s, a woman was stabbed in a fight that broke out in the restroom or hallway. She had enough strength to stagger outside the door before bleeding out. Another story says that a scuffle started in Snuffer's back when it was a biker bar, and a man was stabbed. He made it to the hallway, where he collapsed in a heap in front of the men's room. The door to the men's room occasionally has been seen opening and closing by itself, lending credence to the second story.

Most of the waiters and waitresses at Snuffer's describe its ghost or ghosts as mischievous. They say that something seems to enjoy moving place settings and menus that have been carefully placed on tables. A few employees claim to have felt someone brush past them when they were alone in the dining room. The occasional manifestations at Snuffer's only serve to enhance the allure of the most colorful—and perhaps the most haunted—restaurant in Dallas.

The Lizard Lounge

The Lizard Lounge is thought to be one of the most haunted entertainment spots in Dallas. Located at 2424 Swiss Avenue, in what is known as the Deep Ellum section of the city, the building was originally constructed as a warehouse at the turn of the nineteenth century. After several decades, it fell into disrepair. It was saved from destruction by a theater group, who decided that the old building would be the perfect venue for a playhouse. The Grand Crystal Palace, as the theater was called, featured off-off-Broadway productions for many years, until it closed as a result of financial problems in the 1980s. For a short time, the theater housed the Empire Club. The building was then taken over by the Gold Club Topless Cabaret, which featured adult entertainment. In 1992, the Lizard Lounge became the most recent occupant of the old warehouse. And customers and employees claim that occasionally elements from the building's storied past resurface, sometime in terrifying ways.

Tales of a ghost inside the old building began circulating back when it was still known as the Grand Crystal Palace. People began talking about seeing a man dressed in an old-fashioned black suit, cape, and hat who wandered around the audience area. Playwright Molly Louise Shepard shared several of her ghostly encounters in the Grand Crystal Palace with author Mitchel Whitington. One day, she was in her dressing room when suddenly all the dressing table lights exploded. Another time, she was sitting alone in her dressing room when a hair dryer flew across the room, just as if someone had picked it up and thrown it.

The identity of the Dark Man, as the specter is called, is unknown. However, many people believe he is the spirit of one of several workers who were killed during the construction of the building. The music entertainment offered at the Lizard Lounge today is a far cry from the acts that once walked the stage of the Grand Crystal Palace. Some people believe, however, that the Dark Man—whoever he was—cannot resist the temptation to put on a performance of his own once in a while.

The Lady of White Rock Lake

The Lady of White Rock Lake is a Texas version of the Vanishing Hitchhiker story, versions of which can be found all over the world. White Rock Lake was initially formed in the early twentieth century as a reservoir to supply water to the city of Dallas. After it was no longer the primary water source for the area, it became a recreational lake. Even as far back as World War I, people began building vacation cabins along the lakeshore to escape the hustle and bustle of city life. Between 1930 and 1960, White Rock Lake was known as "The People's Playground" because thousands of Dallas residents flocked to the lake every summer for boating and fishing. Although swimming has been banned here for many years, young couples still drive out to the lake for an evening of necking along its shores—and for the possibility of seeing the ghostly Lady of White Rock Lake.

The story of the Lady of White Rock Lake exists today in several different forms. In one version, a girl standing along the roadside flagged down a passing driver and informed him that she had an automobile accident and needed a ride home. The young man driving the car noticed immediately that the 1920s-era evening dress she was wearing was soaking wet. He drove the car to the address she gave him, but when he arrived, he noticed that the girl who was sitting next to him was gone. The only evidence that she had even been in his car was the water pooled on the car seat. He knocked on the door of the house and was told by the woman living there that he was one of many drivers who picked up the ghost of her dead daughter, who had fallen out of a boat and drowned in the lake years before. One variant of the tale ends with the young man driving to the street address the girl gave him, only to find that there was nothing there but a dilapidated old house. The female specter is also said to have appeared to young couples necking in cars along deserted roads.

Another verson of the tale says that a bootlegger and his girlfriend were partying on a boat in the middle of the lake in the 1920s when they began arguing. After the boat docked, the intoxicated woman ran to the bootlegger's car, started the engine, and drove away at a high rate of speed. She lost control of the car at the intersection of Lawther Drive and Garland Road and plunged into the lake.

In yet another version of the story, a local physician named Dr. Eckersall was driving along White Rock Lake after spending the day at the golf course when he spied a beautiful young girl standing by the road in a sheer evening gown. She told him that her car broke down and she would appreciate a lift to her house, which was only five miles down the road. The doctor agreed to take her to the address she gave him, but when he pulled in the drive, he was surprised to find that the girl sitting in the backseat was gone and the house was shuttered up. Thinking that the girl might have rolled onto the floor, he opened the back door and found nothing but a pool of water on the backseat.

The first version of the Lady of White Rock Lake story appeared in Anne Clark's published account in 1943. In her telling, a young couple picked up the girl, who climbed into the rumble seat. When they drove to her house, the girl's father answered the door. In another account published in 1953, Frank X. Tolbert wrote that Mr. and Mrs. Guy Malloy, who created window displays for Neiman-Marcus, picked up a young lady who was wearing clothes she purchased at their store. When the Malloys drove to her home, her father told them she would never wear anything other than clothes from Neiman-Marcus. The story of the Lady of White Rock Lake gained popularity when it was published in the local newspaper in the 1960s. In fact, a bluegrass group named Country Gentlemen based their 1965 song "Bringing Mary Home" on the legend.

The multiple versions of the Lady of White Rock Lake suggest that this story is probably nothing more than an urban legend, even though some of the older residents living by the lake swear that it's true. Even today a number of individuals have tried to make contact with the spirit of the Lady of White Rock Lake. One Halloween night, a local television station brought a psychic to the lake in an attempt to make contact with the ghost. In 1998, the Southwest Ghost Hunters Association drove to White Rock Lake's eastern perimeter and took a number of EMF readings. The spikes in their readings that occurred around the docks presented the possibility that White Rock Lake might be haunted by more than one ghost—possibly the spirits of two women who committed suicide there in 1935 and 1942.

The Hotel Lawrence

The Hotel Lawrence was built in 1925 by George Scott at 302 South Houston Street, located near Union Station to provide accommodations for passengers who had just gotten off the trains. Originally called the Scott Hotel, it went through several name changes over the years. Today the hotel is still ideally located for guests interested in seeing the local sights. It is also a favorite with people fascinated by ghost stories.

The Hotel Lawrence is said to be haunted by a woman who was staying in the tenth-floor suite in the 1940s. Legend has it that one day, the despondent woman climbed on top of the balcony railing and leaped to her death. Since then, guests and staff have reported hearing disembodied footsteps and the voice of a woman conversing with someone. The most common spectral sound is the clicking of high heels down the tenth-floor hallway and in the lobby. People walking down this hallway occasionally encounter a drastic drop in temperature. Members of the housekeeping staff have seen laundry carts move by themselves.

The Texas Haunted Society detected the presence of a ghost in Room 807. A man named "Smiley" Jackson had just taken a shower in Room 807 when someone—or something—pulled off the towel he had wrapped around his waist. A number of people who have unlocked the door to this room and tried to open it felt as if someone were on the other side pulling on the doorknob, thereby preventing them from entering the room. According to Donna Allen, a man named Brookshire had his throat cut in this room. No one knows for sure whether it is this man's spirit haunting Room 807.

In *A Ghost in the Guest Room*, Olyve Hallmark Abbott tells the story of a woman and her husband who were staying in a room next to the elevator. The woman was having trouble falling asleep because of a strange sound that was coming from the elevator. At first she thought it was the faint howling of a dog or puppy. Her curiosity got the best of her, so she put on her robe and walked out into the hallway. As the elevator moved down to her floor, the sound became louder. Now that she was closer to the source of the sound, she believed it sounded more like the moaning or crying of a human being. When the elevator reached her floor, the door opened. She peered inside and was shocked to find that it was empty. Suddenly, she felt very cold. After returning to her room, the woman told her husband about her strange experience, but he insisted that she had probably been dreaming.

According to Sally Anne Lewis, a casino operated on the second floor of the Lawrence in the 1920s and 1930s. Staff members believe that the ghost of a gambler who lost all his money playing poker still wanders the hallways on this floor. They say that this mustachioed man is wearing a coat, vest, black top hat, and gold watch, and he carries a deck of cards in his hand. When he realizes that he is being watched, he holds up the deck of cards, smiles, and vanishes.

The ghosts reportedly haunting the Hotel Lawrence belong to two different categories. The activity of the apparition haunting Room 807 is an example of what paranormal specialists call an "intelligent haunting," because he interacts with the living. On the other hand, the manifestations of the suicidal woman are what Troy Taylor refers to in *The Ghost Hunter's Handbook* as a "residual haunting." He compares this type of haunting to a loop of film that replays periodically when the spiritual energy is activated. Both types of hauntings may make a night's stay at the Hotel Lawrence an unforgettable experience.

The Stoneleigh Hotel

Around the time that the Stoneleigh Court Apartments opened in 1923, Dallas had become one of the state's financial hubs, and the eleven-story hotel catered to wealthy Texans. The hotel fell upon hard times after the 1929 stock market crash, and its owners soon declared bankruptcy. It subsequently passed through the hands of a variety of owners, until in 2008, it was renovated and reopened as the Stoneleigh Hotel and Spa. Today the boutique hotel offers guests a full-service spa, a signature restaurant, an elegant penthouse—and at least one ghost.

A special room where high-stakes poker games were held is said to be one of the most haunted parts of the Stoneleigh Hotel. Legend has it that oil tycoons, politicians, television and movie stars, and a number of other celebrities won and lost fortunes in these games. A hidden staircase provided a quick and easy exit for card players who wanted to keep their gambling secret. Guests and employees of the hotel claim that some of these poker games have never ended. People have heard the spectral voices of invisible players seated around a card table, raising the stakes and folding.

Most of the paranormal activity at the Stoneleigh Hotel centers around a lounge area called the Bolla Bar, where moguls and movie stars whiled away the time. Sonny Skrakowski had a number of strange experiences during his four-year stint as a bartender in the hotel, especially on dark and stormy nights. One night during a thunderstorm, one of the ashtrays that were stacked on the bar flew across the room and struck a stack of glasses. Sonny asked the two men sitting at the bar if one of them had thrown the ashtray, but they said no.

After the hotel's renovation, the director of marketing, Kate Neu, was given the task of rearranging the photographs on one wall of the Bolla Bar. To complete the design she had in mind, she needed five more photos. She was unable to find any more pictures, so she added five silhouettes of herself, all of which were facing left. The next morning, one of the bartenders asked Kate why the silhouettes were now facing right. No one could have tampered with the silhouettes because the frames were anchored to the wall—no one human, that is.

Other parts of the hotel are said to be haunted as well. Sonny says that a number of guests have called down to the front desk, claiming that a strange man was standing in their room. Several security guards who were sent to the room saw a ghostly figure walk down the hallway and vanish. Robert Stahl, a reporter for the *Dallas Examiner*, reported that one night, a young woman was in the office making copies of a letter describing the upcoming renovations of the hotel when the photocopier stopped printing. The girl replaced the paper and proceeded to make the rest of her copies. At the exact moment when the copier stopped a second time, the office door slammed and the plug was yanked out of the copier by an unseen hand. The terrified girl turned the doorknob to the office, but she was locked in. Her piercing screams caught the attention of a janitor, who quickly came to her assistance.

No one knows for sure if anyone has actually died in the Stoneleigh Hotel. However, rumors of deaths in the hotel are revived whenever lights flicker off and on in the rooms or the elevator goes up and down by itself. The hotel's secret doors and gloomy hallways certainly lend an air of mystery that might make it particularly appealing to wandering spirits in the neighborhood.

Fort Worth

The White Elephant Saloon

Fort Worth came into being in 1849 when troops under the command of Maj. Ripley Arnold were ordered to protect the settlers in the area. It became a real town in 1853 after the fort was abandoned. Before long, the frontier town became a favorite stop for cowboys driving their longhorn cattle through Texas. By the late 1870s, thousands of cattlemen were letting off steam in Fort Worth's bordellos, gambling parlors, and saloons. The most famous of the town's watering holes was the White Elephant Saloon, which started out as a small restaurant owned and operated by F. A. Borodino on the 200 block of Main Street. The food prepared at the restaurant was subpar, however, so the business was converted into a saloon and billiards parlor by Gabriel Burgower. Because the food was short-order fare, the White Elephant became known as a "working man's saloon." It later became a "gentleman's saloon" when it began offering first-class food and a private clubroom for invitation-only poker games and private parties.

Late in 1885, Burgower sold the saloon to John Ward, who ran a tobacconist's shop just inside the front door of the saloon, and his brother, Bill. The brothers completely refurbished the saloon in an attempt to turn it into a haven for high rollers. On opening day, Bill Ward threw the key into the street, a gesture indicating that the establishment would never close. He then set about enhancing the saloon's reputation by screening its customers. He also set up a cigar factory in the rear of the building and turned the upstairs into an upscale casino with public and private rooms. As the business thrived, Bill Ward became a key player in Fort Worth's political scene.

By the late 1880s, Ward's business had expanded to the point that he decided to form a partnership with a former cattleman named Jake G. Johnson and a gentleman gambler named Luke Short, who had arrived in Fort Worth in 1883. Ward not only made Luke one-third owner in the saloon, but also gave him living space in a two-room apartment. Short introduced the game of keno to the saloon, thereby attracting a higher-class clientele. Soon card sharks like Bat Masterson and Wyatt Earp were flocking to the saloon. On February 8, 1887, an incident took place that forever linked the White Elephant Saloon with the violent history of the Old West. A former marshal in Fort Worth known as "Long-Haired Jim" Courtright staggered into the foyer, obviously intoxicated. He called Luke Short out into the street because he wanted to talk to him. The two men began exchanging harsh words on the boardwalk. Suddenly gunfire erupted, and Courtright lay dying in the doorway of a shooting gallery next door to the saloon.

Short later formed a partnership with Johnson in the Palm Royal Saloon, leaving Bill Ward as the sole owner of the White Elephant. In the mid-1890s, the saloon moved to a more spacious building at 604-610 Main Street. The downstairs was reserved for walk-in business, while the upstairs was converted into clubrooms. A telegraph hookup brought in reports of horse races, ball games, and prizefights from all over the country. Even though the White Elephant was still a saloon, it earned a reputation as a comparatively clean establishment, largely because prostitutes were banned from the premises. However, stabbings and fistfights did occur here on a fairly regular basis.

After local businessman Joseph G. Wheat opened a restaurant club at 800 Main Street, Bill Ward gave the White House Saloon a facelift and held a reopening featuring luminaries such as boxers James J. Corbett and John L. Sullivan. In the early twentieth century, a new Sunday closing law restricted the hours of operation for saloons, which were rapidly becoming a thing of the past. The White Elephant saloon operated briefly as a chili parlor but finally closed in 1912, reopening a short time later as a pool hall. After the pool hall closed, a number of other businesses occupied the building for the next sixty years, during which time the original building was destroyed by fire and replaced by the present building. In 1976, a new White Elephant Saloon opened on Fort Worth's historic North Side, two miles from the saloon's original location. Between 1993 and 2001, the saloon was used in the television series *Walker, Texas Ranger*. Apparently, though, the spirits of one of the real cowboys who whiled away the hours in the original White Horse Saloon is still there.

Paula Gowins, the manager of Miss Molly's Bed and Breakfast, had an eerie encounter one night in 2010 while watching a performance on the stage of the White Elephant Saloon. "I was sitting at a table, listening to a band," she said. "During intermission, the man who owns a tattoo parlor down the street was talking to a member of the band, and I took their picture. When I looked at the picture later on, I noticed the transparent figure of a slim man standing behind the man who owns the tattoo parlor. I showed the picture to the two guys in the band, and they said they were sure there were the only two people on the stage at the time."

The owners of the White Elephant Saloon take great pride in its cowboy past. More than a hundred sweat-stained cowboy hats that once belonged to the nation's greatest rodeo stars hang from the walls. Every February 8, Fort Worth's most famous gunfight is reenacted in front of the White Elephant. Sometimes, though, a remnant of the Old West may make a guest appearance at the old saloon.

Miss Molly's Bed and Breakfast

Around the turn of the nineteenth century, Fort Worth was completely transformed by the coming of the railroad. Buying and selling cattle took place at designated towns along the railroad, like Fort Worth. No longer did cowboys have to drive herds of cattle to market. In the early 1900s, Fort Worth had thirty-seven saloons, seventeen blacksmith shops, twenty-four wagon yards, six hide dealers, and seven barbers. In 1910, an imposing boardinghouse was constructed just a block west of the old Fort Worth Stockyards to accommodate the stream of cattle buyers and cowboys who poured into what had become one of the state's primary cattle hubs. The following decade, the proprietor, Amelia Elmer, tried to imbue the hotel with an air of glamour by changing its name to the Palace Rooms. Before long, however, the boardinghouse was converted into a speakeasy called the Oasis. By the 1940s, the once-proud hostelry had become a bordello. Operating under the name the Gayattee Hotel, the bordello's primary clientele consisted of cowboys, cattle buyers and sellers, and a host of unsavory characters. The brothel was operated by an enterprising woman named "Miss Josie" King.

The bordello lasted through Prohibition and World War II but was finally closed in the 1950s, and the building was turned into a boardinghouse once again. In the 1980s, the building was extensively renovated, and it was reopened as Miss Molly's Bed and Breakfast. Today the Star Café occupies the first floor, and the B&B takes up the second floor. Each of the eight guest rooms has its own western theme— and, according to some paranormal investigators, its own ghosts as well.

The testimony of the staff and visitors suggests that Miss Molly's is one of the most haunted sites in Fort Worth. They say that the spirits enjoy tormenting visitors by moving objects from one location to another. Guests occasionally encounter cold spots while walking across their rooms or down the hallway. Ghosts have been blamed for lights turning off and on and toilets flushing on their own. At night, moans, cries, and disembodied footsteps echo through the darkened hallway. One maid quit her job after finding coins in a room she had just cleaned. Not that she minded receiving tips, just so long as the tipper was alive. A guest complained of being unable to open an unlocked door, which seemed to have someone—or something— pushing from the other side. Many people have detected the pungent odor of perfume in some of the rooms.

Two types of full-bodied apparitions have been reported inside Miss Molly's. One is the ghost of a little girl who has been seen in Rooms 8 and 9. Most of the sightings, however, seem to be the spirits of some of the "fallen women" who plied their trade in the Gayattee Hotel. A male guest sleeping in one of the rooms was awakened by the nagging feeling that someone else was in the room. When he opened his eyes, he saw an attractive blond woman sitting on the edge of his bed. On another occasion, an Englishman woke up to find an elderly lady sitting on the edge of his bed. The next morning, he told the desk clerk about her, saying that she was wearing an old-fashioned dress and a bonnet. Guests have also sensed that they are in the presence of the spirits of prostitutes when the distinct odor of perfume wafts through the rooms.

Paula Gowins has had a number of paranormal experiences inside the hotel since becoming manager in 2007. Her first encounter with the ghosts of the old building occurred during her first night in the hotel. "I heard someone call my name," Paula said. "That was kind of creepy, so I thought, 'Oh, well. This is a new place with new noises, and it's down here in the Stockyards, where it's pretty noisy.' I dismissed a lot of it in the beginning because I thought it was just my imagination. I continued hearing voices after a while, and I was getting really concerned that I was losing my mind. I didn't have anyone to talk to about all of the weird stuff that was happening. Doors were opening and closing by themselves, the water was turning off and on, things were moving around during the night. I'd hear things at night and wake up at 4:00 A.M."

Paula's first actual encounter with a ghost in Miss Molly's occurred not long after she moved in. "It was a Monday afternoon, around 1:00 or 2:00 P.M. I came around the corner back there where the laundry room is, and I saw the ghost of a cowboy. He had on a black hat and long, wavy hair. His hair was black and gray. He was wearing a long duster and boots with spurs. He just strolled down the hallway into Room 7. He went in the room, and the door shut and locked. I just stood there with my mouth open and thought, 'How did he get in here?' The doors were locked. I walked over to Room 7 and knocked on the door. I said, 'Hello,' and turned the key. The door opened, and no one was there. That night, I took a big shot of Nyquil because I thought I needed some serious sleep."

When Paula woke up the next morning, she told the ghosts what the boundaries would be: "OK, this here's the deal. I don't want to see you. You stay out of my room, and don't you dare touch me. Then we'll get along just fine." She then tried to resume her normal routines. "I was doing the laundry and went around the corner again at 1:00 or 2:00 in the afternoon. Once again, I saw the same ghost in the same room. I stopped in my tracks and hollered, 'Hey!' at him. He just kept walking. He went into Room 7 and shut the door. He locked it too. I became infuriated because I was being frightened. I went over to the room and unlocked the door. I flung it open, and the cowboy wasn't there, just like before. This time, the overhead light and lamp were on. I knew for a fact that the lights hadn't been on for days."

This was a turning point for Paula because at that moment, she knew that she was not insane. "I called up a girlfriend who had had a near-death experience and asked her to come over here. She walked around here and told me that she felt a presence here." After a few more sleepless nights, Paula contacted psychics and mediums to see if they could answer her questions about the ghostly cowboy. One of the psychics revealed the spirit's identity. "I found out that his name is Jake and that he used to live in the room that he always walked into. He died of natural causes. Once I found that out, I was OK. He just comes and goes. He doesn't really bother anybody. I still hear him walking around now and then."

One of Paula's most frightening experiences occurred in July 2011. "One night around midnight, there were about four or five of us, out here in the parlor talking. Guests had been staying in all of these rooms, but they had all checked out. The five of us had been talking since 5:00 P.M. All of a sudden, the door to Room 7 slammed. These doors don't slam. They have these vacuum arms that keep the doors open. Everyone heard it, but no one saw the door slam. We all agreed that it was the door to Room 7. The other ladies looked to me for answers, so I told them about all of the crazy things that had been happening to me. About a minute later, the door to Room 4 began shaking. I was sure that Room 4 had been locked. The ladies ran over to Room 4 and just stood there, watching the doorknob shake. I had to laugh because they had never experienced this sort of stuff before. These ladies had been to other so-called haunted places where nothing ever happened. I'll admit that I was really scared too."

Some of Paula's guests have booked rooms in Miss Molly's for the express purpose of making contact with the ghosts. One of these amateur ghost hunters was spending the night in the Cowboy Room. "She had put a trash bag down before she went to bed and sprinkled baby powder on it. The next morning, when she got up, there were little boot prints on the bag. They looked like the prints of a Victorian boot with pointed toes, about the size of a little girl's foot. The footprints led to the door to the connecting room. They continued on the other side of the door to another lady's room. Neither of the ladies knew each other."

Other things have happened in Miss Molly's that reflect the playful side of one of the ghosts. "A lady in Room 6 took off her necklace and placed it on the nightstand and went to sleep. The next morning, she couldn't find her necklace. She told me about the missing necklace, so my girlfriend and I went into the room and looked around. I picked up an antique pitcher and found the necklace in the bowl underneath. On another night, a lady woke up in the same room to find her ring missing. I looked under the pitcher, and there it was." Two of Paula's guests have caught a glimpse of the mischievous ghost in Room 6. "In the middle of the night, a woman in a Victorian dress walked through the closed door. She opened the closet door and stood there like she was trying to pick out a dress to wear. Then she shut the closet door and walked through the door to the room. Two of my female friends described the ghost the same way."

Once Paula became accustomed to all the strange activity in the building, she adopted the attitude that the weirdness was funny, especially when it happened to other people. "A young couple was staying in Miss Josie's Room—the madam's quarters," Paula said. "At 3:00 A.M., there were three ladies sitting in the parlor, waiting for something to happen. Suddenly this young couple came running out of the room, screaming. The ladies in the parlor asked them, 'What's wrong?' The couple said, 'There's a ghost in there!' The three ladies got up and went in the room, and then came running out screaming too. All that screaming woke me up, so I got out of the bed and went out into the parlor and said, 'What's going on?' I'd thought maybe someone was sick. They all said, 'There's a ghost in there,' and I replied, 'Is that all?'"

It seems that Jake and Josie are not the only ghosts in the bed-and-breakfast. "There's a male and a female ghost, and a couple of children too," Paula says. Sometimes she can tell which spirits are present by the ghostly smells in the building. "There are lots of cold spots and odors," Paula said. "I smell perfume and cigars now and then. Some of the odors are kind of funky." Some of the ghosts seem to enjoy partying late at night. "Sometimes I wake up at 4:00 A.M., two hours after all in the bars in town have closed. It's really a ghost town at 4:00 A.M., but sometimes I hear partying coming from Jake's room. I walk over to the door, and I don't hear the sounds anymore."

Miss Molly's ghost stories have received so much national attention in recent years that a number of paranormal groups have expressed interest in conducting investigations there. "TAPS has been here," Paula said, referring to the group from SyFy's *Ghost Hunters*.

"We've been on the Travel Channel a couple of times, the Discovery Channel, PBS, and Channel 5. In 2008, a psychic working with the Texas Paranormal Advanced Research Team claimed to have been struck in the chest so hard by an unseen assailant that his lungs ached. Several members of the group who were investigating Room 4 felt someone touch their arms and cheeks. Another member felt long, feminine fingers stroking his hair and leg. Apparently some of the working girls in the old bordello do not know when it is time to quit."

Paula explained that not all the TV shows come here for the ghosts. "Some of them are interested in the history of the place. For a while, I had to turn down all these paranormal groups because so many of them wanted to come. It's kind of calmed down now, though. It goes in phases. Sometimes we're bombarded with ghost hunters, and then it drops off."

A couple of the groups of paranormal investigators told Paula that they could "cleanse" the old hotel. She turned down their offers for fear that removing the ghosts would ruin business. "I don't want to get rid of those things," Paula said. "I just don't want anything in here that's harmful to me or my guests. Everything else can stay—the prankster stuff, the voices, the apparitions, like the guy I saw."

The Texas White House

The Texas White House was originally built in 1910 by a man named Bishop as a residence for his son. However, his son chose not to live there, and Bishop sold the house to Mr. and Mrs. William B. Newkirk, who raised their four sons there and remained in the house for their entire lives. Over the decades after they passed away, several different businesses operated in the old house, including a restaurant called the Texas White House. In 1994, Grover and Jamie McMains bought the house and converted it into a bed-and-breakfast filled with modern amenities, but part of the past persists—a particularly annoying part.

Most of the paranormal activity reported in the Texas White House takes place in the Lone Star Room, which was William Newkirk's room while he was alive. Grover McMains said that three women have had encounters while staying in the room alone. One was sound asleep when she was awakened by feeling someone's back pressed against hers. Petrified, she lay perfectly still while her unwelcome bedmate started to crawl out of bed. Within a few seconds, the lady mustered up the courage to roll over to see who was in bed with her, but the intruder was gone. Another woman sleeping in the Lone Star Room had a similar experience of being awakened when she felt someone get into bed with her. She quickly turned over to see who was there, but she too found that she was all alone. Just a few seconds later, her cell phone began beeping, which it had never done before.

The third encounter occurred in 2009, when a woman who had booked the Lone Star Room returned to the hotel in the evening after a day of shopping. While she was getting settled, she felt the presence of someone standing in the corner of the room. She did not see anyone there, so she went to bed. That night, she felt someone lying in bed with her, but when she turned on the light, she discovered that she was all alone. The next morning, she told Grover that she had shared the room with a "friendly presence." Her eyes grew wide as the innkeeper informed her of the two other women who had had ghostly experiences in the same room.

Guestbooks on the nightstand in another of the bed-and-breakfast's haunted rooms, the Texas Room, are full of stories of visitations and strange occurrences. In February 1997, a woman who had just awakened from a restful night's sleep discovered that the crystal on her watch face was shattered. The watch remained sitting on the nightstand, right where she had left it. The next night, the ceiling fan started turning on its own—there was no air was coming from the vents that could have moved the blades, and the windows were shut. Another woman who stayed at the hotel in September of 2008 said that she was awakened at 3 A.M. by the feeling that something was lifting the covers off her feet.

Most people believe that the ghost in the Texas White House is the spirit of William B. Newkirk. Perhaps he is laying claim to the room where he lived and died. One cannot rule out the possibility, however, that Mr. Newkirk simply craves female companionship.

Grover McMains suspected that something odd was going on in the house after the two women's reports of a ghostly presence climbing into bed with them during the night. However, none of the guests who have had a paranormal experience in the old house has been terrified. "No one has ever been so frightened that they left," McMains said. "It's just the opposite. No one has ever asked to change rooms. They're thrilled if they see the ghost."

McMains said that his wife, Jamie, has also sensed that they are sharing their old house with a ghost: "One time when I was gone, she made the bed [in the Texas Room], and when she came back in, it looked like someone had sat on the bad. She didn't even think about it. She just figured that she hadn't done her job very well, so she went back in and straightened out the bed. Later, when people started telling her stories about things that had happened to them in that room, Jamie remembered that experience."

McMains himself had made contact with the spirit in the house just before this writer interviewed him in July 2011: "Three times this week, I heard someone moving around the house," McMains said in the interview. "I assumed that it was my wife because no guests were staying there at the time. [The first time this happened], I got up from my chair and tried to find her, but she wasn't there. I thought she'd gotten up from her nap and gotten a drink of water and gone out. I walked outside to see if she was out in the yard, but she wasn't there. I went upstairs, and she wasn't there. Finally, I found her in bed, taking a nap. Maybe the ghost is picking up on her habits."

McMains does not mind the publicity the Texas White House has received over the years because of the ghost stories. Like many innkeepers, McMains has discovered that ghosts are good for business. Many of the accounts in the guestbook in the Texas Room are written by people who booked that particular room in the hope of encountering a ghost. Ghost-hunting groups also drop by on a regular basis. "I told the ghost stories to some of my friends who ran bed-and-breakfasts, and they said I shouldn't publicize them because ghosts would be bad for business," Grover said. "Actually, it hasn't been a negative at all. I've been very pleased with my guests' reaction to the ghost stories."

Thistle Hill

Behind the construction of the one of the most magnificent mansions in Fort Worth is the story of a man's love for his family. According to one version, in 1904, William T. Waggoner had the house built for his daughter, Electra, to keep her from moving to Philadelphia with her new husband, Albert Buckman Wharton Jr. In another variant of the story, Waggoner promised Electra that he would build a house to her specifications if she helped him raise her brothers and sisters, as their mother had just died. After her siblings were old enough to leave home, she married Wharton in 1902. Two years later, Electra and Albert moved into the palatial home that her father had built for her on Summit Avenue in the fashionable residential district known as Quality Hill. Over the next few years, Wharton ran the Fort Worth Auto and Livery Stable. Electra and her husband moved to a ranch in 1910 and put their home, known as Thistle Hill, up for sale.

In 1911, the Whartons sold Thistle Hill to Mr. and Mrs. Winfield Scott, who had been friends of Electra's parents. Mr. Scott died before he had a chance to take up residence in his new home, but his wife, Elizabeth, and their son, Winfield Jr., moved in a year later. Elizabeth Scott lived at Thistle Hill for the next twenty-six years. During this time, she honed her skills as both a landscape artist and a hostess. After Elizabeth died, her son found himself low on funds and sold the mansion to the Girls Service League in 1940. In 1968, the league put the house up for sale, but it stood empty until a group of concerned citizens formed a preservation society and raised enough money to buy Thistle Hill in 1976. For years, the organization ran Thistle Hill as a tour home and a venue for special events such as receptions and weddings. In 2005, the house and property were gifted to Historic Fort Worth.

Rumors that Thistle Hill is haunted have been swirling around Fort Worth for decades. Many people claim to have seen the ghost of Electra on the second floor. In the mid-1980s, a bridesmaid at a wedding being held on the first floor of the old house had an eerie experience. Just before the ceremony began, the bride realized that she had left her veil in the upstairs dressing room, and one of the bridesmaids ran upstairs to fetch it for her. As she hurried down the hallway, she happened to look into a parlor room to the right of bridal dressing room.

A woman wearing a Victorian-era dress stepped out of the parlor door and nodded her head. The apparition then proceeded to walk down the hall toward the staircase. The bridesmaid assumed that the woman had been hired by the parents of the bride to add a period flavor the wedding. After the ceremony, the bridesmaid asked the proprietor of house about the woman dressed in the early-1900s gown. The proprietor stared at the girl for a few seconds before replying that she must have seen Electra's ghost, because no one matching that description was in the house at the time.

Since that first encounter, a number of people have seen a woman in white on the staircase. Some have also reported seeing a man with a black handlebar mustache standing at the top of the stairs. *Ghosts of North Texas* reports on an investigation conducted by a paranormal group at Thistle Hill in 1989. The director of the group, Andy Greiser, said that when the members started their investigation, an antique rocking chair and other pieces of furniture were covered in protective plastic sheets. A couple hours later, however, they were surprised to discover that the plastic had been removed from the rocking chair. At 5 A.M., just before they wrapped up their investigation, everyone was standing in the ballroom when they heard the rocking chair creaking. The mysterious behavior of the rocking chair was not the only possible paranormal activity observed by Greiser's group that evening. Earlier in the evening, Greiser had left a flashlight and an envelope containing newspaper clippings on a table downstairs. A few hours later, the objects had been moved to the billiards room, but none of the members had touched the envelope or flashlight.

Despite the growing number of reported sightings at Thistle Hill, most of the staff members deny that the house is haunted. Admittedly, some people still avoid places that are reputed to be haunted. These days, however, more and more museum homes are finding that publicizing their ghostly activity can be good for business.

The Stockyards Hotel

The idea for constructing a lavish hotel in Fort Worth's Stockyards District was conceived in the mind of Col. T. M Thannisch, one of the city's pioneering businessmen, who initially constructed a two-story frame building in 1904 on the corner of North Main and East Exchange Streets. In the early years, the building housed a saloon and billiard parlor, barber shop, confectionary shop, restaurant, and real estate and insurance firms. A few years later, Thannisch built a three-story brick hotel on the eastern side of the property. The new Chandler Hotel had a restaurant and bar, guest rooms on the second and third floors, and physicians' offices on the street level. In 1913, Colonel Thannisch demolished the wooden structure and built a brick addition to the hotel in its place. Over the years, the hotel underwent several changes in ownership and names, and today it is known as the Stockyards Hotel. Located in the heart of the Stockyards National Historic District, the hotel preserves the splendor that has attracted guests like Willie Nelson, Garth Brooks, and an assortment of cowboys and cattle barons. Legend has it, however, that some of the hotel's most illustrious guests never checked out.

Bonnie and Clyde stayed in the hotel in 1933, and their ghosts are said to haunt Room 305. Each year, hundreds of guests visit the "Bonnie and Clyde Room" to gaze at an amazing collection of memorabilia from this infamous couple—and a few guests say that they have encountered the outlaws themselves. One morning at 5 A.M., a guest reported feeling an invisible presence climb into bed. The terrified guest jumped out of bed, got dressed, and checked out. A number of remarkable EVPs have been recorded in Room 305, and a faucet in the bathroom is said to sometimes turn on by itself.

Another of the hotel's seemingly permanent residents is believed to be the ghost of a cowboy who was killed in a gunfight in front of the hotel in 1910. Apparently this cowboy's spirit, whom the staff members have christened as Jesse, has taken a liking to the Stockyards Hotel. The cowboy's full-bodied apparition has been seen wandering up and down the hallways on the second and third floors, on the staircase leading to the second floor, and in the indoor–outdoor banquet area called the Marine Creek Terrace. Some guests reported hearing the jingling of the cowboy's spurs in the hallways.

Room 214 is also thought to be haunted. Guests have complained about feeling unusually cold at specific spots in the room. One guest told management that she was trying to sleep when she heard footsteps pacing back and forth outside her room. The footsteps stopped, but then a few minutes later she heard them again—this time inside her room.

In *Ghosts of North Texas*, Mitchel Whitington tells the story of a former employee named Jake, who worked at the hotel for twenty years. As the hotel "houseman," Jake's job was to knock on the doors of the guest rooms and deliver messages. The ghost of the former houseman has been credited with a number of strange occurrences at the Stockyards Hotel. For example, desk clerks have reported receiving mysterious phone calls from an unknown extension late into the night. Jake is also said to take the elevator up and down at odd hours. In 2010, two sisters were using the telephones behind the elevator when the floor started to shake. At first the girls thought that the hotel was being rocked by an earthquake. When they reported the incident to the desk clerk, he told them about Jake the houseman, who frequently rode the elevator as he delivered messages to the guests.

The Stockyards Hotel is still the premier hotel within the Stockyards area. It is walking distance from a number of historic saloons, such as the White Elephant, Booger Red's Saloon, and Billy Bob's Texas Saloon. Inside the Stockyards Hotel, one can find suites named after some of the outlaws who might have spent the night in the hotel after a hard night's drinking in the local watering holes. And according to some of the witnesses to paranormal activity, a few of these old Western types might still be making themselves right at home at the Stockyards Hotel.

The W. E. Scott Theatre

The W. E. Scott Theatre at 1300 Gendy Street is known as one of the best public events theaters in the entire state. Since its construction in 1966, financed by a trust left by its namesake, William Edrington Scott, the theater has hosted concerts, plays—and an occasional public appearance by an apparently stage-struck ghost.

The night cleaning crew has identified the ghost as the spirit of Ken Yandell, said to have been either a young actor or a lighting designer who hanged himself from a pipe in the basement. Many people have seen a shadowy figure stride across the stage when no one else was present. Some have heard the echoes of disembodied footsteps in the stairwells just off the stage or on the stage itself. In one well-publicized account, a wardrobe woman was standing near the stage late one night when she heard weird laughter. She was so certain she was the only living person in the theater that night that she dashed out the front door and never returned.

Late one afternoon, a female employee was walking past the janitor's office when she noticed that the tap was turned on in the sink. She turned off the water and was shocked to see the tap slowly turn itself back on. Terrified, she fled the area and returned a few minutes later with another employee, who also witnessed the tap turning itself on. A male employee who heard the commotion in the janitor's closet walked into the room and exclaimed, "OK, Kenny! Cut it out." The water immediately stopped flowing out of the faucet.

Ken's mischievous spirit sometimes ventures into the costume shop as well. Employees have seen objects falling off a shelf for no apparent reason, looking as if they had been swept off the shelf by an invisible hand. On one occasion, several young women who had been working inside the costume shop left for a few minutes. When they returned, they were surprised to see wet footprints leading in and out of the doorway.

On July 22, 2006, the Stockyards Paranormal Investigation team conducted an investigation of the W. E. Scott Theatre. Several members of the group started investigating the "dungeon" area under the stage where Ken is said to have killed himself. One of the investigators was walking around with dowsing rods when suddenly the rods crossed themselves. During the night, the group collected a number of interesting EVPs, including a voice saying, "Let me out of here," and several popping and clicking sounds in the dressing room. In the Green Room, the group recorded a spectral voice saying, "It's cold again." If Ken Yandell's spirit did indeed make his presence known that night, it would seem that he is not particularly happy to be wandering around the theatre.

The Jett Building

Built in 1902, the Jett Building at 400 Main Street was originally the home of the Northern Texas Traction company office, and the first "inner city" rail line, connecting Fort Worth and Dallas, was operated from this building. Over the succeeding years, the building's occupants included a candy company and a tile company. In the 1940s, the U.S. Sandwich Shop served lunch from the Jett Building. Legend has it that during this time, two women were taken to an upstairs room and murdered. Some people say that the stains in a sink in the bathroom upstairs are residue from the killer's attempt to wash the blood from his hands and clothing. However, no factual evidence can be found in newspapers or court records to corroborate this story.

The Jett Building stood vacant for a while in the late 1970s but was home to four different restaurants over the following decade. During this period, artist Richard Haas painted a mural called "The Chisholm Trail" on the building to commemorate the cattle drives of the 1800s. The managers of one of the restaurants, Mi Cochina's, told Robert and Anne Powell Wlodarski, authors of *A Texas Guide to Haunted Restaurants, Taverns and Inns*, a number of stories about supernatural phenomena in the Jett Building. Employees reported hearing a woman walking in high heels upstairs. Sometimes people experienced drastic drops in temperature when they passed through a specific section of the building. Frozen-drink machines were said to turn on by themselves. Women who entered the powder room reported hearing the bone-chilling laughter of a woman. One night, the owner gave a woman permission to tour the third floor. After she returned to the first floor, she informed him that she had enjoyed the view of Main Street from one of the windows on the third floor. With a look of confusion on his face, he informed her that there was no view of Main Street from the third floor, because the windows had been boarded up.

In *Ghosts of Fort Worth*, Brian Righi says that a bartender was closing up one Halloween night when he looked up at the mirror and saw the image of a woman standing behind him. When he turned around, she was gone. In 1983, a plumber who was working in the basement quit his job when he saw a spectral woman floating down the stairs. A few months later, a bookstore opened up in the basement of the building. A clerk who was stocking shelves late one night heard music and the sound of a metallic ball rolling around a roulette wheel. He looked through the store but eventually reached the uneasy conclusion that he was the only one there. Other employees claimed to have heard the sound of a child's ball rolling around on the floor. Several mornings, the manager of the bookstore opened the door in the morning and was shocked to find science-fiction books scattered all over the floor.

In 2000, Jamba Juice began operating inside the Jett Building. The manager, Jessica Canavan, said that many customers and employees have witnessed lights turning off and on by themselves. The apparitions of a cowboy with alabaster skin and a transparent woman on the upper floor have also been sighted in Jamba Juice.

Additional evidence that the Jett Building was haunted came to light in 2005, when a construction crew was hired to do some remodeling for the building's new occupant, radio station KEWR-FM. Workers soon discovered that tools they had left in a specific place mysteriously had disappeared when they returned the next morning. Sometimes the workers would find the tools again in an entirely different location. They also reported seeing "shadow people" in dark corners of the building. Most of the workers refused to climb down the stairs to the basement, where people had encountered a large number of strange shadows. After the radio station moved in, the ghost sightings continued. The station's Internet director, Gabriel Arrequin, said that one day, two of his coworkers were walking down the hallway. When they stopped at one of the rooms, the sound of footsteps continued past the doorway that the two young women had just entered. Other employees claimed that ghostly footsteps sometimes walked right into a wall.

As a rule, answers to why a site is haunted are supplied by folklore or history. In the case of the Jett Building, science might be able to provide the answer. The large number of radio and television stations across the country that are said to be haunted suggests that the high levels of radio frequency energy could be either the cause or the catalyst of the paranormal activity. Or the hauntings could be attributed to the fact that many broadcasting stations are housed in old buildings, like the Jett Building—which was considered haunted long before the radio station took up residence.

The Mitchell–Schoonover House

The Mitchell-Schoonover House at 600 Eighth Avenue was built in 1907 by jeweler James E. Mitchell. A friend of the Mitchell family, Charles Simmons, bought the home in 1920. Twenty-five years later, Dr. Simmons gave the house to his daughter and her husband, Dr. Frank Schoonover. The house was sold in 1979 and converted into a savings and loan. Two years later, a group of architects set up their offices inside the old building. The building was home to a number of different businesses in the 1990s, including a doctor's office, a beauty parlor, and an advertising firm. In 1995, the Mitchell-Schoonover House was purchased by attorney Art Brender, who renovated it. Some locals believe the restoration Brender did on the interior of the house might have awakened one or more of the former owners.

No one knows much about the spirit that haunts the Mitchell-Schoonover House except that it seems to be a poltergeist. One occupant of the house said that the spirit enjoyed turning up the thermostat. Another said the ghost turned the water on in the kitchen during the night and turned the chandelier in the main reception room off and on. People have placed objects in one place in the afternoon and found them moved to another location the next morning. On several occasions, people have answered the doorbell and found no one there. A shadowy figure has been seen moving outside the side windows.

In *Phantoms of the Plains*, Docia Schultz Williams writes of the experiences of architect Fred Cauble in the early 1980s. Soon after purchasing the house, Cauble was walking down the basement when he felt icy fingers grasp his shoulder. He expected to see one of his colleagues standing behind him, but when he turned around, no one was there. Cauble said a real estate agent had a similar experience in the basement not long thereafter. The resident ghost showed its helpful side when Cauble was carrying a heavy box upstairs. He was about to set the box down and open the door, but it opened all by itself. While Cauble was doing some remodeling, a softball-size ball of light bounced around the attic.

Most of the people who have worked in the Mitchell-Schoonover House have had experiences that can best be described as disturbing.

Nevertheless, despite the bizarre incidents that have occurred over the years, the old house is not a creepy place to work in. In fact, most of the owners have said that the Mitchell-Schoonover House had the same homey atmosphere as a family home.

Log Cabin Village

In the 1950s, the Pioneer Texas Heritage Committee formed to save some of the nineteenth-century log cabins that were rapidly disappearing from the North Texas countryside. After collecting six log cabins, each representing a different style, the group created a log cabin village at a wooded spot near the Trinity River in Forest Park, where they restored and furnished the cabins. In 1965, the city of Fort Worth took responsibility for the little cluster of cabins, and the following year, Log Cabin Village was opened to the public. The living-history museum has grown over the years, with the acquisition of several other log houses dating from the 1800s, as well the 1870s Marine School and an 1860s smokehouse. It seems that the Pioneer Texas Heritage Committee did such a good job restoring the old cabins that some of the original owners have moved back in.

The most haunted cabin in Log Cabin Village is undoubtedly the Foster Cabin. Built of hand-hewn oak and cedar timbers by slave labor in 1853, this two-story cabin is one of the oldest surviving plantation homes in Texas, as well as one of the state's largest nineteenth-century dogtrot cabins. In its early days, the Foster Cabin was used by tenant farmers, but it was completely abandoned in 1939 and soon fell victim to the ravages of time, weather, and neglect. Eventually the home was dismantled and moved to Log Cabin Village for preservation. Today the Foster Cabin is a house museum and also houses the museum store and staff offices—and apparently one or more ghosts.

Its most well-known ghost is thought to be that of Miss Jane Holt, the widow of a local doctor, who gave medical attention to one of the Fosters' sons after he returned injured from the Civil War. The staff can usually tell when she is around by the smell of lilac perfume, which is strongest in the upstairs room where she treated the son. Ivette Ray, the curator at Log Cabin Village, claims to have smelled the perfume and detected cold spots in the cabin. The creaking of a rocking chair and disembodied footsteps are often heard on the second floor. An employee who works at Parker Cabin said that she was inside the Foster Cabin one day after closing time when she felt someone touch her arms, but all the other park employees had gone home. According to Gary Freeman, who worked in the Marine School, a teenage boy was walking through the Foster Cabin when he felt a presence on the other side of the door. Freeman concluded that the young man was one of those sensitive souls able to sense presences in places where no one else can feel them.

A few staff members have reported seeing a female apparition in the upstairs part of the Foster Cabin, and they all describe her in the same way. She is a middle-aged woman around forty years old, with long dark hair, a long black dress, and a blouse with a high collar. The female specter has appeared downstairs only twice. Most staff members believe that it is the ghost of Jane Holt, primarily because of the special bond she shared with the Foster family, although some think it is the spirit of Martha Foster.

Over the decades the Foster Cabin has been at Log Cabin Village, a number of people, including both employees and visitors, have reported eerie experiences there. A college student named Margaret Shaw worked in a small office in the cabin while she was conducting genealogical research on the village's cabins in the 1970s. In an article published in the *Fort Worth Star-Telegram* on August 21, 1991, Shaw told staff reporter Mary Rogers that she never really felt she was entirely alone in the old cabin: "I felt that if I scooted back from my desk and looked across the hall, someone would be there." She also reported catching glimpses out of the corner of her eye of a long skirt trailing around the door. Shaw's most frightening experience in the Foster Cabin occurred one morning when she discovered that several rolls of microfilm that she had set on her desk the night before had been moved to a different location. Thinking that a burglar may have broken in and ransacked her desk, she checked all the other items on her desk, but nothing else had been disturbed, and the doors and windows were locked.

A woman who claimed to have psychic abilities approached staff member Betty Register one day and said that the ghost of a woman was hanging around one of the upper bedrooms. Register gave the woman permission to return to the cabin the next day and attempt to contact the spirit. Afterward, the woman told Register that she had indeed spoken to the woman's ghost, who told her that she was waiting for her husband to come home.

On October 3, 1992, several groups of students investigated some of the village's cabins, including the Foster Cabin. According to an article by Jeff Gunn, a reporter for the *Fort Worth Star-Telegram* who participated in the investigation, one girl claimed that something was upstairs in the left-hand room with her, and that a pungent odor wafted through the room. Gunn and some of the others immediately followed the distraught young woman into the room. They did not see anything unusual, but they did detect the strong odor of lilacs. Later that night, two students investigating upstairs sensed an invisible entity in the right-hand room. They too smelled lilac perfume. At 3 A.M., a group of boys decided that playing Stephen Foster songs on the electric piano they had brought with them might get the ghost's attention (the legendary songwriter has no connection to the cabin). While the boys were playing "Jeanie with the Light Brown Hair," other students on the first floor heard footsteps that continued as long as the music was playing. The next morning, the students left the Foster Cabin, convinced that the old building was haunted.

In an article appearing in the *Fort Worth Star-Telegram* on October 31, 2004, park managers Ivette Ray and Kelli Pickard discussed the weird experiences they had had in the Foster Cabin. The previous month, they had been working in their office on a day when the park was closed. Suddenly, they heard the doorbell ring and someone walking toward their office. When no one entered their office, their got up to investigate. No one was there. Pickard also said that in 1999, she was working upstairs in a storage area of the Foster Cabin when she felt someone brush against her back. She quickly turned around, expecting to see another employee standing behind her. No one was there, but in front of her on the floor was a straw hat. At the time, no straw hats were being stored away upstairs.

What was perhaps the most bizarre incident in the Foster Cabin occurred when a director of Log Cabin Village was taking photographs of the display case. After the film was developed, she noticed a blue dot in the upper left-hand corner of one of the photographs. The director had the dot enlarged and was shocked to see the smiling face of a woman.

Supernatural phenomena has been reported in some of the other cabins as well. The oldest building in the village is the Parker Cabin, which was built in 1848 in the "dogtrot" style, consisting of two separate sections connected by a breezeway. It is thought to be haunted by the spirit of Cynthia Ann Parker, who had been taken captive by a band of Comanches at Fort Parker on May 19, 1836, when she was nine years old. In 1860, the Texas Rangers raided a band of Comanches camped by the Pease River and forcibly took Cynthia, who had become the wife of a tribal leader named Peta Nocona, and her little girl, Topsannah. The rangers delivered them to the Parker Cabin, the home of Cynthia's uncle, Isaac Parker, where she remained briefly before being sent to her other relatives in East Texas. After her daughter died of pneumonia, Cynthia starved herself to death, just four years after being "rescued" from her Comanche captors. Some employees at Log Cabin Village believe that her restless spirit might be responsible for some of the poltergeist-like occurrences inside the cabin. Employees say that this particular ghost enjoys moving objects around. One former employee said that the lye soap in the sink inside the cabin was constantly found in different parts of the room. If someone placed it in the sink early in the morning, the soap might end up on the floor later in the afternoon. Maybe Cynthia is expressing her displeasure at having been cooped up here by vexing the park staff.

A number of ghost stories have also been reported from the Howard Cabin. One night, park managers Ivette Ray and Kelli Pickard were cleaning up after the tourists who had passed through during the day. Before locking up the Howard Cabin for the night, both women noticed that a baby's photograph and an oil painting were hanging over the fireplace mantel where they belonged. When the women returned the next morning, however, they discovered that the oil painting was on the floor and the photograph was on the dresser. Another time, a museum intern who had been cleaning the Howard Cabin was sweeping when she felt a hand on her shoulder. No one was there when she turned around, so she informed the spirit that she was there to clean and would be leaving very soon. As soon as she finished speaking, the invisible hand lifted from her shoulder. Pickard also told of an incident that occurred when she was leading a woman and her granddaughter through the cabin. All of a sudden, the girl exclaimed, "I see them!" The grandmother asked the girl what she was seeing, and she replied, "The ghosts," adding that they smelled like oranges.

Log Cabin Village's haunted reputation is so well known in Fort Worth that a large percentage of the park's visitors are children, who walk through the cabins in hopes of having a ghostly experience. If the stories people tell about Log Cabin Village can be believed, a number of children have gotten their wish.

The Downtown Grocery Market & Deli and Back Door Bookstore

In many Texas cow towns, boardinghouse was a polite term for "house of prostitution." The building at the corner of Eighth and Throckmorton Streets in Fort Worth had a legitimate boardinghouse on the first floor but a bordello upstairs. The old building stands on the western edge of what was once Fort Worth's red-light district, which was referred to by locals as Hell's Half Acre around the turn of the nineteenth century. Like many old bordellos, this building is said to be haunted by the spirit of a prostitute who once worked there.

Most of the haunted activity was reported in the 1970s through the 1990s, when the building housed Barber's Bookstore. Brian Perkins, who purchased the old building in 1969, said that he sensed from the very beginning that the building was haunted. He soon became accustomed to the "clump-clump-clump" sound of phantom footsteps climbing the staircase and resounding throughout the building. Sometimes he was awakened late at night or early in the morning by the sound of someone flipping through the pages of books. When he got out of bed and investigated the noise, he discovered that he was the only one inside the building. Perkins never felt threatened by the entity sharing his business, but apparently his pet cat did. After living in the building for only two weeks, the cat refused to go upstairs.

The only person who ever reported seeing a ghost inside the bookstore was Perkins's son. One night, he was sleeping in one of the upstairs rooms and awoke just in time to see a strange man walking past his doorway. The young man immediately grabbed his gun and ran through the building, looking for the intruder, but it turned out he was the only one there. Some people believe that this was the ghost of a young man who was shot to death on the staircase by his girlfriend's irate father. Although the only apparition ever sighted in the bookstore was that of a man, Perkins and his son believed that the building was also haunted by the spirit of a prostitute who fell in love with a cowboy, but the man was eventually killed in a gunfight. Unable to live without him, she took her own life.

Perkins's last supernatural encounter occurred in the early 1990s, just before he closed the store. He passed through the entire day thinking he was alone in the building, when suddenly he heard the sound of boxes moving around on the upper floor. He looked up the staircase and could clearly tell that someone was blocking the sunlight streaming through the windows in one of the rooms upstairs. The person was also making a lot of noise as he walked through the room. Perkins knew that no one else was inside the building, so he left the store in a hurry. "I had a bad feeling about that," he said.

Today the old boardinghouse houses the Downtown Grocery Market & Deli and Back Door Bookstore. The ghosts may still be there as well, but they seem to have kept a pretty low profile in recent years.

Peters Bros. Hats

Jim and Tom Peters were Greek immigrants who started out shining shoes in Waco. After they had saved up $600, the brothers moved their business to Fort Worth in 1911 and bought a small building near Ninth and Houston Streets. The pair then set about remodeling the building into a shoeshine parlor. During World War I, to accommodate their growing business, the Peters brothers had to add on to their building and increased their staff from four to thirty-six men, who shined shoes in two shifts. At this time, Jim and Tom also began refurbishing hats. In 1921, Tom traveled to Philadelphia and began working for John B. Stetson. After learning how to make hats, he returned to Fort Worth and began making hats at the downtown store. Amon G. Carter, publisher of the *Fort Worth Star-Telegram*, was so impressed with the Peters brothers' hats, which he called the "Shady Oaks," that he gave them to movie stars and dignitaries who visited Fort Worth.

Tom took over the business after his brother died in 1933 and moved the store to 909 Houston Street. He discontinued the shoeshine business and began making hats full-time. Decades later, following Tom's death in 1991 at age ninety-eight, the hat shop was passed down to his grandson, Joe Peters, who runs the business today, assisted by fifth-generation hatter Thomas Bradley Peters. The store has a Wall of Fame featuring photographs of its most famous customers, including President Lyndon Johnson, actor Jimmy Stewart, evangelist Billy Graham, and Clayton Moore, who played the Lone Ranger on television. In 2011, the business celebrated its centenary with a special hundredth anniversary hat. Nowadays, Peters Bros. Hats is also known for its resident ghosts.

The most commonly reported ghost at the hat shop is the spirit of Tom Peters. Joe believes that Tom's ghost is a vigilant spirit who walks through his old store to make sure the business is being run properly. In *Ghosts of Fort Worth*, Brian Righi reports that objects have been mysteriously moved around the store. Joe has also found hats that had been placed on long hooks were found lying on the floor the next morning. For years, employees have heard moans coming from the basement, which they have attributed to the spirit of a former employee who tripped and tumbled down the stairs, and subsequently died from his injuries.

According to Righi, a pizzeria next door to the hat shop is haunted as well. Shortly after the funeral of a dishwasher named Jack Martin, the door of Eli's Pizza opened and closed by itself for several days. The phenomenon always occurred precisely at 4:15, the time when Jack left work every day. Jack Martin's ghost was also said to torment new employees by spraying them with water every time they walked past his dishwasher. So if you visit the hat store, stop in next door for a slice of pizza as well. You just might end up getting a taste of the supernatural.

The Swift and Company Building

Originally a meatpacking plant, the building that housed the Spaghetti Warehouse from the 1970s until recent years was—and still is—reputed to be haunted. In the early twentieth century, two meatpacking companies, Swift and Armour, opened plants in Fort Worth, making the city the country's fifth-largest livestock market. During the 1950s, however, the meatpacking industry in Fort Worth entered a decline as the result of a drought in West Texas and decreased demand for its products. Armour and Company closed its Fort Worth plant in 1962, and the Swift and Company plant eventually shut down in 1970. Most of the Swift plant was destroyed, but the office portion was transformed into a restaurant that was part of the Spaghetti Warehouse chain. Before long, the building had gained a reputation of being haunted.

Almost immediately after the restaurant opened, employees began talking about hearing strange noises in the unoccupied upper rooms. Soon stories began circulating about a former employee of Swift and Company who had died in the plant many years before. In *Ghosts of Fort Worth*, Brian Righi tells the story of a night manager who was preparing to lock up at 2:30 A.M. when he heard some noise coming from the bar. His curiosity was aroused because he was the only one in the building at the time, so he walked slowly over to the bar area and peered in through the doorway. Inside the bar was the figure of a man sitting on a bar stool.

Not long thereafter, a different night manager was walking through the restaurant, turning the lights off and the burglar alarms on. After locking the front door, he walked over to his car in the parking lot. Suddenly he was overcome with the feeling that someone was watching him. He turned around and saw a man gazing down at him from one of the windows on the upper floor. Instead of going back inside the restaurant and confronting a possibly dangerous intruder, the manager decided to go home and deal with the problem the next morning. The next day, he found no signs of forced entry in the building.

The Spaghetti Warehouse closed in 2003. Today the old building has been converted into corporate office space. However, employees who work late at night still report feeling as if someone is standing in the darkness, watching them from the shadows.

Texas Wesleyan University

If you are in Fort Worth, be sure to pay a visit to Nicholas Martin Hall, the auditorium in Texas Wesleyan University's Ann Waggoner Fine Arts Building, where you can catch a performance by the university's theater students—and, if you are lucky, the ghost of a woman known around campus as Georgia. Legend has it that the building was erected on the site of an old graveyard. People say that the tombstones were removed before construction began, but the bodies were not. According to the historical account, however, the university physician, Dr. W. C. Dobkins, owned the adjacent property, and several of his family members were interred on the grounds. When the property was developed, all but three of the corpses were exhumed and moved to different burial plots. One of these bodies that were left behind was that of Dr. Dobkins's disabled sister, Sarah. Perhaps it was Sarah's spirit that interrupted the production of the musical *Brigadoon* in the theater in 1955.

According to Brian Righi in *Ghosts of Fort Worth*, director Mason Johnson was sitting in one of the seats toward the back of the theater during rehearsal when he got the feeling that he was being watched. Peering into the darkness, he caught sight of a strange woman sitting a few seats down from him. She had turned around and was staring straight at him. Rehearsals were closed to the general public, so the director walked down the aisle with the intention of telling the woman she would have to leave when suddenly she vanished. Wondering if his eyes were playing tricks on him, Johnson returned to his seat. A few minutes later, he noticed that the woman was sitting in the same seat, Seat 13, watching the actors. Exasperated, he started walking back down the aisle, but the woman disappeared before he reached her seat. Johnson immediately christened the ghost Georgia, and the name stuck.

Since this first sighting, Georgia has been seen many times in the old theater, usually during the production of musicals. Witnesses describe the specter as a woman around sixty years old, dressed in the fashions of the 1890s. They say she wears a brooch around her neck and a shawl draped over her shoulders. Georgia usually appears in Seat 13, although occasionally she has been seen gliding along the balcony. Georgia's most dramatic manifestation occurred during a rehearsal for *Cabaret*, when Johnson and the entire cast stopped performing to gaze at Georgia's ghost, who, as usual, was staring intently at the stage from Seat 13.

Many college theater departments develop an affection for their resident ghosts. Texas Wesleyan University's theater department is so attached to Georgia that when the theater's seats were reupholstered, Seat 13 was left unchanged so that Georgia would still feel at home.

Fort Worth Zoo

When the Fort Worth Zoo first opened in 1909, its only attractions were an alligator, a coyote, two bear cubs, a lion, and a number of rabbits. As funds were raised over the years, the zoo was able to purchase additional animals and build exhibits, from earlier ones like Monkey Island and a sea lion pool to today's Parrot Paradise, World of Primates, Raptor Canyon, Texas Wild, Great Barrier Reef, and penguin and cheetah exhibits. But perhaps the Fort Worth Zoo's most fascinating—though least publicized—exhibits are its ghosts.

Two ghosts are believed to haunt the zoo. One of these spirits is thought to be that of a zookeeper who was crushed to death by an elephant in the 1980s. People have reported seeing his restless spirit wandering around the elephant and zebra enclosures. The identity of the second ghost is unknown. Witnesses have usually described seeing a woman who appears to be in her thirties, wearing a white Victorian-era dress and holding a matching parasol in her right hand. This phantom female has been seen many times walking back and forth in front of the café.

The Castle at Heron Bay

Inverness Castle, on Heron Drive in west Fort Worth, appears at first glance to be a relic from the Middle Ages. However, it was constructed in several stages. The original wing of the structure was built as a stone farmhouse in 1860. Over the next half a century, several different families lived there, until the city of Forth Worth purchased the estate for the Lake Worth project in 1911. The city then leased out the land as waterfront property. In the 1920s, Samuel E. Whiting reportedly won the property in a poker game. It was Whiting who added the two round, three-story towers that give the structure its castlelike appearance. In 1939, the main house was extensively renovated following a fire that gutted the building. In the 1970s, Tony and Marian May converted the building into a center for self-improvement training programs and renamed it Castle St. Michael. Today the old building, now called the Castle at Heron Bay, stands abandoned—except perhaps for the spirits of two of its former occupants.

The earliest ghost story dates back to the construction of the stone farmhouse in 1860. It is said that a young man built the house as a gift for his fiancée. The wedding ceremony was scheduled to take place inside the house, but on the day of the wedding, the bride's lifeless body was found floating in Lake Worth. The cause of the woman's death was never determined. The grief-stricken young man found consolation in the arms of his bride's sister, whom he eventually married. For many years, people reported seeing the ghostly figure of a woman running into the lake. The apparition always vanished just as she reached the water's edge.

Another ghost was sighted walking the halls of the castle. He is thought to be the spirit of Samuel Whiting's son, who committed suicide in the house in the 1930s. This ghost has been described as the spirit of a very handsome but morose young man. In 2006, Carmen Montoya, who had recently moved into the area with her family, decided to drive out to the castle with her husband to investigate that stories they had heard. The couple drove through the gate and parked just outside the entrance to the castle. While her husband was adjusting the car radio, Carmen gazed up at the castle and saw the image of a young man looking out of one of the upper-story windows. She turned to her husband and said, "Oh my God! Look!" But when she turned back to the window, the strange figure was gone.

Today the Castle at Heron Bay is even more ominous-looking than it was when it was occupied. All of the windows have been boarded up, and the property is enclosed by a razor-wire fence. Signs warn intruders that the property is protected by video surveillance. Trespassing past the front gates is strictly forbidden. For the present time, curiosity seekers will have look for the castle's spirits with telephoto lenses or high-powered binoculars from the road.

Del Frisco's Double Eagle Steak House

Beginning in the 1870s, the lower end of Fort Worth was called Hell's Half Acre because of the dens of vice located there. Thousands of cowboys who rode into town on Saturday nights to blow off steam washed off the trail dust in the area's bathhouses before spending their hard-earned money in the town's bordellos, saloons, and gambling parlors. Many of these cowpokes ended up dead or incarcerated in the local jail following their late-night escapades. One of these unfortunate drovers ended his life in a bathhouse that is now one of Fort Worth's finest restaurants, Del Frisco's Double Eagle Steak House.

According to legend, a cowboy was soaking in an iron tub in the bathhouse late one evening. The warm water was so relaxing that he drifted off to sleep in the tub. As the sun dipped below the horizon, a man slowly opened the door to the room, sneaked up to the front end of the bathtub, and shot the sleeping cowboy in the back of the head. The murderer dashed out of the room before the other occupants of the bathhouse could be alerted. Neither the motive for the murder nor the identity of the cowboy's assailant was ever discovered.

For many years, people have reported seeing the cowboy's ghost wandering from the banquet room to the upstairs bar. Footsteps have been heard in the upper level of the restaurant and on the staircase after hours. Servers and customers occasionally run into cold spots in different areas of the restaurant. In *Ghosts of Fort Worth*, Brian Righi tells the story of a server who was on the second floor late one night cleaning tables when she detected a sudden drop in temperature. She then felt invisible hands grasping her shoulders from behind. As a rule, though, the cowboy's ghost makes his presence known in much less obtrusive, less frightening ways.

Today no vestiges of the old bathhouse's unsavory past are readily apparent in the elegant steakhouse, with its subdued lighting and mahogany-paneled walls lined with photographs of hundreds of the restaurant's guests. Alas, no image of the building's most notorious guest—the murdered cowhand—is displayed in Del Frisco's.

Galveston
and Houston

Bolivar Point Lighthouse

Although the Bolivar Point Lighthouse has been closed and its light has remained darkened for decades, its ghost stories continue to live on to this day. The lighthouse was constructed at Bolivar Point at the entrance to Galveston Bay in the early 1850s. Between 1852 and 1858, a third-order Fresnel lens was installed, and twenty-four sections were added to the tower. During the Civil War, however, the lighthouse was completely dismantled, probably so that the iron framework could be used as armor plating for ships. In 1865, a thirty-four-foot wooden tower was erected on the site of the original lighthouse.

This tower served as a temporary lighthouse until 1870, when a second iron tower was built at Bolivar Point, modeled after the lighthouse at Louisiana's Pass a l'Outre. Two years later, the lighthouse was illuminated for the first time. After a dispute between the lighthouse keeper and his assistant, the keeper was replaced in late 1894 by Harry C. Claiborne, who became the best-known lighthouse keeper at Bolivar Point. Claiborne's relatively humdrum existence at the lighthouse was disrupted by two disastrous hurricanes in 1900 and 1915. More than 120 people sought refuge at the lighthouse during the Great Hurricane of 1900. Harry Claiborne and his wife fed the refugees until their food supply was depleted. When the hurricane of August 16–17, 1915, struck Galveston, sixty people made their way to the safety of the lighthouse. After the storm had passed, the Claibornes were dismayed to find that the two lighthouse keeper's dwellings had been completely destroyed and the outbuildings and oil house had been washed away. When new dwellings were constructed, this time they were placed on pilings. Harry C. Claiborne served as Bolivar Point's lighthouse keeper for twenty-four years. After his death, the U.S. Coast Guard named one of its 175-foot buoy tenders the *Harry Claiborne*.

The lighthouse was closed by the lighthouse commissioner in 1930, but it became operational once again as the result of public outcry. However, just three years later, because of the Great Depression, the Bolivar Point Lighthouse closed for good. The historic structure was sold to E. V. Boyt for $5,500 in 1947 and has remained in the Boyt family ever since. The fact that the lighthouse tower is not open to the general public may account for the aura of mystery surrounding its signature ghost story.

The 1970 movie *My Sweet Charlie* was filmed at the caretaker's house next door. After filming ended, rumors began circulating that the stars, Patty Duke and Al Freeman Jr., had seen a ghost. Before long, other people reported seeing a ghostly figure standing in the window. Some people believe that the spirit of a boy who was the son of a lighthouse keeper still haunts the lighthouse. One night, it is said, he slipped into his parents' bedroom and choked them to death while they slept. In another variant of the tale, he crushed their skills with a large, jagged rock. Other people believe that the apparition is the ghost of Harry C. Claiborne, whose sense of duty has compelled him to stay on at the lighthouse long after his death.

Ashton Villa

Ashton Villa is one of the most famous antebellum homes in Galveston, not only for its history, but also for its paranormal phenomena. James Moreau Brown, a merchant whose thriving hardware business had made him a very wealthy man, had the three-story Italianate villa constructed in the 1860s. Built of brick and iron, the house withstood the blasts of the Great Storm of 1900. To reduce the pressure on the outside walls, Brown opened the front and back doors of the mansion, thereby allowing the floodwaters to flow through the house. According to the folklore of the Brown family, one of the youngest daughters sat on the main staircase and watched the water rise up to the tenth step.

The most dominant of Brown's five children were Bettie and Mathilda. Bettie, who never married, was much more assertive than most of the genteel young ladies in Galveston. She was a serious artist who traveled through Europe, looking for fine furnishings for the house. Mathilda, the youngest child, returned to Ashton Villa in 1896 with her three children after divorcing her husband. Bettie took possession of the home after the death of her mother in 1907. When Bettie died in 1920, Mathilda inherited Ashton Villa. She passed the house down to her daughter Alice in 1926. The house was then sold to the Shriners, who occupied the mansion until 1970. The following year, Ashton Villa was spared from the wrecking ball when it was purchased by the Galveston Historical Society and turned into a house museum. Today thousands of visitors tour the old home each year to gaze at the nineteenth-century antiques, Bettie Brown's original artwork, and the family heirlooms—and perhaps catch a glimpse of its ghosts.

Tours occasionally have been disrupted by the ghosts of Ashton Villa. Guests being led through the house by one of the guides sometimes report feeling as if an invisible entity has joined them on the tour. One tourist said he had just left one of the rooms when he heard a very loud sound, as if a large pane of glass had fallen out of a window and broken. Oddly, the tour guide had not heard the mysterious sound.

The most well-known ghost at Ashton Villa is said to be that of Bettie Brown. It seems that Bettie was so enamored of the house where she spent so much of her life that she has never really left. Her ghost has been seen standing in the Gold Room, where the fans she collected on her travels are on display. Staff at the old house have seen furniture move when no one else is around, and clocks that have just been wound up stop working. People also have heard spectral piano playing echoing through the Gold Room. Some have credited this ghostly activity to Bettie, but she was a painter, not a musician. Her sister, however, played both the piano and violin. Could it be that her spirit is haunting the house as well?

One night, a substitute caretaker had a very eerie experience in the Gold Room. He was sleeping in the caretaker's home when he was awakened by a dog barking. Thinking someone was trying to break into the mansion, he got dressed and entered the house. He immediately heard a man and woman arguing in the Gold Room. When he reached the doorway, he peered into the moonlit room, where he saw a woman sitting on the piano bench with a bearded man looking down at her. Both figures were dressed in fashions of the late nineteenth century. As the woman softly wept into her handkerchief, the man complained that she paid more attention to her personal belongings and her appearance than she did to him. She replied that she could no longer listen to him and proceeded to play the piano. The caretaker felt uneasy because he was intruding on a private scene, so he hid behind a Chinese screen. Suddenly he heard the creaking of floorboards behind him. He turned around but no one was there. When he looked back into the Gold Room, the woman now was all alone. She laid her head on the piano and cried. Then she stood up and walked over to her fan collection. She picked up a fan, walked over to the wall mirror, and asked, "Mirror, mirror, on the wall, who's the fairest of them all?" A few seconds later, she slowly faded away.

Bettie Brown's ghost has also been sighted in the hallway on the second-floor landing and at the top of the central stairway. One day, a docent was standing on the landing when all at once a beautiful woman wearing a turquoise evening gown appeared before him. In her hand was a lovely fan dating back to the Victorian era. Paranormal activity has also been reported inside Bettie's dayroom. A chest of drawers that she brought back from the Middle East locks and unlocks itself fairly frequently, and ceiling fans turn on by themselves. Tour guides who walk into the room just after the house has opened up have found the covers on one of the beds rumpled, as if someone had just woken up and climbed out of bed.

John Zaffis, host of the Syfy television show *Haunted Collector*, believes that spirits can attach themselves to various objects. If this theory is true, then in many cases, the source of a haunting could possibly be traced back to a book or piano, for example, and not to the house itself. Many residents of Galveston believe that Bettie Brown loved her lavish possessions so much that her spirit will remain in Ashton Villa as long as they do.

Hotel Galvez

Built in 1911 and named after the first Spanish colonial governor of Texas, Hotel Galvez is listed on the National Register of Historic Places and has had a number of well-known guests over the years, including Frank Sinatra, Gen. Douglas Macarthur, and Presidents Franklin D. Roosevelt, Dwight D. Eisenhower, and Lyndon B. Johnson, but it may be best known for another kind of guest—a spirit called "the Lovelorn Lady." In the late 1890s, a young lady checked into Room 501. She was waiting for her fiancé, a sailor whose ship was expected to dock at the Galveston port soon. After a couple days, however, she received word that her fiancé's ship had gone down off the coast of Florida. Her lover's name was not listed among the survivors. When the impact of the message finally sank in, the young woman hanged herself in her hotel room. Tragically, it turned out that her fiancé was not really dead and arrived in Galveston a week later.

It seems that the spirit of the young lady who took her own life in the Hotel Galvez never really checked out. Guests have felt an invisible presence throughout the hotel, but especially in Room 501. Dishes have broken by themselves, and candles have been extinguished when no breeze was wafting through the hotel. The young suicide's spirit has made its presence known on the entire fifth floor. Jackie Hasan, an employee at the hotel, says that the Lovelorn Lady's ghost walks around the entire hotel. In the downstairs ladies' restroom, sinks have turned on by themselves, toilets flush on their own, and an unseen hand has been known to rattle the doors of the stalls. Guests have heard heavy breathing coming from inside one of the stalls. Hasan says that after the Great Storm of 1900, a photographer inadvertently caught the image of an armless, headless figure that could have been the ghost of the Lovelorn Lady.

On November 9, 2005, a formal investigation of the Hotel Galvez was conducted. The paranormal team focused its investigation on Room 501. Around midnight, the doors up and down their wing of the hotel began to slam shut. Because the members of the team were the only ones staying in that particular wing, the loud slamming was particularly significant. They also heard footsteps running up and down the hallway. One of the members, Anna, was assigned the task of watching through the peephole to see if she could catch sight of anyone. After thirty minutes, she said that she saw no one in the hallway, even though she could hear someone running outside the door the entire time. A few seconds later, the team heard the door to Room

505 shut. The team proceeded to search every room in the wing, including Room 505, but all of them were empty. By the end of the investigation, the group had photographed a few orbs, apparitions, and what appeared to be ectoplasm.

The "Queen of the Gulf," as the Hotel Galvez is called, has retained its grandeur over the years, despite the toll that storms and the passage of time have taken on the structure. But the hotel's most enduring feature may be its ghost story—the legend of the Lovelorn Lady.

The Samuel May Williams House

In 1838, Samuel May Williams built a house that reflects both the Creole plantation and New England architectural styles. In addition to being Stephen F. Austin's secretary, Williams also helped establish the Galveston City Company, became the first banker in Texas, and founded the Texas Navy. After he died, his family sold the house to a relative. The house remained in the Tucker family until the early 1950s, when it was sold to the Galveston Historical Foundation. The Samuel May Williams House was operated as a house museum until 2007, when it was closed because of a decline in the number of visitors. It is now a private residence, but even though the general public can no longer visit the house to learn the history of one of Galveston's most important residents, they can get a sense of his personality from the ghost stories that are still passed around.

Samuel May Williams's reputation as a penny-pinching banker seems to have survived his physical body. According to Shirley Holmer, who worked for the Galveston Historical Foundation, Williams's penchant for foreclosing on the mortgages of Galveston residents made him the most hated man in Texas. Docia Schultz Williams, author of *Ghosts along the Texas Coast*, believes that the banker's cruel side is responsible for the "bad vibes" that still resonated through the historic home when it was open as a museum. In 1995, the former director of the house museum told a reporter for the *Houston Chronicle* that one night, after she turned off a lamp inside the house, it immediately began rattling, as if in protest.

Mario P. Ceccaci Jr., who lived next door to the Williams house, told Docia Williams that once a psychic paid admission to the house museum and was about to step over the threshold when she was overcome by a feeling of dread. When a docent asked her what was wrong, the psychic said she could not enter the house and walked away. Ceccaci had an eerie experience of his own inside the Williams house. After the last member of the Tucker family passed away, but before its sale to the historic foundation, Ceccaci checked on the house periodically to make sure that no one had taken any of the family's antiques. One day, he discovered that someone had built a fire in the fireplace. The fire was out but the embers were still glowing. He walked through the house but could find no sign of forced entry.

People who toured the Samuel May Williams House still talk about the strange presence they detected in the old house. On the second-floor landing just outside the children's bedrooms, visitors experienced a drastic drop in temperature. Some wonder if the cold spot has anything to do with the death of Williams's son, Little Sam, who died of an unknown sickness when he was ten years old. The Williams family, it seems, has left an indelible print on the house they once called home.

The Tremont House

The Tremont House hotel was built in 1839 at Tremont and Post Office Streets. The official grand opening of the hotel was marked by a gala ball on April 19, 1839, in honor of the Battle of San Jacinto, and it saw quite a bit of history over the years to come. On April 19, 1861, Gen. Sam Houston delivered his last public speech from the north gallery of the hotel, warning the crowd of the bloodbath that would surely ensue if Texas seceded from the Union. The following year, Union soldiers were quartered inside the hotel. In the summer of 1865, the first of many fires that ravaged downtown Galveston reduced the Tremont to a pile of ashes. Seven years later, it was rebuilt as an even more luxurious hotel on a block of land bounded by Tremont, Church, and Twenty-fourth Streets. The Tremont House entertained a number of illustrious guests during the nineteenth century, including Buffalo Bill Cody, Edwin Booth, Clara Barton, Stephen Crane, and Presidents Ulysses S. Grant, Grover Cleveland, Benjamin Harrison, Rutherford B. Hayes, and Chester A. Arthur. During the

Great Storm of 1900, the hotel served as a temporary refuge for disaster victims. By the late 1920s, however, the ravages of time and nature had taken their toll on the old hotel, and it was demolished. Over half a century later, in 1980, the Tremont House reopened in its third incarnation, this time in the former Leon & H. Blum Building, which had earlier housed a dry goods company, a department store, and the offices of the *Galveston Tribune*. Today people interested in the paranormal would insist that the pleasure of staying in this elegant hotel is enhanced by the presence of several ghosts that guests and staff encounter from time to time.

The most commonly sighted ghost in the Tremont House is the spirit of a Civil War soldier. Most witnesses describe the apparition as a Confederate soldier who marches up and down the lobby in front of the elevator shafts and back toward the office area. Front desk clerks have heard the stomping of heavy boots leading from the bathroom into the lobby. Guests and staff members have also reported seeing the ghostly soldier in the bar and dining area.

A ghost fondly called Jimmy, who often hangs around the lobby and seems to enjoy playing with bottles and glasses in the bar, is thought to be the spirit of a little boy who was run over in front of the building in the late 1880s. Some guests have even reported seeing the little phantom outside the hotel, usually in the alley. A former manager of the hotel named the ghostly boy after Jimmy the Hand, a street urchin from one of Raymond E. Feist's novels.

Another ghost, known as Sam, is said to be the spirit of a murder victim who was killed in the hotel in the late 1800s. One night, a salesman who had had a lucky night in one of the city's gambling houses returned to his room on the fourth floor of the Tremont House and was shot and killed by an unknown assailant, who made off with the poor man's winnings. Some people say that the ghost of the unfortunate salesman still walks the hallways of the fourth floor and also rattles glasses in the bar area.

Another spectral entity sometimes torments guests staying in Room 219. Guests staying in this room have reported going to bed at night and awakening the next morning to find the contents of their suitcases scattered all over the floor. Paranormal investigators have suggested that the spirit of a disgruntled employee of the dry goods store that was once housed in the building could be responsible for the disturbances.

The Tremont House is said to be a charming and commodious blend of the past and present. And the ghosts from the hotel's past seem to be determined to remain a part of its present.

The Galveston Railroad Museum

The Galveston Railroad Museum is housed in a yellow Art Deco-style building at 120 Twenty-fifth Street. The museum has one of the largest restored railroad collections in the Southwest, with more than twenty thousand railroad items, including forty train engines and cars. The building is an appropriate location for the museum, because it served as the Santa Fe Union Station when it was built in 1913. Not only was the building the central passenger station for Galveston's railway system, but it also housed the general offices of the Atkinson, Topeka, and Santa Fe's Gulf lines. In 1932, the eight-story north wing and eleven-story tower were added. Half a century later, the old train station was transformed into the Railroad Museum. Brief histories of Galveston are shown in a series of theaters contained in the former Railway Express building. The original Santa Fe carpentry shop was converted into a replica of an 1875 Victorian-era railway station. The old freight offices are now the museum offices. The waiting room of the terminal looks much as it did in the station's heyday. Sitting on the benches are full-size plaster models of passengers dressed as they would have been in the 1930s. Legend has it that the railway lines' former passengers exist in a more spectral form as well.

The oldest known haunting in the building is said to date back to a horrible accident that occurred on September 1, 1900, just a few days before the Great Storm of 1900 made landfall. Legend has it that a thirty-two-year-old engineer named William Watson was standing on the cowcatcher of a locomotive as it was moving out of the railyard behind the present-day museum. Watson had performed this reckless act many times before, so he must have been shocked when he felt his feet sliding off the cowcatcher. He flailed his arms in the air but was unable to find anything to clutch on to. He didn't even have time to scream as he fell under the train. Watson was immediately decapitated, but his head was not recovered until the train finally came to a halt a quarter mile down the line on Fourteenth Street. Many believe that a poltergeist that has been making strange noises and moving objects in the building for decades is Watson's spirit.

The spirit of a distraught woman is also said to haunt the old terminal. In the early 1980s, a woman was said to have jumped from a fourth-floor window in a wing where mental patients were being treated. Since then, the apparition of a woman running down the hallway on the fourth floor has been sighted many times. One day in 1990, a couple of women who were working in an office on the fourth floor walked into the ladies' room and were surprised to see a woman sitting on the windowsill with one leg dangling outside the window. The strange figure gave them a taunting look, as if she were daring them to try to grab her before she jumped. A few seconds later, the woman vanished.

In 1998, the police department received several telephone calls from the third and fourth floors of the building. The officers who answered heard nothing more than heavy breathing. However, when the phone call was played back on the answering machine, the policemen heard the tinny sounds of music dating from the 1920s. It seems that the ghosts who are trapped inside the old building are trying to make contact with the outside world.

The Ghost of Jean Lafitte

Jean Lafitte arrived on Galveston Island in 1817 with hopes of setting up a colony. Galveston was perfectly suited to his purposes because it protected a large inland bay. Lafitte and his crew immediately set about tearing down the existing buildings and replacing them with two hundred new houses. Within a year's time, one hundred to two hundred men were living in the seaside village known as Campeche. A two-story house served as the headquarters of the colony, but day-to-day business transactions were conducted aboard Lafitte's ship, the *Pride*. Lafitte's smuggling operations benefited immensely from a poorly written law, passed in 1818, that prohibited the import of slaves but gave privateers permission to capture slave ships. For several years, Lafitte and his pirates seized treasures from ships and coastal towns all across the Caribbean and the Gulf Coast. In 1821, however, Lafitte committed the fatal error of attacking an American ship. A few months later, sailors aboard the American warship *Enterprise* ordered Lafitte and his pirates to evacuate the island. Before leaving, Lafitte and his pirates threw a huge party, during which they consumed gallons of rum and whiskey and burned down the entire village of Campeche. The next morning, Lafitte and his crew sailed away, never to be heard from again. Some people insist, however, that Lafitte never really left.

Treasure hunters were the first people to report encountering the ghost of Jean Lafitte. Not long after Lafitte abandoned Galveston Island, people began digging for treasure that he was rumored to have quickly buried on the island. Throughout the nineteenth century, treasure hunters in LaPorte, directly across the bay from Galveston, claimed they had been choked during the night as they sought refuge in an abandoned house. One of these men described the ghost who rudely awakened him as wearing a red coat and breeches. The apparition pointed to a place on the floor and said, "Take the treasure. It is mine to give you. I earned it with the forfeiture of my immortal soul. But the money must all be spent in charity. Not one penny may you spend in evil or in selfishness. What was taken in selfishness and evil must be spent for good." As soon as the spirit vanished, the man pried up the floorboards, but he found nothing there.

In recent years, sightings of Lafitte's ghost ship have been reported. Legend holds that Lafitte sails up and down Galveston Bay in search of a lover who fell overboard. Workers on offshore oil rigs have claimed they saw the billowing sails of a nineteenth-century wooden ship on the horizon, just before sunset. Crews of offshore supply ships say they have heard phantom shouting and the flapping of sails. A ghostly fleet of ships has been blamed for nearly swamping small boats. Because the ghost of Jean Lafitte was reportedly sighted just before Hurricane Katrina swept through the Gulf Coast, the appearance of Lafitte and his pirate fleet is usually taken as a bad omen. Another possibility, however, is that Lafitte has returned to Galveston Island to retrieve his hidden treasure.

Luigi's Italian Restaurant

Luigi's is a Tuscan-style Italian restaurant that opened its doors in an old bank building in 1997. A historical marker outside the pink and gray granite Neo-Renaissance-style structure at 2328 Strand Street identifies it as the Sealy-Hutchings Building. According to employees and customers alike, this popular dining spot is haunted by the ghost of a woman who became a heroine during the city's greatest natural disaster.

At 2 A.M. on September 8, 1900, a great wind blew in from the north, creating a gigantic wall of water that surged toward Galveston. When the wind shifted from the north to the southeast, the city was doomed. Houses built near the beach began to crumble. Men and women tried to escape the fury of the storm by moving to higher ground or seeking refuge in sturdy-looking buildings. Many people evacuated the city in wagons, by boat, and on foot. Some of the lucky ones were able to make their way to the sturdy Tremont House. At 3 A.M., Galveston was submerged when the waters of the gulf and the bay converged. The cyclone-force winds hurled boards, timbers, and other objects through the air like missiles. Roofs were ripped from buildings and telephone poles were knocked down. A Santa Fe train was lifted from the track two miles north of Alvin. Huge ocean steamers were tossed from their moorings. The combination of 140-mile-an-hour winds and a 17-foot storm surge devastated Galveston. Approximately six thousand of the city's thirty-seven thousand residents were dead, and more than thirty-six hundred homes were destroyed. Thirty thousand people were left homeless. The damage amounted to a loss of $30 million. The Great Storm of 1900 was the deadliest natural disaster in U.S. history.

One of the hardest-hit parts of the city was the Strand. The water level at the building that now houses Luigi's was seventeen feet high. One of the many acts of heroism that took place that day was performed by a schoolteacher who raced up the steps to the third floor of the bank building in an effort to escape the storm's fury. Witnesses say that she climbed out of one of the windows and perched on the ledge, grabbing at people as they floated by and hauling them into the room. She placed the injured people on one side of the room and the dead on the other. She did her best to care for them over the next several days, until she contracted a fever and died.

For more than a century, people have reported seeing the ghost of the brave schoolteacher in various parts of the Sealy-Hutchings Building. In 2002, a group of five women who had just gotten off work were walking down Strand Street when something attracted their attention to the first-floor window of Luigi's. They all saw the figure of a woman, dressed in the fashion of the early 1900s, standing on the stairway. The woman vanished in just a few seconds, but she was visible long enough for all five women to see her. After this unnerving experience, they all became believers in the paranormal.

In 2006, an employee named Steve Havlock had closed the restaurant and was in the process of sweeping and rearranging the chairs when he heard a woman's voice call his name: "Steve! Steve!" At first he thought that one of waitresses was still inside, but after walking through the building, he realized that he was alone. His growing suspicion that Luigi's might really be haunted was confirmed a few months later when his three-year-old son told him that he had been speaking to a lady upstairs on the second floor, which had been vacant for years. After a customer showed Steve a photograph of a misty female figure that she had taken in Luigi's, he had no doubt that there must be some truth to the tales he had heard about the ghost of the schoolteacher.

Not all the disturbances inside Luigi's are as dramatic as the ones experienced by Steve and his son. Some of the strange things that happen here are just annoying. For example, a waiter says that every night before he and the other waitstaff leave, they place silverware on the tables. Some mornings, they find that the knives have been turned outward instead of in toward the plates. Perhaps the spirit of the schoolteacher wants to make sure no one forgets what she did for the city of Galveston.

The Mediterranean Chef Restaurant

The Mediterranean Chef is one of Galveston's favorite Greek restaurants. The building at 2402 Strand Street in which it has been located since 1991 was originally constructed in 1877 and housed the Smith Brothers Hardware Store for many years. Today customers flock to the restaurant because of its delicious gyros and other ethnic cuisine, as well as its supernatural phenomena.

As the story goes, a robbery occurred near the old hardware store in 1920. A man who had just withdrawn a considerable sum of cash from the Hutchings, Sealy and Company Bank across the street was accosted by two men, who demanded that he hand over the money. The man refused and began resisting the robbers. A young policeman about twenty-five to thirty years of age named Daniel Brister witnessed the altercation. He ran up behind one of the two men and began hitting him in the head. The men fell to the ground and struggled in the dirt until finally the policeman was able to put handcuffs on the robber. Brister had just stood up when the other robber shot him in the chest. Somehow he was able to run down his assailant and handcuff him as well. After the two robbers were hauled away in a paddy wagon, the heroic policeman sat on a bench in front of the Smith Brothers Hardware Store to catch his breath. Suddenly he keeled over and fell dead to the ground.

Not surprisingly, the ghost of the policeman seems to still be haunting the scene of his death. He is often credited with throwing pots and pans in the restaurant for no apparent reason. His apparition has also been seen standing in the back of the building. Apparently he also seems to enjoy attracting the attention of female customers, as women have complained of feeling someone breathing down their necks, even though no one is there—at least, no one human. A female tour guide reported that she was telling the story of Daniel Brister to a group of tourists standing in front of the restaurant when she felt someone pinch her backside. Because no one was standing behind her, she thought it was Brister's ghost getting fresh with her.

The Thomas Jefferson League Building

The Thomas Jefferson League Building is one of the most impressive structures on the Strand, which was the central business district of

Galveston in the nineteenth century. In 1869, a fire set by robbers in the Cohn Brothers Clothing Emporium destroyed an area a mile wide. One of the businesses that burned to the ground was an upscale bar called Moro Castle. In 1871, an attorney named Thomas Jefferson League began construction of a large commercial building on the site of the bar. This Renaissance Revival-style structure is typical of many mid-nineteenth-century buildings that used cast-iron arcades on the first floor. The first businesses to occupy the three-story building were a clothier called Isaac Bernstein & Company, a cotton factor and commission merchant, and a stationer and bookseller. Over the years, attorneys, insurance agents, and clothing manufacturers also had their offices here. The Ben Blum Hardware Company occupied the building from 1923 to 1973.

In 1976, Cynthia and George Mitchell, who were strong advocates of historical preservation in Galveston, purchased the old building for development. It was recorded as a Texas historic landmark three years later. The couple first suspected that the building might be haunted in 1998, when two security guards from the nearby Tremont House hotel were summoned to the Thomas Jefferson League Building to investigate complaints from hotel guests that someone inside the building was playing the piano late at night. The men opened the door and saw that it was a woman in a white dress who did not appear to be "quite real." The men turned around and raced back to the Tremont House. Three weeks later, two security guards were summoned to the old building once again to investigate the strange piano playing, but when they opened the door this time, no one was there.

In 2011, restoration began on the iron façade and structural supports of the old building. One wonders if these additional restoration efforts will produce more paranormal sightings at the Thomas Jefferson League Building in years to come.

The University of Texas Medical Branch

The University of Texas Medical Branch was established in Galveston in the late nineteenth century to help meet the state's need for doctors. At the time, only 80 percent of the state's physicians had any formal training. When the school's doors opened in 1891, it had just one building and fifty students. Today it consists of six on-site hospitals, the Shriners Burns Hospital, research facilities, medical libraries, classroom buildings, and one of the state's largest medical libraries. Not surprisingly, the oldest medical school in the state of Texas is said to be haunted.

The school's best-known ghost can best be described as a "displaced spirit." Legend has it that one of the buildings on campus, Ewing Hall, was constructed on the site of a shack owned by a retired sea captain, who had lived there so that he could look at the gulf from his window. Because he did not own the property where he lived, his shack was torn down. He died during the construction of Ewing Hall.

In another version of the story, the property was owned by a wealthy man. When he became too old to take care of his business concerns, his family sold the property to the university. He became irate when he found out what his family had done without his knowledge and vowed to make life miserable for all of them.

The old man's threat may have been fulfilled in 1972, when the huge image of the face of a bearded old man appeared on the back wall of Ewing Hall. A sandblasting crew was hired to remove the strange-looking "stain" on the wall. During the two days it took to blast away the face, the work crew was beset by accidents, including the collapse of the scaffolding. The accidents became so frequent that the work crew, fearing that the project was cursed, quit, and the job had to be completed by the owner of the company. Three weeks later, the face reappeared on a panel at the next lower level. It remains there to this day.

Captain Mott's House

The large Victorian house at 1121 Tremont Street in Galveston was built by Capt. Marcus Fulton Mott for his family in 1884. Mott fought for the Confederacy in the Civil War and later became a lawyer. In 1943, Tommy Witwer bought the old house. After his death, one of Witwer's sons took over the upper rooms. The first floor has been occupied by a variety of small businesses for many years. Evidence from various occupants of the house suggests that Captain Mott has never left—and, indeed, seems to have no intention of leaving.

Tommy Witwer's family members apparently were the first to encounter the captain's ghost. Witwer's daughter told her father that late at night, she could hear voices in the attic. His granddaughter said that one night while she was lying in bed, an old man walked into her bedroom and talked to her. His son Joseph said that when he was twelve years old, he actually saw the captain's ghost.

John Implemence, a navy veteran of the Vietnam War who lived for a while as a tenant at the Mott House, had a number of bizarre experiences. One night, Implemence heard a disembodied voice order, "Get out of here!" A few minutes later, Implemence and his mattress were lifted off the floor and thrown across the room. During a session with a Ouija board, Implemence learned that Captain Mott's son had murdered three women and dropped their bodies down a cistern on the property. However, Implemence was never able to locate the well. During another session, the Ouija board indicated that something was going to come after him with a wet rope.

After John Implemence moved away, another of Tommy Witwer's sons, Neil, moved into the house with his wife, Cathy. They had not lived in the old house for very long before Cathy began to suspect that it was haunted. One night, she heard heavy footsteps in the attic. She also said she saw the image of a man in a mirror. Neil's four-year-old daughter told her parents that she also saw the captain inside the house. The paranormal activity inside the Mott house seems to have died down since 1995—much to the relief, one imagines, of the current owners of the house.

The Spaghetti Warehouse

One of the scariest places in Houston is not an abandoned prison or mental hospital—it is another Italian restaurant that is part of the Spaghetti Warehouse chain. This restaurant is housed inside the old Desel-Boettcher Warehouse, which was built in the Market Square Historic District at 901 Commerce Street in the early 1900s. Over the years, the building as served as a produce warehouse, a storage facility for the Southern Pacific Railroad, and a pharmaceutical warehouse. In 1972, the Spaghetti Warehouse opened its doors in the old building. Before long, employees and customers alike began telling stories about the ghost of a former owner of the building.

As the story goes, the owner of the warehouse was working late one night in his office. When the man glanced up at the clock, he realized that his wife was probably getting worried about him. He grabbed a handful of papers that he was working on and headed out of his office. He stepped inside the elevator and began riding it down to the first floor. Suddenly the cable snapped, and the elevator crashed to the bottom floor. The young man broke his neck in the fall and died instantly.

At approximately the same time that the fatal accident took place, the man's wife was sitting in a chair in the living room when she saw her husband open the front door, hang up his hat and coat, and walk to the back of the house. Looking up from her newspaper, she asked her husband how his day went. When he did not reply, she searched the entire house but was unable to find a trace of her husband. She looked at the coat rack by the front door and noticed that his hat and coat were gone, as if he had never returned home at all. She immediately sensed that something was terribly wrong, so she grabbed her coat and hurried to the warehouse.

The distraught woman rushed inside and immediately noticed a crowd of men standing around the elevator shaft. After nudging her way through the crowd, she peered into the darkness and could see the wreckage of the elevator car in the dim light. She knew without being told that her husband's corpse was inside. After the funeral, the woman stayed inside her house, refusing to see anybody. About a year later, a friend of her husband's came by to check on her. When she did not answer his knock, he forced his way in. He walked into the bedroom, where he found the woman's corpse lying in the bed. He could find no signs of physical trauma. The next day, the medical examiner concluded that she had died of natural causes. Her friends and neighbors were certain that she had died of a broken heart.

Some people believe another source of the haunted activity inside the Spaghetti Warehouse resulted from the unsafe working conditions inside the old building during the 1880s. Several workers were said to have been killed while unloading crates of merchandise. Like the ghosts of many victims of accidental deaths, some say, their spirits are trapped inside the place where they died, confused about what happened to them. Or perhaps the ghosts are the spirits of the families of the men who died in the warehouse, still roaming around the building looking for their loved ones. Several employees have reported seeing the apparition of a woman walking through the restaurant as if she were searching for someone.

So many people have inquired about the hauntings inside the restaurant that customers are given a photocopied synopsis of the ghost story. Sandra McMasters, general manager of Houston's Spaghetti Warehouse, has said that paranormal activity occurs there daily. "For example, someone hears their name being called, yet no one is there," McMasters said. Many customers have photographed orbs in one of the restrooms. "Folks hate to use this restroom," Sandra said, because of the cool breezes that sometimes waft through. "Nobody stays in there very long."

In *A Texas Guide to Haunted Restaurants, Taverns and Inns*, Robert and Anne Powell Wlodarski tell the story of a waitress who was taking a nap upstairs. She was awakened by the sound of someone walking around. She sat up in bed and listened as the footsteps came closer and closer. Just as she was about to scream, the footsteps stopped. The terrified woman turned on the light and was both relieved and puzzled to find that she was the only one in the room.

Other employees have also had strange experiences. A busboy was cleaning upstairs when all at once, several plates seemed to leap off the shelves and smash on the floor. After that incident, he refused to work upstairs by himself. Another night, a waitress saw a wicker basket floating in the air near the wooden staircase. A few seconds later, the basket floated gently to the ground, just as if someone had set it there. Yet another waitress was talking to a couple of customers at their table, when suddenly a bottle of wine floated into the air and then landed upright on the table.

The most active part of the Spaghetti Warehouse is the dining area on the second floor. On many occasions, waitstaff have cleaned up the dining area before closing up and returned the next morning to find that the chairs and tables have been rearranged and the silverware has been scattered all over the tables. One night, several guests who were dining inside the trolley car on display complained to their waitress that something had caused their salt and pepper shakers to vibrate and slide across the table.

The Spaghetti Warehouse remains one of Houston's most popular Italian restaurants, even though customers frequently have their hair tugged and their shoulders touched by an invisible hand. Either the ghosts are the restaurant's main attraction or the food is so good that having one's meal interrupted by a ghost is viewed as just a minor inconvenience.

Julia Ideson Building

Named after the city's first librarian, the Julia Ideson Building opened its doors in 1926, replacing the Carnegie Library at 500 McKinney Street. During Julia Ideson's tenure as the chief librarian of the Houston Public Library system, she oversaw the opening of six branch libraries and the purchase of a bookmobile. Oddly enough, however, the ghost haunting the building is not the spirit of Julia Ideson, who passed away in 1945. Rather, it is thought to be the ghost of another library employee named Jacob Frank Cramer.

Cramer began working as a janitor in the new library shortly after it opened. Over the next ten years, he also served as gardener, night watchman, and handyman. Cramer and his German shepherd, Petey, lived in an apartment in the basement of the library. Every night, Cramer and his faithful companion walked up the stairs to the top floor and sat near the balustrade of the library's inner court, where he played his beloved violin for hours. On a chilly morning in November 1936, librarians found Cramer lying on the floor. He had died during the night of a lung hemorrhage. Although his body was buried in Hiawatha, Kansas, it seems that his spirit has never left.

Cramer and his dog were fixtures in Houston's central library, and some employees and visitors believe that the inseparable pair still are. People have heard the clicking of the paws of a dog walking through the library. Sheet music has been found scattered around in different parts of the library. Orbs have appeared in photographs taken inside the building. Lights have been known to turn off and on by themselves. On several occasions, the rickety elevator has climbed up to the top floor of the library when nobody was inside. The strangest thing about this phenomenon is that ordinarily the elevator will not move unless someone inserts a key inside the mechanism.

However, the most frightening paranormal occurrence inside the old library is when the lilting sounds of a ghostly violin echo through the cavernous building. Caroline Reeder, who was a member of the library's fund-raising staff, was returning to work after her lunch hour when she heard someone playing the violin. She looked all around, thinking that a street musician was in the vicinity. Then she realized that the music was coming from inside the library. Another library employee named Douglas Weiskopf has sensed an invisible presence on the second floor and has seen a shadowy figure out of the corner of his eye. In the 1970s, a patron named Robert Beekman was reading in the children's section when suddenly he heard the unmistakable sound of stringed instruments.

In 1976, the Central Library moved to its new location in the Jesse H. Jones Building. Today the Julia Ideson Building is the repository for the archives, manuscripts, the Texas and Local History Department, and the Houston Metropolitan Research Center. Some people believe that it is also the permanent home of a former night watchman and his dog.

The Post Rice Lofts

In 1881, Col. A. Groesbeck built the Capitol Hotel on Texas Avenue in Houston, on the site of the old capitol building of the Republic of Texas. Two years later, William Marsh Rice, the founder of Rice University, bought the hotel, renamed it the Rice Hotel, and added a five-story annex. A new hotel was erected on the site in 1913. The Rice was known as one of Houston's finest hotels, and its Capitol Club was a meeting place for some of state's most influential power brokers. At the top of the list of lawyers, businessmen, judges, and celebrities who visited the hotel is President John F. Kennedy, who stayed there the night before traveling to Fort Worth and Dallas, where he was assassinated by Lee Harvey Oswald. In 1962, the Rice Hotel gained national attention as the meeting place for NASA Astronaut Group 2. The hotel closed in the 1970s, however. Two decades later, it was renovated and reopened as an apartment complex called the Post Rice Lofts. Today the former Rice Hotel is said to be one of Houston's most haunted sites.

A number of spirits have been sighted in the old hotel over the years. Phantom dancers have been seen on the roof where the dance pavilion used to be. A spectral woman has been sighted walking where the balcony once was. According to Robert and Anne Powell Wlodarski in *A Texas Guide to Haunted Restaurants, Taverns and Inns*, people have felt an icy wind blowing from the elevator when it rises—unoccupied—to the fourth floor. Maids made the beds in vacant rooms and left, only to return a few minutes later to find that someone—or something—had messed up the blankets. Closet doors in some of the rooms open and close by themselves. Disembodied voices calling people's names have been heard in both rooms and hallways.

The old Rice Hotel's most famous ghost is the spirit of President John F. Kennedy, who is said to haunt the room where he spent his last night in Houston. Guests who stayed in the former president's room reported seeing balls of light, feeling cold spots, and hearing the doors rattling. Some claimed that in the middle of the night, the bed shook and the closet doors opened and slammed shut on their own. A number of guests became so terrified that they checked out of Kennedy's room only a few hours after checking in. Today the room is an unrented loft. Apparently the building owners got tired of having to field complaints of paranormal disturbances.

North Texas

The Hotel Turkey

Turkey

Located a hundred miles southeast of Amarillo and a hundred miles northeast of Lubbock, Turkey is about thirty miles off Highway 287. It was first called Turkey Roost when people began settling the area in the 1880s because of the flocks of wild turkeys living in the trees there. When the village got its first post office in 1893, the postmaster shorted the name to Turkey. Turkey achieved national fame as the home of Bob Wills, known as the "King of Western Swing." Like many old-time fiddlers, Bob worked as a barber, which he claimed enhanced the flexibility of his fingers.

The importance of the settlement was elevated with the arrival of the Fort Worth and Denver Railroad, and in November 1927, the Hotel Turkey was built at Third and Alexander Streets to accommodate the hundreds of salesmen and travelers who were stopping over at the little town each year while passing through on the newly constructed railroad. In 1989, the old hotel was renovated after it was purchased by Jane and Scott Johnson. Eight years later, Scott sold the Hotel Turkey to his cousin Gary Johnson, who made additional improvements in the structure. Gary and his wife, Suzie, soon discovered that their most loyal customer is apparently a deceased one.

Legend has it that the Hotel Turkey is haunted by the ghost of a cowboy who usually returns to his favorite room—Room 20—during storms. He announces his presence by ringing the desk bell—unseen, of course. The ghost prefers to book a room on nights when the hotel is empty. According to Docia Schultz Williams in *Phantoms of the Plains*, Jane Johnson told her that during her first winter storm as proprietor of the Hotel Turkey, she heard the desk bell ring. She was puzzled when she walked over to the front desk and nobody was there. The next morning, she opened Room 20 and was surprised to find the impression of a body that apparently had been lying on top of the blankets. The mysterious occupant seems to have crossed his ankles and arms. The impression of a single boot heel was visible on the blanket.

It seems that another ghost also enjoys spending the night at the Hotel Turkey. In *A Texas Guide to Haunted Restaurants, Taverns and Inns*, Robert and Anne Powell Wlodarski tell the story of a woman in her twenties who was staying in one of the other rooms in 1998. In the middle of the night, the young woman was awakened by what appeared to be a flashing light. When her eyes adjusted to the darkness of the room, she saw a man standing in the doorway close to the bathroom. He was dressed in old-fashioned railroad attire and swinging a lighted lantern. Within a few seconds, he vanished.

Most residents of Turkey believe that the primary attraction of the little town, population 500, is still Bob Wills. Indeed, hundreds of people travel to Turkey each year to gaze at the fiddles, boots, hats, recordings, and photographs at the Bob Wills Museum. The annual Bob Wills Day music festival is also a big draw. However, the Hotel Turkey also attracts its share of visitors—not just because it is listed on the National and State of Texas Historic Registries, but also because of its resident ghosts.

Stampede Mesa

Crosby

For almost as long as people have been riding horses, there have been legends of phantom riders sitting astride ghostly horses and galloping across the night sky or just above the ground. Although the riders are demons or fairies in some tales, they are usually associated with the dead. Often these phantoms are said to have appeared just before a catastrophe. In many of these tales, people unfortunate enough to find themselves in the path of the ghostly riders are caught up in the air and transported to the land of the dead. The setting for one American version of this myth is Stampede Mesa, wedged between the forks of the Blanco River just outside Crosby.

The word *mesa* is of Spanish origin and refers to a large hill with a flat top and steeply sloping sides. Cowboys liked to use Stampede Mesa as a grazing ground for their cattle, driving their herds to the top and bedding down there for the night. Because of the steep slopes, which also served as a natural barrier to predators, only one or two cowboys were required to watch over the cattle at night.

Stampede Mesa derives its name from an incident that allegedly took place in 1889. As the story goes, an old trail boss named Sawyer was driving fifteen hundred steers across the nearby Dockum Flats one afternoon on his way to Colorado. As he made his way across a plot of land occupied by a homesteader, forty or fifty of the farmer's steers joined Sawyer's herd. The farmer rode up to Sawyer and pleaded with him to cut out his steers from the herd. Sawyer shook his head, telling the man that he and his cattle were "plumb tuckered out" and he was not going to subject them to any more stress. He added that even if he wanted to grant the homesteader's request, he did not have enough men to do the job. The homesteader swore profusely and told Sawyer that he would be sorry.

Later that night, as Sawyer, his cowboys, and his cattle were bedded down on top of the mesa, the homesteader silently crept up the steep slope. When he reached the top, he waved a blanket and whooped. He also fired his pistol into the air several times. The cattle panicked and began to stampede. After only a minute had passed, all but three hundred steers had plummeted off the south side of the mesa to their death. Two night riders were caught up in the rush, and they and their mounts perished as well.

As he watched his fortune disappear before his very eyes, Sawyer swore that the farmer would pay for his crime. He and his remaining herders rode out to the homesteader's place and lifted him up onto a horse or mule, depending on the version of the tale. They all rode out to the place where the homesteader had stampeded the herd. Sawyer blindfolded the animal while another cowboy tied the farmer to the horse with a lariat. Sawyer then walked behind the horse and fired a pistol so close to the animal's rump that it singed the hairs. The horse whinnied in pain and took off in the direction of the south slope of the mesa. Sawyer and his men cheered as the homesteader met the same fate as their two companions.

Before long, rumors had spread that every herd that was held on the mesa stampeded during the night. Some people claimed to have seen the ghost of the murdered homesteader sitting on a horse and racing behind a herd of phantom cattle over the south side of the mesa. Cattlemen began avoiding Stampede Mesa, even though it was the best grazing ground for miles around. In an article titled "The Special Charm of Stampede Mesa" in the *Lubbock Avalanche-Journal* on March 16, 2000, Tanner Laine tells the story of an old cowhand named Pancho Burall, who was keeping watch on a herd of cattle on top of Stampede Mesa in 1900 when he saw a man on a blindfolded horse that seemed to be running above the ground. The horseman fired a gun, which startled Pancho's cattle. He and another cowboy barely had enough time to divert their stampeding steers away from the south side of the mesa.

Stampede Mesa still maintains its forbidding aura. Texas author and historian C. F. Eckhardt says that years ago, before the Blanco Canyon dam was constructed, one could still walk around the base of the mesa and kick up cattle bones and strands of barbed wire. Today campers in the area sometimes report hearing the thundering hooves of stampeding cattle around Stampede Mesa, and sightings of the phantom herd occasionally make the local news around Crosby.

The Screaming Bridge

Arlington

Several stories surround a pair of bridges—both now closed—in Tarrant County, a few miles from Arlington. One was said to be haunted by the ghosts of six girls who were killed in a car wreck on the bridge. After watching a movie on the night of February 4, 1961, three high school girls and three other girls from Arlington were driving down Arlington-Bedford Road, which has since been renamed Greenbelt Road. Driving at a speed of forty-five miles per hour, they had just crossed the railroad tracks and began their approach over the wooden bridge spanning the West Fork of the Trinity River.

But unbeknownst to the girls, a group of boys had set fire to the bridge several days earlier to prevent blacks living in Mosier Valley from crossing the river into Arlington. The car flew in the air across the ravine and hit the bank on the other side. The car landed upside down, killing two of the teens, Mary Lou Goldner and Claudia Jean Reeves, the daughter of a highway patrolman. Another passenger, Kathy Fleming, was dead on arrival at Baylor Hospital. According to newspaper articles published two days later, a young man, Bill Young, had skidded to a halt just three feet from the ravine shortly before the girls arrived. He tried to signal to the girls' car by honking his horn while he was backing up. The authorities speculated that the sight of his taillights coming toward the girls' car might have frightened the driver and actually caused her to speed up as she passed Young's car. Immediately after Young saw the car plummet into the ravine, he notified the police. Later, County Fire Marshal Mason Linkford said that the police had erected barriers over the remains of the bridge at both ends, but the barriers had been removed the night of the accident.

Following the accident, the remains of the bridge were removed and replaced with large concrete drain tunnels. The tunnels were paved over with asphalt, thereby creating a means of crossing the Trinity River. In 1994, however, this stretch of road was closed after two women, Rayelynn Jonston and Tammy Lynn Dodson, tried unsuccessfully to outrun an oncoming train.

High school students who had been partying in this area generated another ghost legend about a bridge about a half mile away that crossed the Trinity River at the end of Trammel Davis Road. According to locals, a group of students were celebrating near the site of the burned-out bridge after an Arlington High School football game in 1977. At 10 P.M., the party was disrupted by the sound of a loud crash coming from the other bridge. When the students arrived at the scene, they found that two cars had had a head-on collision on the narrow bridge. Four teenagers are said to have perished in the crash on the bridge now known as Screaming Bridge.

This bridge is now closed to traffic. However, the wire barricades stretching across each end of the structure are not enough of a deterrent to prevent young people from climbing around the wire and walking and partying on the bridge. The sides of the bridge are covered with graffiti proclaiming that this is the true Screaming Bridge. For decades, walking across this bridge has been a rite of passage for local teenagers, who have an entire body of ghost stories chronicling their experiences. As one story goes, one night in 2008, three teenage boys were lured to the bridge by rumors of a demon lurking around the structure. While they were there, the bridge started shaking. When they got back in the car, one of the boys found fresh scratches on his arm. Another tale holds that in 2009, several girls were sitting in the middle of the bridge late at night when they heard a woman's scream and a male's voice saying, "OK. Time to go." They heeded the warning of the disembodied voice and left immediately. Some young people who said they heard the scream claimed that it originated a half mile away, at the site of the old wooden bridge. One young man was walking on the bridge when he saw a black, shadowy figure standing at the end of the bridge, screaming. A misty, humanlike shape has been sighted on the bridge as well.

But the ghost story that gave the Screaming Bridge its name harks back to the 1977 collision. Teenagers bold enough to venture onto the bridge on the night of the anniversary of the tragedy say that around midnight, a dense fog rolls from the river onto the bridge. At the same time, glowing headlights appear momentarily from either end of the bridge. A few people even claimed to have seen tombstones engraved with the names of the deceased teenagers rising from the river.

River Legacy Park

Arlington

River Legacy Park may look like typical modern park, with hiking trails, picnic areas, and a playground, but the ghost stories people tell reveal dark episodes from its past. The most notorious area in the park is called Hell's Gate, which can be accessed by entering the gate on Northeast Green Oaks and taking the first left turn. A foot trail leading from the cul-de-sac takes curiosity seekers to the One Mile sign. After turning left at the sign, visitors who have not lost their nerve walk up to the bench area, where two fence posts mark the entrance to Hell's Gate. Legend has it that this is the place where a number of Union prisoners were taken to a hanging tree and summarily executed. People walking up to the gate have reported hearing the disembodied cries of phantom soldiers being marched to their death. A red-haired general wearing a Confederate uniform has been seen walking away from Hell's Gate.

Another story surrounds a hobo who had jumped off a passing train in the late 1970s or early 1980s. He was trying to go to sleep in the woods near River Legacy Park when he heard the screams of a woman. The screams seemed to come from a car parked on the edge of the woods. When he had walked close enough to peer through the windows of the car, he could see a man hitting a woman in the head. The hobo opened the door and grabbed the man, who pulled out a pistol and killed the hobo. The woman, who had been knocked unconscious, did not regain her senses until the next morning, when she was found, half naked, staggering through the park. Today, lovers who park along the woods for a romantic interlude sometimes report seeing the ghost of the old hobo wandering around. Some people claim that their privacy was interrupted by a ragged-looking old man tapping on their car's window. He always disappears after a few seconds.

Thanks to the Internet and chat rooms, River Legacy Park has become a favorite haunt of thrill seekers eager to have a paranormal encounter. However, getting lost in the park likely poses more of a threat to the amateur ghost hunters than the ghosts do.

Bruce Hall

Denton

Bruce Hall, which opened in 1947, is the oldest dormitory on the campus of the University of North Texas. Two spirits have sent chills up and down the spines of the residents of Bruce Hall for more than half a century. One of these specters is known as "Boiler Room Bill." Legend has it that Bill was an African American student who attended the university in the 1950s. After he moved into the dormitory, a group of white students began harassing him. One night, Bill's tormentors sneaked into his room while his was asleep, gagged him, and dragged him down to the basement, where they hanged him from one of the steam pipes that run along the ceiling in the boiler room.

Residents of the dormitory believe that Bill was hanged from one particular pipe that has a dent in the middle. Bill's ghost has been credited with opening the boiler room's heavy, metal industrial doors after they have been shut. Adonias Wondwessen, a music education junior, said he believes that Boiler Room Bill primarily haunts black students to save them from the same fate that he suffered.

Bruce Hall's most famous ghost, however, is a female apparition named Wanda, the spirit of a student who lived on the fourth floor of Bruce Hall and usually manifests in the attic. According to campus lore, Wanda hanged herself from the rafters in the attic when she learned that she was pregnant. Even though no record of the incident has ever been discovered, the high levels of paranormal activity detected in the attic tend to lend credence to the story. In 1999, two contractors were hired to remodel the bathrooms on the fourth floor. At the time, they were the only ones in the building, and all the rooms were open. As the men walked down the hallway, every door slammed shut on its own. The contractors also reported that several of the showers turned on by themselves while they were working in the bathroom.

On January 2, 2011, the Texas Paranormal Advanced Research Team and Palo Duro Area Paranormal Society conducted a joint investigation of Bruce Hall. Late that night, the group sat down in the hallway on one of the floors and began an EVP session. In an effort to acquaint the spirit with the recording equipment, one of the members said, "You'll have to talk into these microphones, or we won't be able to hear you." Almost immediately, all of the members heard a throaty voice say, "Yeah." Two of the voice recorders recorded the same EVP. Bruce Hall's resident ghost seems to be just as comfortable with technology as most college students are.

Northeast
Texas

The Grove

Jefferson

The Grove, a beautiful Greek Revival home built in the 1860s, is known today as the most haunted house in Texas. Stories of the hauntings of the Grove date back to 1983, when Daniel McKinley Grove Jr. and his wife, Lucile, purchased the property. One night, Mrs. Grove took a Bible to bed with the intention of reading scripture and praying for her husband. However, she was so tired that she soon fell asleep before she could pray. A few hours later, she sensed a presence in the room and woke up. She turned on the lights and was horrified by what she saw: an amorphous black cloud swirling around the bedroom. Before she could exit the room, it had vanished. Over the next few years, strange noises that resonated through the house—spectral voices, ghostly footsteps, sounds of objects moving around—convinced the Groves that they were sharing their home with something not of this world.

When the building housed a restaurant between 1990 and 2002, guests and employees soon realized that the stories the Groves had been telling about their house were true. Patrick Hopkins, the owner of the restaurant, said that he and his family heard someone moaning in upstairs rooms that were unused at the time. Mirrors fell off the walls and landed several feet away from where they had originally been hung. The pungent odor of sweat sometimes permeated specific parts of the old house. One day, a waitress who was on her way into a hallway from the kitchen was attacked by a large, black dog. The dog lunged at her and knocked her on her back. Screaming, the girl ran into Patrick Hopkins's office. Sobbing uncontrollably, she told him about the vicious canine that was loose in the house. Patrick searched the restaurant and house for a good hour, but no trace of the dog was ever found.

Patrick had his own encounter with one of the restaurant's best-known ghosts, the lady in white, who is said to be the spirit of the original owner, Minerva Fox Stilley. One morning, he was getting ready to open the restaurant when he saw a lady in white walk down the hallway and into the ladies' room. Later, Patrick found out that the lady in white has been seen by neighbors as well. One night at 9 P.M., a woman who lives across the street was on her porch when she saw a white figure standing on the eastern side of the Grove. The apparition seemed interested in the progress the workmen had made on the new house. No one was living in the Grove at the time.

While the restaurant operated in the Grove, sightings of the lady in white became common. During this time, a number of dinner theater productions were presented here. One night during rehearsals for the play *Angel Street*, a lighting technician was standing on the front porch, looking through a window, when she sensed someone staring at her. She cast her eyes to the right and saw a woman in a Victorian-era dress walking down the eastern side of the house. The technician ran after the woman to tell her that there was no door on that side of the house. As soon as the lady in white rounded the corner, she disappeared. That same night, the actress portraying the heroine was walking down the stairs when she saw a woman dressed in period costume standing in a corner on the first floor. The actress attempted to strike up a conversation with the mysterious woman, but she disappeared almost immediately.

One usually associates ghosts with dark, gloomy spaces, but at the Grove, even the garden seems to be haunted. A man who was renting out the cottage said that he saw a little girl picking the flowers in the garden. Concerned that she might have wandered away from her parents, he walked outside and went to the little girl. She stared up at him and slowly faded away. A pleasant-looking young gentleman has also been seen strolling through the garden. A spirit thought to be that of Minerva Fox Stilley has been seen walking through a place in a wall where there was once a door leading to her beloved garden.

Mitchel and Tammy Whitington have been operating the Grove as a tour home since they became the latest in the series of owners in 2002. Mitchel's first encounter with the spirits in the house occurred in October of that year, when he was hosting a party at his new house.

An hour before the party was scheduled to begin, he turned on the oven to preheat it before placing a tray of chicken wings inside. After a few minutes, he realized that the oven was not warming up. He opened the lower front panel of the oven and, with lighter wand in hand, knelt down on the floor. As soon as he found the pilot light, he noticed the pungent odor of gas. He reached for the lighter wand, but it was gone. Tammy could not find the lighter wand either, so she handed her husband a lighted candle. Mitchel lit the pilot light and Tammy placed the chicken wings in the oven. By the time the guests arrived, the chicken wings were ready, and the party was a huge success. A few days later, Tammy opened a buffet cabinet and was surprised to find the missing lighter wand sitting on a pile of dishes. The Whitingtons are convinced that one of the Grove's protective spirits had hidden the lighter wand to keep Mitchel from accidentally igniting the gas fumes in the kitchen.

Most people would probably shudder at the prospect of living in the most haunted house in Texas. However, Mitchel Whitington is glad he is sharing his home with ghosts. He feels they are protective spirits who love the Grove so much that they have no plans to leave.

The Excelsior House Hotel

Jefferson

Built in the 1850s, the Excelsior House Hotel is the second-oldest hotel in Texas. Its register bears the signatures of some of the most famous names of the nineteenth and twentieth centuries, including Oscar Wilde, Ulysses S. Grant, Rutherford B. Hayes, and Lady Bird Johnson. One of the hotel's most legendary guests was railroad tycoon Jay Gould, who signed the register by drawing a bird in place of his first name. When the city turned down Gould's offer to run his railroad through Jefferson, he wrote, "The End of Jefferson," on the hotel register. Gould's angry prophecy turned out to be true. After the natural log dam on the Red River broke, Jefferson's days as a port town ended abruptly, causing the population to dwindle from thirty-five thousand to three thousand.

According to the cleaning ladies and a number of guests, the Excelsior House is always occupied—even when no one has checked in. The second floor is said to be haunted by a woman in black. Many guests have seen the forlorn spirit aimlessly walking the halls with a baby in her arms. She has been blamed for the disappearance of objects in guestrooms as well. Some people also claim to have smelled perfume in the hallways when no women were present.

The most famous sighting in the Excelsior Hotel occurred when Steven Spielberg stayed there during the filming of *Sugarland Express* in 1974. It is said that the director was awakened in the middle of the night by the creaking of a rocking chair, which seemed to be rocking itself. Spielberg immediately knocked on the rooms where the members of his crew were sleeping and woke them up. They all checked out of the hotel at 2 A.M.

Several of the ghosts in the hotel seem to have made their identities known. In recent years, weird noises have been heard in the rooms where President Ulysses S. Grant stayed in 1883 and where President Rutherford B. Hayes stayed in 1878. One morning in 1970, a woman staying in the Rutherford B. Hayes Room told the desk clerk that someone had tried to pull the covers off her four-poster bed sometime during the night. She insisted that the door to the room had been locked the entire time.

The Jay Gould Room has also been the scene of paranormal activity. The pungent odor of cigar smoke has been detected in the room. Some people have reported seeing a rocking chair in the room rock by itself. A cleaning woman named Ruby Britton claimed that she always felt a presence in that room whenever it rained. One day, she entered the room and almost walked right into a headless apparition that was standing in the middle of the room. After that encounter, Ruby refused to go into the Jay Gould Room unless she was accompanied by someone else.

In the 1970s, newspaper columnist Frank X. Tolbert decided to test the validity of the ghost stories he had heard about the Excelsior Hotel by spending the night in the Jay Gould Room by himself. A couple times during the night, the bathroom door slammed shut. Despite the rude awakening, he was able to return to sleep. Tolbert reported that at 3:35 A.M., he was awakened by the siren at a nearby fire station. As his eyes were blinking awake, he noticed that the door to the wardrobe was open. Tolbert shut the door and went back to sleep. When he awoke at 6 A.M., the door to the wardrobe was standing wide open again. In 1976, Tolbert returned to the Excelsior Hotel, this time with his family in tow. He said that his family was awakened during the night by the sounds of conversation that seemed to be coming from the attic. Tolbert could tell by their vocabulary that they were fairly cultured. The next morning, the hotel manager told them that no one had been staying in the attic the previous night.

The Excelsior Hotel is one of those southern inns whose history has become intertwined with its ghost legends. Frank Tolbert is one of hundreds of people who have spent the night at the hotel to see for themselves if there is any truth to the tales guests and employees have been telling for years. At the Excelsior Hotel, the term "living history" has acquired an entirely new meaning.

The Jefferson Hotel

Jefferson

The building that is now the Jefferson Hotel was originally constructed in 1851 as a cotton warehouse. After the town's steamboat port closed in 1875, the warehouse served a variety of purposes for the remainder of the nineteenth century. A Chinese laundry operated out of the back of the building for a while, and according to locals, a bordello and dance hall were located here as well. At the turn of the century, the building was converted into a hotel. In the 1920s, when it was known as the Crystal Palace, gambling was offered in the back room. The hotel has changed hands as well as names a number of times since the 1940s. To ghost hunters, however, it is known as the most haunted place in Jefferson.

Employees have been talking about the ghosts in the Jefferson Hotel for many years. In the late 1990s, a night clerk was working on the first floor when she heard loud noises coming from upstairs. She said that she heard people talking and doors opening and closing. The young woman was terrified because no one had booked any of the upstairs rooms that evening. After the noises stopped, she walked upstairs to investigate, but no one was there. One morning in the early 2000s, a maid placed fresh towels in a bathroom and changed the sheets on the bed. She then walked out into the hallway to get some clean glasses. When she returned to the room, she was stunned to see the impression of a body on the bed. She looked into the bathroom and noticed that one of the face towels had been used. While she was trying to think of a rational explanation for the disturbances in the room, she felt someone touch her shoulder. The maid ran out of the room and informed the owner that she was quitting.

Most of the reports of supernatural manifestations inside the Jefferson Hotel have come from guests, however. People walking up the staircase have felt an invisible hand pulling at their hair and touching their shoulders. Some have also heard the creaking of boards as if someone—or something—is walking up or down the stairs. Guests have photographed orbs in the upstairs hallway. In Room 5, a little boy complained to his parents that a strange man was waking him up during the night. In Room 19, guests have seen a dark, shadowy figure standing in a corner of the room. Many people have felt somebody lie down next to them on the bed. When they turn on the light, the unwelcome visitor is gone. This invisible presence has also been known to touch people during the night. In Room 20, a man and his wife who had just checked into the hotel tried to put their clothes in the armoire but found the task to be extremely difficult because the handles were gone. While they were sitting on the bed talking, the doors of the armoire slowly swung open. A few years later, an elderly lady standing in the hallway early one morning saw a tall man walk through the closed door into Room 20. A woman was asleep in Room 21 when she felt someone pull the sheets down to the foot of the bed. A few seconds later, she felt someone stroke the back of her head.

Hotel guests are not the only people who frequent the Jefferson. Locals as well as visitors enjoy dining at Lamache's Italian Resturant, located inside the hotel. The food and service are so good that people do not seem to mind walking through cold spots or hearing disembodied footsteps and voices.

1895 Tarlton House

Hillsboro

John and Frances Tarlton moved to Hillsboro in 1873. The couple had two sons, Benjamin Dudley and Greene Duke, who both became lawyers. Benjamin Dudley served as a Texas Supreme Court justice and on the faculty at the University of Texas Law School. Greene Duke married Sarah Elizabeth Scott and built a three-story Queen Anne Victorian mansion at 211 North Pleasant Street in 1895. The couple had five children. Sarah died in 1907, and three years later, Greene Duke married Elizabeth Millard. Because Elizabeth did not get along with her stepchildren, Greene Duke built a second house next door to his former residence, where his children lived. Elizabeth died of cancer in 1931, and her husband followed her in death that same year. Some people say that he died of influenza, but others claim that he hanged himself in the attic. Today the 1895 Tarlton House is a bed-and-breakfast that is reputed to be haunted by the old man's ghost.

Greene Duke Tarlton is said to be a restless spirit who wanders the halls of his former home. Witnesses have encountered cold spots and heard footsteps in the hallway, usually late at night. An attic door opens on its own. A few guests have even felt soft kisses on their brow while they slept. In *A Texas Guide to Haunted Restaurants, Taverns and Inns*, Robert and Anne Powell Wlodarski report that members of the Morris family, who lived in the house in the 1970s, claimed that something pulled on their blankets while they slept and sat on their bed. After the Rhodes family turned the old house into a bed-and-breakfast, a housekeeper said she was making one of the beds when she looked up to see an old man smiling at her.

The 1895 Tarlton House is one of the state's best-preserved bed-and-breakfasts. A number of celebrities have stayed here, including President Calvin Coolidge and television host Art Linkletter, and First Lady Laura Bush held a reception at the Tarlton House to promote literacy. None of the guests seem concerned that they might be paid a visit during the night by the friendly spirit of the original owner of the house.

The Baker Hotel

Mineral Wells

In the early 1900s, Mineral Wells was a popular spa resort town. For years, people traveled hundreds of miles to partake of the mineral water, which was reputed to have curative powers. A woman was said to have been cured of insanity by drinking the water, which was nicknamed "crazy water" and gave the resort's guest facility the name of Crazy Water Hotel. When this hotel burned to the ground in 1925, Texas hotel magnate Theodore Brasher Baker built the Baker Hotel on the same site. It was a luxury hotel that was twice the size of its predecessor. The Baker Hotel opened in 1929, two weeks after the stock market crash, but it managed to survive and even thrive during the Great Depression. Its guest list included such luminaries as Will Rogers, Jean Harlow, Judy Garland, and Marlene Dietrich. By the end of the decade, however, physicians began to question the medical benefits of drinking mineral water, and the fortunes of both the hotel and the city began to decline.

After the Fort Wolters military base opened in late 1940, the Baker Hotel served as a military dependent quarters for several years. When the base closed at the end of the war in 1945, the hotel began a downhill slide from which it never totally recovered. There were a few bright spots, such as when it hosted both the Texas Republican and Democratic Conventions several times in the 1950s. By the 1960s, many health resorts across the country were losing money, and although the Baker closed briefly, local investors managed to keep it open until 1972. Since then, the Baker Hotel's rooms have remained vacant except for rats, pigeons—and possibly ghosts.

Today, the manager of the building, Ronny Walker, gives tours on the weekends for people eager to catch a glimpse of the Baker's permanent residents. One of locations in the Baker Hotel that's said to be haunted is the Brazos Room on the first floor. Some people have smelled the aroma of sweet chocolate in this room. Lights are said to turn off and on by themselves. A number of visitors have photographed orbs in this room. In the 2000s, a group of World War II veterans took a tour of the hotel and were walking through the Brazos

Room. Late in the evening, they all reported hearing the clanking of dishes and silverware. They also heard the faint strains of orchestral music. Some people believe that the noises might be attributed to the ghosts of Bonnie and Clyde, who stayed in the Brazos Room in the 1930s.

A number of strange incidents have been reported on the seventh floor as well. A former maid at the hotel said that on a number of occasions, she found drinking glasses with red lipstick on the rims in a vacant room. Ronny Walker said that one night during the Christmas season, he was trying to locate a breaker switch when he heard the soft footsteps of someone walking up to his left. Ronny thought someone was sneaking up on him, so he snapped his head around. No one was there. A woman's ghost was first sighted on the seventh floor by a porter in the 1960s. Other people have smelled her perfume in a suite on the southeast corner of this floor. She is said to be the spirit of the hotel manager's mistress, who committed suicide by jumping off the top of the building. In the early 2000s, a male member of a local paranormal group was taking readings in the seventh floor all alone when he felt himself being groped by a female hand. The entity stopped making advances when a female investigator entered the room.

Not surprisingly, the one place in the hotel that has seen the most foot traffic—the lobby—is also believed to be haunted. Ronny Walker said that he was walking through the first floor when he heard the clicking sound of someone in high heels passing through the main lobby. Thinking that another employee, Jane Catrett, was in the lobby, Ronny called out her name. Later, he discovered that Jane had not been in the hotel at all that day.

The kitchen is said to be haunted by the victim of a grisly murder. One day in the 1930s, a maid got into a heated argument with her lover, a cook. When the maid threatened to tell the cook's wife about their affair, he grabbed a butcher knife and stabbed her several times. The woman collapsed to the floor and lay in the blood that was pooling around her. Members of tour groups claim to have heard a faint female voice say, "Leave!"

In the early 1990s, a teller who was working in the bank across the street from the abandoned hotel noticed that several windows were open. She pointed this out to her coworkers, who told her they had seen a number of different windows open in the hotel a few days ear-lier. The tellers decided to amuse themselves by keeping track of which windows were open each day. It continued to vary, and after a while, the tellers began to notice a pattern.

With all of these ghostly goings-on, it's no wonder that paranormal investigators consider the Baker Hotel one of the best places to record supernatural activity in the entire state.

The Catfish Plantation

Waxahachie

The Catfish Plantation is one of the most famous restaurants in Northeast Texas, made so by the paranormal reputation of the house in which it is located. The history of the house, built in 1895 at 814 Water Street, reportedly was rife with tragedy and death. Locals say that in the 1920s, Elizabeth Anderson, the nineteen-year-old daugh-ter of the original owner of the house, was strangled in the bathroom either by a former lover or by her groom's ex-girlfriend on her wed-ding day. Two other people are said to have died in the house of nat-ural causes in subsequent years: a farmer named Will, who died in the 1930s, and a woman named Caroline Jenkins Moody, who died of a stroke in 1970. The house stood empty for much of the next decade. Then in 1984, Tom and Melissa Baker purchased it with the intention of turning it into a restaurant. Before long, the couple found that the former owners apparently had not quite accepted the fact that their house was no longer their home.

Melissa was the first to arrive at the conclusion that the old house might be haunted. One morning, she walked into the kitchen and was surprised to find that a large coffee urn, which had been on the table, was now in the middle of the floor. The urn was full of coffee cups, which had been sitting on a shelf the night before. On another occa-sion, she entered the kitchen and found that someone had made a fresh cup of coffee. Her husband swore that he did not do it.

Melissa's suspicions that there was a ghost in the house were con-firmed by her employees, who began having experiences of their own. One of the cooks said that a fry basket floated up in the air while he was in the kitchen. Another reported that a blue light was emanating from an empty room. A third employee saw the figure of a woman in a wedding dress staring out of the front window. Refrigerator doors opened and slammed shut on their own, and lights turned themselves off and on. Employees frequently reported running into cold spots in the house.

Tom and Melissa received so many reports of haunted activity inside the house that they consulted a psychic, who conducted a séance at the Catfish Plantation. The psychic told the owners that they were sharing their house with three entities, all of whom were former residents. One was the spirit of the old farmer, Will, who wears overalls and seems to enjoy flirting with customers by stroking their hair and touching their knees. One day, the police were driving by the house when they saw a man dressed in overalls standing on the porch. After they parked the car and walked toward the house, the figure of the man slowly dematerialized.

The second ghost is the spirit of Elizabeth Anderson, who is thought to have made her presence known during the séance by rattling the dishes, tapping the walls, lighting a candle, and appearing in the kitchen doorway as a filmy female figure wearing a wedding gown. People say they know she is around when they smell the sweet scent of roses or feel cold all of a sudden.

The spirit of Caroline Jenkins Moody seems to be the most active of the three ghosts at the Catfish Plantation. By the time she died in 1970, Caroline had lived in the house with her husband and children for seventeen years. The temper tantrums that she seems to occasionally throw in the house suggest that she still considers herself to be in charge. She is credited with slamming doors and throwing coffee cups in the kitchen. She is even said to have struck one of the "strangers" who was standing in her kitchen.

Change came to the Catfish Plantation after the turn of the twentieth century. In 2003, the house was partially burned in a fire, but the damage was repaired, and the restaurant was once again open for business the following fall. In 2007, the Landis family bought the Catfish Plantation from Tom and Melissa Baker. The new owners seem excited about their restaurant's haunted reputation. They have invited paranormal investigators to spend the night in the old house and even threw a "ghost party" in 2010.

A number of newspaper and magazine reporters have traveled to Waxahachie to find out more about the town's most haunted house. Television shows have filmed here as well. When a film crew from the Travel Channel visited the restaurant, an investigator was sitting in a side room, talking about the haunted history of the Catfish Plantation, when a transparent figure was seen entering the room and standing behind him for a few minutes before disappearing. In October 2010, Brad and Barry Klinge, the hosts of the Discovery Channel's *Ghost Lab*, conducted a "ghost hunt" at the restaurant. It's clear that the Catfish Plantation offers guests much more than the best in Cajun-style cuisine.

The Rogers Hotel

Waxahachie

Emory W. Rogers, the founder of Waxahachie, built the first log cabin in the area in 1847. After Waxahachie began to grow, he built a hotel on the site where his log cabin had stood. The hotel was rebuilt twice after being destroyed by fires. The last incarnation of the hotel, built in 1913 of reinforced concrete and dark, mottled brick, was promoted as being "absolutely fireproof." The architect also added two towers to set this building apart from the other hotels in the area. For the next several decades, the Rogers Hotel operated as a "gentlemen's hotel" where traveling businessmen whiled away the hours by gambling and paying for the services of prostitutes. After World War II, however, hotels like the Rogers were no longer profitable. It nevertheless continued to operate until 1964. In 2000, the building was restored and reopened as a hotel. Today the Rogers Hotel has a "spooky" reputation that seems to be due to more than just its appearance.

The paranormal activity that has been reported inside the Rogers Hotel might have been generated by the building's violent past. Stories are told of several people dying here tragically. A man is said to have hanged himself in Room 409. In the 1920s, a little girl supposedly drowned in the swimming pool. Legend has it that not long after the hotel opened, the owner's son hanged himself in the elevator shaft. And a few years later, after the hotel closed, a vagrant reportedly jumped out of one of the upper-story windows.

In the early 2000s, a maintenance man who lived in the hotel was awakened by an insistent knocking sound. He got out of bed and opened the door. Standing in the doorway was a strange-looking man dressed in dirty, old-fashioned clothes. The man asked the maintenance man to follow him downstairs. When they reached the basement, the strange man said, "Weird things have happened down here. Don't ever come down here again." As soon as the man finished talking, he faded away. The maintenance man was so terrified that he ran back to his room and locked himself inside.

The fourth floor where the hanging is said to have occurred is the creepiest floor in the entire hotel. Many employees claim to have felt very uneasy on this particular floor. Maids have investigated the sounds of voices and footsteps in rooms that were supposed to be vacant. When they opened the door, no one was inside. One staff member reported being touched in her room by a cold, invisible hand. Guests have also had very unnerving experiences on this floor. A woman who was sleeping in bed with her husband was awakened by the feeling that she was being watched. When her eyes finally focused, she saw a man dressed like a cowboy standing at the foot of her bed. She turned over to awaken her husband. When she looked back, the ghostly cowboy was gone.

A night clerk had a particularly harrowing experience. She was sitting at the desk, reading a magazine, when the elevator went up to the fourth floor. After the elevator returned to the lobby, the clerk was surprised when the door opened but no one was inside. Suddenly a young girl in a white dress appeared in front of the desk. The night clerk asked the girl if she could help her, but instead of answering, the girl turned around, ran a few feet, and vanished.

Area ghost hunters investigated after hearing about the old hotel's ghost stories. One group of paranormal investigators informed the owner that there was a malignant entity in the basement but all the ghosts on the fourth floor were benign. During another investigation, a woman who left a tape recorder running in one of the rooms on the fourth floor picked up movement. She said it sounded as if someone were walking back and forth across the room. The Rogers Hotel, it seems, has a special appeal for spirits who have no other home.

Demons Road

Huntsville

From all appearances, Huntsville, home to Sam Houston State University, is a typical college town, but one of its roads is anything but typical. The town was founded in 1836 and was the home of Samuel Houston, who served as president of the Republic of Texas and governor of the state of Texas. Today Huntsville's reputation lies in more than its university and its historic buildings. Huntsville is also known for "Demons Road," which runs through the city.

The road's real name is Bowden Road. People living in Huntsville first realized that something was wrong with "Demons Road" in 1890, when a farmer plowing his field was dragged into the woods by a dark entity enveloped in mist and subsequently murdered. The fact that the historic road leads to Martha's Chapel Cemetery has not helped its reputation. People driving along the road at night claim to have driven past old houses that were not there in the daytime. Shadowy figures wrapped in fog have been seen lurking in the woods. People who drove along Demons Road have discovered that they drove ten more miles than the actual length of the road. A few people have picked up hitchhikers along the road, only to discover that they have vanished a few minutes later. Drivers have also seen red lights flickering in the woods along Demons Road. The number of lights always corresponds to the number of people in the car. More than a hundred drivers have reported finding handprints on their cars. It seemed as if someone were trying to grab onto their cars on Demons Road. Once again, the number of handprints is the same as the number of people riding in the car. A child with glowing eyes, riding a tricycle, makes an occasional appearance on the road.

Some people swear that the spectral figures they encountered on Demons Road and in the cemetery followed them home. Writer Dana

Goolsby tells the story of a woman and her husband who drove down Demons Road to Martha's Chapel Cemetery in May 2010. While they were looking at the tombstones, she saw a man walking through the cemetery. A few days later, the woman was getting ready to take a shower. She was just about to shut the curtains when she saw a strange man standing in her bedroom. He was the same man she had seen roaming around the cemetery.

In the mid-1980s, people began spreading rumors that satanists were performing rituals in the woods along Demons Road. Reports of slaughtered animals lying on the ground and robed figures running through the woods eventually reached the ears of the local police, who, for a while, cautioned people against stopping along the road. The road's evil reputation has not stopped young lovers and teenage boys eager to prove their manhood from venturing onto the road late at night. Actually, it seems that Demons Road's primary attraction is not so much its alleged links to the devil as it is the aura of mystery that hangs over the old road at every turn.

Andrews–Taylor House

Karnack

In 1843, Cephas "Milt" K. Andrews wanted to construct a mansion that would dwarf all the other dwellings in Karnack. The classic Revival house, which is located three miles southwest of town on State Highway 43, is one of the finest nineteenth-century buildings in Northeast Texas. In 1902, the "Big House," as it was known in the area, was purchased by Thomas Jefferson Taylor, who converted the property into a ranch. Taylor was the father of Claudia Alta Taylor, known affectionately as Lady Bird. The future wife of President Lyndon Baines Johnson was born and raised in the house. After Taylor's death, his wife, Ruth, became owner of the mansion.

Lady Bird Johnson's birthplace and childhood home is said to be haunted by the ghost of Milt Andrews's nineteen-year-old daughter, Eunice, or "Oonie," as she was called by her parents. According to writer Bob Bowman, Oonie was sitting in one of the upstairs bedrooms on a dark and stormy night in the 1880s when a lightning bolt struck the roof and raced down the chimney. She was struck by the lightning bolt and burned to death.

For more than a century since then, Oonie's ghost is said to have been haunting the bedroom where she died. People have reported hearing weird noises and seeing full-body apparitions, which many believe is Oonie making her presence known. Years after moving from the "Big House" to the White House, Lady Bird Johnson said that she never had a personal experience with Oonie's ghost. She did admit, however, that she had always felt uneasy in the old house when she was a little girl.

Stephen F. Austin State University

Nacogdoches

Stephen F. Austin State University was founded in 1923 on 640 acres, part of which was the homestead of one of the state's founding fathers, Thomas Jefferson Rush. The university is named after another Texas founding father, Stephen F. Austin. It is one of only four public universities in Texas that are not affiliated with one of the state's six university systems. The university offers more than eighty undergraduate majors and over fifty graduate degrees. And according to campus lore, it also offers students an opportunity to have a brush with the paranormal in several buildings that are thought to be haunted.

According to writer Dana Goolsby, one of the dormitory buildings, Mays Hall 11, was originally a hospital. The campus clinic was located on the first floor until the 1960s, when the "short wing" was constructed. At this time, the clinic was completely renovated into dorm rooms. The basement houses a bomb shelter, which was built in the 1940s. Students who have somehow managed to break into the bomb shelter end of the basement have experienced feelings of deep depression. Some students say that the false wall in the basement projects a great deal of dark energy. No one knows what lies behind the false wall.

According to the Twilight Paranormal Society, the third floor of Griffith Hall is haunted by the ghost of a female resident assistant who leaped out a window while playing with a Ouija board. Lights in the shower are said to flicker at the exact time she died. Women living in the south end of the building have heard someone running down the hallway around 2 A.M., and the specter of a young woman in a tattered dress has been seen at the end of a hallway. The building ceased to function as a dormitory in 2005.

The most famous haunted building on campus, however, is the Turner Fine Arts Building. Some people say that the building is haunted by the spirit of a Caddo Indian who died in one of the battles fought on this site. Others say he could be the ghost of a soldier killed in the Texas Revolution. But many students, faculty, and staff believe that the ghost, nicknamed Chester, is the spirit of the architect who designed the building. As the story goes, the foreman read the building plans incorrectly, and as a result, the auditorium was built backward. The architect, whose first name was Chester, killed himself in disgrace. An equally large number of people believe that the ghost haunting the building is a drama student. Whoever this young man was and however he died, his ghost seems to be very active around the theater. In the 1960s, the drama department was staging a production of Shakespeare's *Hamlet*. On the evening of the first performance, the actor portraying the ghost took ill, so the director replaced him with a young man who seemed to know the ghost's lines. That night after the performance, the cast posed for a group picture. When the film was developed, the director was shocked to find only a faint glow at the spot where the actor who had portrayed Hamlet's ghost was standing.

Stephen F. Austin State University, like many colleges and universities, seems to be a hotbed of paranormal activity. And the memories of the unfortunate individuals whose spirits are thought to haunt the buildings are kept alive by the stories students tell in the dorms at night.

The Ghost of Chief Popher

Burke

Bradley Prairie, which lies in Angelina County, was named after Tom Bradley, who started a trading post in the area in 1835. Bradley traded primarily with the Shawnee Indians who lived along the Neches River.

One of the small towns encompassed by Bradley Prairie was Burke, founded in the 1880s after the construction of the Houston, East and West Texas Railway. The friction that invariably resulted when whites and American Indians lived in close proximity to each other is memorialized in a legend that harks back to life on Bradley Prairie in the nineteenth century.

In the 1830s, a young man named Hughes Bradley worked as a clerk in Tom Bradley's trading post. One day, Tom left Hughes in charge of the store while he traveled to McIntosh for supplies. During the course of the day, Hughes quarreled with a Shawnee named Harry Popher, who was the son of the tribe's chief. When Hughes refused to sell whiskey to the young Indian, Harry stormed out of the store. Later that day, Harry returned to the trading post to find Hughes asleep on the countertop. Hughes had locked up the trading post while he took a nap, so Harry removed some of the mud plastered between the logs and shot the clerk where he lay, killing him instantly.

A week later, two settlers stopped by the trading post for supplies. Their suspicions were aroused when they found the door locked and the cattle penned in the back, sorely neglected. The two men rode off to nearby St. Augustine for assistance. They returned with twenty-five armed men, who broke into the trading post and discovered Hughes Bradley's decomposing corpse. The men interrogated the local Indians and learned that Harry Popher had committed the murder. For two days, a posse combed the region in search of Harry but could not apprehend him. On the third day, Harry's father, Chief Popher, approached the head of the posse and offered to allow the men to hang him instead of his son. According to writer Bob Bowman, the chief said, "I am an old man, and my son is still young with his life still before him. Please let me take my son's place."

Six men were given the task of hanging the Indian chief. Chief Popher was hanged along Popher Creek, which is said to have been named after him. Locals say that the ghost of Chief Popher wanders up and down the creek in silent protest of his treatment at the hands of the mob.

The Beckham Hotel

Mineola

Mineola, a city in Wood County, owes its birth to the railroad. Located between Dallas and Longview, Mineola hosted a branch line terminal for the Missouri Pacific Lines and Missouri-Kansas-Texas Railroad. In fact, the railroad was so important to Mineola that its downtown district was built around the depot. Although Mineola's importance as a railroad town has declined since then, a number of buildings in the historic business district that once provided services for the railroad are still standing. Today most of them have been put to different uses, and they now hold specialty shops, cafés, and antique stores.

One of the town's two railroad hotels, the Beckham, is said to be haunted by a number of different ghosts. The original Beckham Hotel was erected in the 1880s across the street from the train station to house passengers and railroad employees laying over between runs. After a fire, the present hotel was built in 1927. In the 1920s and 1930s, the Beckham Hotel was a popular nightspot. A number of big bands played in the upstairs ballroom, and rumor has it that the hotel was frequented by bootleggers and poker players before World War II. These days, the Beckham Hotel is a destination for people interested in the supernatural.

People have reported seeing a number of ghosts in the Beckham for many years. The best known is the spirit of a lonely woman known as Elizabeth, who has been sighted walking down the stairway, usually in a long dress. Legend has it that she died years ago after falling down the stairs. She has also been seen dancing by herself in the ballroom. The ghosts of a little girl and a gambler carrying a deck of cards have also made frequent appearances. A few people said they saw mists and moving lights on the third floor.

John and Nancy DeFoore have owned and lived in the Beckham Hotel since 1993. The DeFoores consider the old hotel to be a great place to live, even though they may be sharing their home with ghosts.

Granbury Opera House

Granbury

When the Granbury Opera House was built in 1886, it shared space with a saloon. In 1911, it became one of several businesses forced to close down by the Women's Christian Temperance Union. By the time the restoration of the Opera House was initiated in 1974, the building was almost beyond saving. The roof had fallen in and the interior was almost gutted. But the following year, the old theater opened its doors once again. Because of the close attention given to period detail, patrons of the newly restored opera house felt as if they had walked through a portal into the nineteenth century. Some people say that the ghost of the most notorious American actor of that century also makes an occasional appearance.

Many employees and patrons of the Granbury Opera House believe that it is haunted by a male apparition wearing a white shirt, black waistcoat, black pants, and high black boots. Some people claim that the ghost has suddenly appeared on the stage and recited lines from some of Shakespeare's plays. The managing director, Marty Van Kleek, says that a number of performers and stagehands have heard footsteps walking back and forth along the balcony.

One man who worked here in the early 2000s had some very strange experiences, according to his wife, Laura Thykeson. Several times, he encountered cold spots in certain parts of the building. Sometimes the urinal in the men's room flushed when no one was there. The "last call" light turned itself off when he made his final walk-through. A production of *Dracula* was disrupted by the stage lights when they went on and off by themselves during the play. His most frightening encounter with the resident spirit occurred one night when he was in the opera house all alone. He was closing up when he distinctly heard someone call his name, although he could not tell if the voice belonged to a man or a woman.

Some say that the ghost that haunts the Granbury Opera House is the spirit of a handsome, dark-haired man who went by the name of John St. Helen when he arrived in the nearby town of Glen Rose in 1865. St. Helen was a schoolteacher who also operated an acting school for the children of upper-class families. He became engaged to the daughter of a local politician, but he left town as soon as his fiancée showed him the guest list, which included a number of soldiers and the U.S. marshal for the Eastern District of Texas. A year later, St. Helen showed up in Granbury, where he worked as a bartender in a saloon adjoining the theater. St. Helen stood out because of his distinctive limp, southern accent, and predilection for Shakespeare. He was never known to take a drink except on April 15, the anniversary of Lincoln's assassination, when he became roaring drunk. He is even said to have performed in several Shakespearean plays at the Granbury Opera House.

St. Helen had lived in Granbury for several years when he became gravely ill. A local doctor examined the man and informed him that he would die of the disease. One day, St. Helen gave a deathbed confession to his best friend, a lawyer named Finis L. Bates. In a barely audible voice, he confessed that he was John Wilkes Booth, the assassin of Abraham Lincoln. When it became clear that he would recover from his "terminal" illness, St. Helen left town. A few days later, Bates was looking through St. Helen's belongings when he discovered a Colt single-shot pocket pistol wrapped in the front page of a Washington, DC, newspaper dated April 15, 1865, the day after Lincoln's assassination.

The story of Granbury's mysterious visitor picks up again in 1906, when an alcoholic named David George died in Enid, Oklahoma. As he lay dying, George admitted that he was John Wilkes Booth. As soon as Finis Bates found out about the death of David George, he traveled to Enid. After examining the dissipated corpse, Bates concluded that this was indeed the body of his former friend, John St. Helen. Bates had the body embalmed and invited government officials to look at it. When they declined, Bates kept the now-mummified body in storage for many years. Between 1920 and 1960, the mummy traveled the country as a sideshow attraction. By the 1970s, however, the mummy had disappeared. Could it be that the man's spirit continues to haunt the Granbury Opera House to this day?

McDow Hole

Alexander

Three miles north of the ghost town of Alexander lies a creekbed with a natural bedrock bottom. This innocuous-looking spring-fed stream supplied life-sustaining water to settlers for miles around and is said to have been surrounded by ghostly activity for many years. Called McDow Hole, the creek was named for Jim McDow, who built a cabin near the creek in 1860. As the legend goes, that spring, a few weeks before Jim's death, his nephew, Charlie Papworth, settled nearby in a suitable location with his wife, Jenny, and their infant son, Temple. McDow's son, also named Jim, helped the Papworths relocate. The Papworths lived in their wagon for a year before finally building a cabin only two hundred yards away from the creek.

By 1865, Charlie and Jenny had another child. A few months after the birth of their second child, Charlie received word that his parents had died in Texarkana and they had willed all their furniture to him. Charlie reluctantly climbed into his wagon, kissed his wife and children good-bye, and set off on the two-hundred-mile journey. Each night, Jenny and her children slept in the homes of their neighbors because of an outbreak of cattle rustling and thievery in the territory.

One month after Charlie had left, Jenny and her children did not show up at the McDow cabin to spend the night. Sensing that something was terribly wrong, the McDow family headed for the Papworth cabin the next morning. When they entered the cabin, they found only a couple overturned chairs and a small pool of blood. A faint whimpering sound led them to look under the bed, where they found little five-year-old Temple hiding underneath. The child was too traumatized to tell what had happened to his mother and his sibling.

The next morning, a search party was organized to find Jenny Papworth and her abductors. Their first stop was at a cabin five miles away, which was owned by a suspicious character named W. P. Brownlow. He insisted that a band of Comanches had attacked the cabin. The search party left Brownlow's cabin and began looking for the Comanches, but they did not find a single Indian. In fact, no Comanche war parties had been reported in the area for some time.

When Charlie Papworth returned to his cabin two weeks later and discovered that his wife and one of his children were missing, he was devastated. He and Temple moved back into their cabin and tried to piece their life back together. Charlie vowed not to rest until the culprit was brought to justice. He suspected that Brownlow was somehow involved, but he had no proof. Knowing that he was under suspicion, Brownlow began spreading rumors about Charlie Papworth, claiming that he was a robber and a horse thief. Charlie's closest friends knew that the charges were groundless, but neighbors who did not know Charlie well took Brownlow's words seriously. One fateful night in 1867, a group of vigilantes began knocking on the doors of houses near the town of Putnam, not far from the Papworth cabin, and dragging off the men. The last man to be arrested was Charlie Papworth. On the morning of his arrest, Charlie and six other men were told that they were to be hanged as horse thieves. As soon as the men were hanged, the vigilantes rode off. After the vigilantes had ridden out of sight, the young Temple climbed the pecan tree and began cutting away at the ropes with his pocketknife. Only his father had survived the hanging. As soon as Charlie was well enough to ride, the pair rode off to the Oklahoma Territory.

Rumors that the Papworth cabin was haunted began spreading throughout the area not long after Charlie and his son left. The first new occupants were a Mr. Keith and his thirteen-year-old son, who had planned to spend just a single night in the abandoned cabin. The pair had just fallen asleep when they awoke because of a sudden drop in temperature and a knock at the door. Mr. Keith opened the door, and there in the doorway was the figure of a sad-faced woman holding a baby. While he was trying to decide whether or not his imagination was working overtime, the spectral woman vanished. Their curiosity aroused, Mr. Keith and his son decided to spend a second night in the cabin. Nothing happened, so the pair decided to stay a third night. Once again, they were awakened by a knock on the door. Inside the doorway was the same female apparition. When he attempted to talk to the woman, she let out a scream that was so bloodcurdling that Mr. Keith and his son ran out the front door and never returned.

The next person who was bold enough to move into the apparently haunted cabin was a coffin maker named Charlie Atchinson, who took up residence there in 1880. The first year he lived in the cabin was totally uneventful. One day, three farmers arrived at the cabin to see if Atchinson had any information regarding some missing cattle. One of the farmers knocked on the door, but no one answered. Concerned that something must have happened to Atchinson, they broke down the door. Lying on the bed was the corpse of Charlie Atchinson, his glazed, lifeless eyes staring at the ceiling. One of the farmers speculated that Atchinson looked as if he had been scared to death.

About five years later, Alabama's most famous train robber, Rube Burrow, and his brother, Jim, were drinking in a saloon in Alexander, Texas. They struck up a conversation with a couple of cowpokes, who told the Burrow boys about the haunted cabin. At the end of their story, they bet Rube and Jim that they could not spend a night in the haunted cabin. Standing up straight, Rube announced that he and his brother were not afraid of anything, and they took the cowboys up on their offer. Three days later, the cowboys rode out to the Papworth cabin to see how Rube and Jim were doing. Not only were the brothers not in the cabin, but they seemed to have fled the entire state.

Several years later, when Jim Burrow lay dying in an Arkansas prison, he told the story of what happened that fateful night. Jim said that on their first night in the cabin, they fortified themselves with whiskey to help them pass the night. They saw a phantom woman standing in the doorway, but they assumed that her appearance had been generated by alcohol, so they decided to stay there a second night without whiskey. Around midnight, the spectral figure of a woman passed through the wall by the door and flew upward into the ceiling. The two men fired their pistols at the apparition and then fled the cabin.

Jenny Papworth's ghost reportedly continued to make appearances in her former home up through the early 1900s. About that same time, W. P. Brownlow lay dying of an incurable disease back east. As he gasped his last breath, Brownlow admitted that he had murdered Jenny Papworth because she had seen him talking to a group of cattle rustlers. Perhaps her spirit finally found rest after the truth about her murder came out.

The Wright Place

Cleburne

In 1870, the twenty-five-room Hamilton House Hotel was constructed in Cleburne to accommodate the passengers who traveled to and from Cleburne and Fort Worth. After it was almost completely destroyed by fire in 1916, A. J. Wright bought the property and constructed an upscale general store on the site. The store occupied only the first floor of the two-story building that extends the entire block from Main Street to Caddo Street, just a block south of the courthouse. After Wright closed his store, a number of different businesses were housed in the building, including a restaurant. For years, every October, the second floor was the site of a "haunted house" called the Faustus Sanitorium. According to the locals, however, so much paranormal activity has occurred at the Wright Place that converting it into a haunted house seems almost superfluous.

The ghost that haunts the Wright Place is known only as Lillie. It is said that when she arrived in 1882 on the first passenger train to pass through Cleburne, she was an attractive twenty-seven-year-old whose family had died in the Civil War. She is rumored to have found work as a prostitute at the Hamilton House Hotel. Either she got into a heated argument one night with one of her customers and was thrown out of an upper-story window, or she became despondent and jumped out of the window. She broke her neck when she hit the ground and died instantly. Eager to close the case, the authorities ruled her death a suicide. The man who reportedly was with her the night she died was never brought to trial.

Many people believe that after the Hamilton House Hotel burned down, Lillie's spirit simply took up residence in the next building to occupy the site, the Wright Place. Her ghost has been sighted upstairs many times. A psychic told the manager of the hotel that Lillie's spirit is usually seen floating above the floor because she has a phobia about dirt. As a rule, witnesses catch only a fleeting glimpse of the woman's spirit as she glides by.

Donna Davidson, a former proprietor of the Wright Place, believes that the second floor of the building is haunted by a number of different ghosts besides Lillie's spirit. Many people have heard the laughter of children echoing down the hallway. An elderly, hunchbacked woman occasionally manifests on this floor. The ghost of an amiable young man reportedly told a psychic that he really enjoyed dancing on the second floor. The ghost of a German cobbler has been heard tapping nails on shoe leather, and many employees and visitors have smelled his cigar smoke. The ghosts of his wife and their young niece, Joy, have been sighted as well.

Today the Wright Place is a far cry from its days as a general store in the early twentieth century. Shoppers peruse the specialty shops in the minimall on the first floor. The second floor has been converted into office space. No fake ghosts wander the hallways on the second floor anymore at Halloween—just the real ones.

The Crying White Lady of Marshall

The story of the Crying White Lady of Marshall is similar to the widespread legend of La Llorona, or the Weeping Woman, which can be found in many variants all over the American Southwest and anyplace where there is a large Hispanic population. In most versions of the tale, a beautiful young woman falls in love with an attractive, powerful man. The woman sacrifices her reputation by moving in with him and having several children by him. Eventually her lover abandons the mother of his children for another woman. Driven by anger and a thirst for revenge, the woman decides to get back at her husband by taking from him that which he loves more than anything else. She leads her small children down to the creek and drowns them. With tears streaming down her face, she drowns herself as well. As punishment for her crime, her spirit is condemned to wander the creekbank forever in search of her lost children. Marshall has its own version of this well-known story.

The Hispanic version of Marshall's "Weeping Woman" story is fairly conventional. A woman named Maria married a handsome man. Within a few years, the couple had three children, two boys and a girl. Some people say that her husband went to another town to find work, and when he returned to visit his children, he had another woman with him. Others say that Maria found out her husband had been seeing other women on the side. Maria became furious when her husband introduced his children to their "new mommy" and retaliated by drowning her children in the creek. When her rage simmered down, she realized what she had done and took her own life. After her funeral, people in the community heard Maria's spectral voice calling out to her children.

Interestingly enough, the Anglos living in the area added their own touches to the legend. In this version of the story, just after the Civil War, a Confederate widow moved to Marshall from New Orleans with her three children, two boys and a girl. Some say that the woman had served as a nurse for the Confederate army. When she lived in New Orleans, she became the mistress of a high-ranking official. After a while, he became tired of her and sent her off to Marshall to get rid of her. Overcome with shame and grief, the widow drowned herself and her three children in the Sabine River. She was buried in Greenwood Cemetery. God forbade her to enter the gates of Paradise without her children, so the spirit of the Confederate widow still walks the banks of the Sabine River, looking for her kids.

African Americans have also added fascinating twists to the old tale. The Confederate widow-nurse is said to have lived just west of downtown in what is now one of the oldest African American neighborhoods in Texas. Locals say that after she drowned her children, her neighbors were so outraged that they burned down her house. Her restless spirit wanders the neighborhood where she once lived, including the campus of Wiley College, the first historically black college west of the Mississippi. Although the story of the Crying White Lady is well known on campus, students speak of her in hushed tones, as if the mere mention of her crimes might make her more real.

Another unique quality of the Crying White Lady of Marshall is her tendency to interact with the living. For many years, people have claimed they were led by her spirit to the grave where a murder victim was secretly buried. As a rule, the specter cried loudly as she did so. Ghost enthusiasts who envy these witnesses should take warning: people say that anyone who sees the Crying White Lady more than three times in a single year is likely to die the following year of natural causes.

San Antonio

Spanish Governor's Palace

The Spanish Governor's Palace, also known as the Military Presidio de Béjar, was constructed in the early eighteenth century and became the capitol of the region known at the time as Tejas. No Spanish governors ever actually lived here. The building was the home of the Presidio captain, who was also the acting governor of Tejas. The Governor's Palace was established to protect the Mission de Valero, also known as the Alamo, as well as the community at large. Treaties with the Indians were negotiated here, and an assortment of dignitaries, including politicians and military officers, stayed at the Spanish Governor's Palace, which continued to serve as the capitol of the Tejas region for more than a century until the declaration of Texas independence. This is the last surviving example of an early aristocratic Spanish house in Texas. And in the twentieth century, the National Geographic Society proclaimed it the most haunted building in downtown San Antonio.

One of the spirits who haunt the old building is said to be that of a little girl. In the 1860s, the daughter of one of the officials was playing in back of the palace. The maid who was caring for the child became concerned when the girl did not come inside after a few minutes. The presidio captain and his servants conducted an intensive search of the grounds, but they could not find the missing girl.

About twenty years later, a gang of ruffians broke into the palace with the intention of robbing it. The only person inside the palace was a maid. They insisted that the young woman tell them where the family had hidden their valuables, but she said she did not know. The angry robbers tied up the poor girl and threw her down the thirty-seven-foot well in the back, where she drowned.

In the 1930s, workmen who were restoring the complex discovered the bones of a little girl behind the altar. No one knows for certain whether these were the remains of the child who disappeared seventy years earlier. For years, staff at the Spanish Governor's Palace have seen small footprints on top of the bed in one of the bedrooms. Apparently the ghost of the little girl still enjoys jumping up and down on the bed. In the early 2000s, a maintenance man named Jessie Rico claimed to have heard wailing noises coming from the well. He also said that some mornings when he arrived at the palace, he found chairs moved all around the building.

Some people say that a large, old tree in the back of the building is also haunted. Known as the "Tree of Sorrow," it was used as a hanging tree in the eighteenth and nineteenth centuries. Reportedly, forty-six men were hanged from this tree. In recent years, visitors and employees say that they have seen the agonized faces of several men in the trunk of the tree. Some of the faces appear to have bulging eyes.

No one knows for certain the identity of all of the spirits inhabiting the Spanish Governor's Palace. According to local historians, twelve battles were waged in and around the area where the building is located, and hundreds of soldiers died on what is some of the bloodiest land of Texas. It would be surprising if the Spanish Governor's Palace were *not* haunted.

The Sheraton Gunter Hotel

In 1836, the Frontier Inn opened its doors at what was then the center of San Antonio's business district: the corner of El Rincon and El Paso Streets. Because of its prime location, the Frontier Inn became a favorite with cattlemen and settlers who stopped over at San Antonio on their way west. By the early 1900s, the corner of what by then was St. Mary's Street and Houston Avenue had become the bustling heart of the city. An entrepreneur named Jot Gunter convinced a group of investors that buying and renovating the Frontier Inn would net them huge profits in the future. After the Gunter Hotel's grand opening in 1909, it became popular with businessmen and visitors. The hotel thrived over the remainder of the century, thanks in part to clever promotional schemes. For example, in 1912, the owners invited the National Association of Advertising Men to spend several days at the hotel for free. The special guests were so pleased with the arrangement that they coined the phrase "The Gunter Hotel is at the center of everything." The Sheraton Gunter Hotel is still one of the most popular hotels in San Antonio today. The hotel promotes itself as a blend of the best that the past and present have to offer. However, the Sheraton Gunter Hotel understandably does not publicize the most infamous episode from its storied past.

On February 6, 1965, a man checked into Room 636 at the Gunter Hotel. He signed the hotel register as "Mr. Knox." The maids described him as being around thirty years old with blond hair. For several days, the man was seen entering his room with a tall, blond woman. On the afternoon of February 8, one of the maids, Maria Luisa Guerra, ignored the "Do Not Disturb" sign on the door and entered the room with her passkey. She had just taken a couple steps into the room when she beheld a sight that would haunt her dreams for years to come. The man she knew only as Mr. Knox was standing by a blood-soaked bed with a surprised expression on his face. When the maid let out a bloodcurdling scream, the man put his finger to his lips as if to say, "Be quiet." He then gathered up a bloody bundle and bolted from the room.

The police detectives arrived about fifty minutes after the maid's discovery of the body, primarily because the hotel maids and desk clerks had spent some time discussing the murder among themselves instead of notifying the authorities. The detectives were unprepared for the grisly scene that confronted them in Room 636. Blood splattered the walls, carpeting, and furniture. The entire bathroom was covered in blood as well as with small pieces of flesh. The detectives deduced that the man had tried to dispose of the body by dismembering it and grinding it up in a meat grinder.

A few days later, the police followed the trail of Mr. Knox to another hotel, the St. Anthony. When they knocked on his door, they heard a shot inside the room. They barged into the room to discover that the suspect had shot himself. Afterward, the police learned that the man's real name was Walter Emerick. On the day of the murder of the blond woman, Emerick had attempted to book Room 636 at the St. Anthony Hotel. They also found that the week before the murder, Emerick had bought a meat grinder at a local department store. Neither the body of the murder victim nor her identity was ever discovered. Green dye staining his shoes, similar to the dye used to color cement, led police to conclude that Emerick had deposited his victim's remains in wet cement, possibly in a sidewalk.

According to the staff at the Gunter Hotel, negative energy from the grisly murder has imprinted itself on the walls of Room 636. Hammering and grinding sounds have emanated from the room. Photographs taken in the room have revealed the image of a tall, blond woman. Maids claim to have seen the apparition of a blond woman walking toward them with her arms outstretched. Some people believe that the old hotel is haunted by another spirit as well, that of an elderly woman who has been seen roaming the hallways. Not surprisingly, a number of maids have quit their jobs at the Gunter Hotel after working only a short while.

Villamain Railroad Tracks

Paranormal activity has been reported for years at a crossing over the railroad tracks near the intersection of Shane and Villamain Roads, and it is one of the most visited haunted sites in San Antonio. It is said that in the 1930s or 1940s, a school bus loaded with children was heading toward the intersection when it stalled at the railroad crossing. The front wheels of the bus had crossed over the tracks without difficulty, but the rear wheels became stuck between pieces of wood that had been placed between the tracks to accommodate trains. The driver made several attempts to gun the engine and drive over the tracks, but the bus stalled. The driver's concern escalated dramatically when he heard the shrill whistle from an approaching freight train. The panic-stricken children tried to open the windows of the bus so that they could climb out, but the windows were difficult to open, even for adults. By the time the engineer became aware of the plight of the school bus sitting on the tracks in front of him, it was too late. He pulled on the brake but could not stop the train in time. Ten children and the bus driver are said to have died in the resulting crash. Since then, people say that the spirits of the children who died will push any car that stops near the tracks to safety.

For decades, drivers have reported that if they drove halfway over the railroad tracks at this crossing, and then stopped the car and put it in neutral, the car would move—against gravity—up the incline and over the tracks. When they got out of the car to see who pushed them over the tracks, they found tiny handprints on the trunk. To test this story, some people have sprinkled baby powder on the back of the car beforehand and said they found little handprints in the powder after their car had stopped moving. Some people who have parked at the crossing claim to have heard voices and childish laughter. Many people have photographed orbs at this site.

The ghosts of children killed in the bus crash have been seen as well. A woman who lived near the site said that one spring day, she was sweeping the floor in her house when she noticed a little girl about eight years old standing at her screen door. She opened the door, and the girl told her that something terrible had happened at the railroad crossing. The lady was about to ask her what had happened, but the girl immediately bolted around the corner and disappeared. The next week, the lady was sitting in front of her house when the same little girl walked up. She said that her name was Emily and asked if her mother were home. The lady asked where her mother lived, and the child pointed to the house the woman was renting. The little girl warned the lady to be careful at the railroad crossing. She then vanished before the lady's fear-stricken eyes. A few days later, one of the woman's neighbors told her a little girl of about eight years old had also appeared at her doorway and warned her to stay away from the railroad crossing.

Some have said that the odd phenomenon of a car defying gravity to travel uphill while in neutral is just an optical illusion. However, the young people of San Antonio continue to congregate at the site of the accident at Halloween and other times of the year to see for themselves if the ghosts are real.

The Emily Morgan Hotel

Emily Morgan, whose real name was Emily West, is generally regarded as one of the state's great folk heroines. In April 1836, six weeks after the fall of the Alamo on March 6, the armies of Texas and Mexico were marching toward a small prairie town called San Jacinto. James Morgan, manager of an investor group called the New Washington

Association, which was building a town on a peninsula overlooking the San Jacinto River, was commissioned by his friend Sam Houston into the Texas Army and stationed in Galveston. Emily West, a young woman of color, was an indentured servant who had signed on to work for Morgan at the association's hotel as a housekeeper, and some believe that as a servant, she took on his last name, which has been perpetuated in folklore. When Col. Juan N. Almonte's Mexican cavalry captured the town of New Washington, the soldiers took possession of one of Morgan's warehouses, along with Emily and other servants, as well as some workmen and local residents.

Legend has it that Emily's beauty caught the attention of Mexican general Santa Anna, who invited her to his tent for the night. While the general was enjoying a romantic interlude with the attractive young woman, Sam Houston's army routed Santa Anna's troops at San Jacinto. The Mexican general was captured by Houston's troops while trying to escape. Many people believe that Emily Morgan was the inspiration for the song "Yellow Rose of Texas." Some historians suggest that Emily allowed herself to be captured by Santa Anna's troops at the warehouse to give her an opportunity to spy on and maybe even distract the general.

The hotel that bears Emily's name was once the Medical Arts Building, the first doctors' office complex in San Antonio. The Gothic Revival structure is known for its terra-cotta gargoyles, which are depicted as being plagued by a number of medical ailments. In 1976, it was converted into a modern office building. Eight years later, it became a hotel. Many of the furnishings from the Medical Arts Building, such as the marble wainscoting and porcelain fixtures, were sold when the renovations were made. But apparently one feature of the old building could not be removed—its ghosts.

The seventh and twelfth floors in the Emily Morgan Hotel are said to be the most active. Shadowy human shapes have been seen walking down the hallway on the seventh floor. Most witnesses have claimed that the apparitions vanished after walking through a wall or door. One night, a family staying in one of the rooms on the seventh floor said that all the electrical devices suddenly turned themselves on at 2:30 A.M. Family members also reported seeing an amorphous shape walk across the room and into a wall. The twelfth floor is said to have retained the "psychic residue" from all the operations that took place there. Guests have complained of hearing strange noises and smelling rubbing alcohol in several of the rooms on the twelfth floor. A few guests have even said they were touched during their sleep.

Not surprisingly, the basement of the Emily Morgan is also said to be haunted. For more than fifty years, it served as the medical complex's morgue and cemetery. People have heard strange footsteps and disembodied voices down in the basement. A few guests have photographed orbs inside the room.

The elevator seems to be haunted as well. Desk clerks have received calls from the phones inside the empty elevator. Some guests believe that the elevator has a mind of its own. It has occasionally ascended to the sixth and seventh floors when no one was inside. One young woman had a terrifying experience inside the elevator. She stepped inside on the first floor and pushed the button for the third floor. Instead of stopping on the third floor, however, the elevator continued moving up to the seventh floor. After the lady made her way back to the third floor, she and her friend put away their luggage and went out for a day of shopping. That night, the young woman was asleep in bed when she was awakened by a sudden drop in the room's temperature along with a strange humming sound. She sat up in bed and was shocked to see a young girl sitting on her bed, swinging her feet. The little girl asked the woman, "Do you want to sing? Do you want to play?" before slowly fading away.

Today the elegant Emily Morgan Hotel is listed on the National Register of Historic Places as part of the Alamo Plaza Historic District. Along with its history, it offers its guests a comfortable stay with modern amenities—and the possibility of encountering its ghosts. Employees and guests who have had paranormal encounters inside the hotel describe it as one of the most haunted sites in San Antonio.

San Fernando Cathedral

The history of San Fernando began on March 9, 1731, when fifty-five settlers arrived at the Presidio of San Antonio de Béjar from the

Canary Islands. King Philip V of Spain had hoped that these immigrants would set up a permanent settlement in this remote area to prevent the French from moving in. Once the settlement had grown into a village, the residents decided they needed a proper cathedral. The cornerstone was laid in 1738, but the church was not completed until eleven years later. The walls of the original church now enclose the sanctuary of the present-day church. In 1836, the battle of the Alamo was initiated when Mexican troops raised a flag of "no quarter" from the bell tower of the San Fernando Cathedral. Col. Juan Seguin, who controlled San Antonio after Texas won its independence, is said to have buried the corpses of the defenders of the Alamo under the sanctuary railing of the old church. The discovery of a box of charred bones and bits of uniforms when the cathedral was being renovated in 1936 seems to support this legend, even though the inscription on a sarcophagus inside the cathedral indicates that this is where their bones were placed. The first bishop of San Antonio, Anthony Dominic Pellicer, is buried under the central aisle. Between 1868 and 1873, the front part of the cathedral was removed, and a French Gothic structure was erected in its place.

Over the years, a number of dignitaries and celebrities have visited San Fernando Cathedral. Mountain man and explorer Zebulon Pike stopped here during his exploration of the lands acquired in the Louisiana Purchase. In 1831, one of the heroes of the Alamo, Jim Bowie, married Ursula de Veramendi at the cathedral. Pope Pius IX named the cathedral as a diocese in 1874. President Lyndon Johnson toured San Fernando Cathedral in 1966. In 1987, Pope John Paul II spoke to a group of students here.

San Fernando Cathedral's haunted reputation seems to have grown along with the popularity of the town's ghost tours. Tourists have photographed orbs hovering around the façade of the cathedral. Some people claim that the sarcophagus and floor where the bishop's body is interred are cold to the touch at times. The most bizarre incident at the cathedral took place in 2007 on Halloween. At the time, workmen had removed the original plaster down to the stone and replastered the walls. A visitor who was touring the cathedral with his video camera is said to have captured the image of a man kissing a skull on the head.

San Fernando Cathedral is much more than a historic landmark. Each year, many weddings, funerals, and baptisms are performed there. Special events, such as concerts and symphonies, are also held in the cathedral. And, like many old buildings that are repositories of history, it has become a popular stop on tours—especially those that focus on ghosts.

Victoria's Black Swan Inn

Victoria's Black Swan Inn is located in an area that is teeming with history. Archeological evidence, such as pottery shards and arrowheads, indicates that Indian tribes inhabited this area for thousands of years, between 5,000 BC and 1,000 AD. In 1842, a Mexican force under Gen. Adrian Woll engaged Texans in battle at Salado Creek, not far from where the inn is located today.

Henry and Marie Mahler built a house on the site in 1887. A second house was built in 1901, following the purchase of more land. In the twentieth century, the house was owned by the Holbrook and Woods families. During this time, two wings were added to the house, which was named White Gables. After Mr. Woods died, his widow lived in the house with Park and Joline Street, who added a second story. In the 1950s, Erle Stanley Gardner stayed at the house while writing a number of scripts for the *Perry Mason* television series. When Park Street died in the house, it was labeled a suicide, although rumors circulated that the prominent San Antonio lawyer was actually murdered. In the early 1990s, Jo Ann Rivera bought the house and turned it into an inn. Today Victoria's Black Swan Inn harks back to a more genteel time in San Antonio's history. Some people say that visitors to the old house can interact with the past on a more personal level as well.

Starting in the 1990s, a great deal of paranormal activity has been reported at the Black Swan Inn. Guests and staff have reported seeing lights flicker off and on and doors open and close by themselves. People walking through the house have experienced a considerable drop in temperature in certain parts of the house. Weird noises have been heard in hallways and guest rooms. A few people have even seen full-body apparitions inside the house.

On March 24, 2005, a group of paranormal investigators, Psy Tech of Kentucky, conducted a formal investigation of Victoria's Black Swan Inn. Over the course of the night, the team's dowsing rods detected paranormal activity in the ballroom, men's room, and Park Street's former office. The group also found cold spots in the men's room and Street's office. A few of the members reported feeling that an unseen presence was watching them in these two rooms. After midnight, the members of the group blew up their air mattresses and went to sleep. At 3 A.M., one member, named Doreen, suddenly flew off her air mattress and landed on the head of the nearest investigator, five feet away. Doreen believes that a small person, likely a child, jumped on her mattress, causing her to bounce up into the air.

Doreen's experience, along with the team's recordings of one female and two male voices, led the group to believe that at least four spirits are haunting the inn. The group's findings and the coverage the inn has received in television shows like *Sightings* have given visitors another reason to visit Victoria's Black Swan Inn.

The Menger Hotel

A German immigrant named William Menger set up a brewery in San Antonio with Charles Phillip Degen in 1855. In 1859, Menger also opened a hotel. The new hotel was so popular that Menger soon added a forty-room annex. The new addition had a tunnel leading to the nearby brewery, and Menger is said to have led hotel guests on tours through the tunnel to his brewery. Following Menger's death in 1871, his wife and son managed the hotel for the next decade, until they sold it to J. H. Kampmann in 1881. The Menger Hotel became even more important to San Antonio after the railroad's arrival in 1877, and it remained the city's social hub until the 1930s, when it entered a period of decline. It was renovated in the late 1940s and again in the 1980s, after being listed on the National Register of Historic Places. Today not only is the Menger San Antonio's most famous hotel, but with at least thirty-two reported ghosts, it is said to be the most haunted as well.

The Menger's most illustrious ghost is said to be the spirit of Teddy Roosevelt, who stopped at the luxury hotel in 1892 during a javelina hunt. In 1898, Roosevelt visited the Menger again while recruiting cowboys for the Rough Riders. He is reputed to have sat in the bar at the hotel, plied cowpokes just off the Chisholm Trail with drinks, and then invited them to join his newly formed detachment of soldiers. Legend has it that when Roosevelt needed assistance from the hotel staff, he walked over to the front desk and tapped out a message in Morse code on the buzzer. Twenty years after his death, employees at the hotel continued hearing the tapping of Morse code on the buzzer. After the hotel was remodeled in the 1940s, the strange buzzing ceased. However, Roosevelt's ghost is still occasionally seen sitting at the bar.

Another well-known ghost at the Menger Hotel is the spirit of Capt. Richard King, entrepreneur and owner of the King Ranch. King was so rich and powerful that he had his own suite in the hotel. When King's personal physician informed him in 1885 that he had only a few weeks to live, the cattle baron decided to spend his final days at the Menger. During this time, he wrote his will and said good-bye to his friends. His funeral was also held at the hotel. King's apparition has been seen in the King Suite, passing through the wall where a door was once located.

Most of the reports of ghostly activity at the hotel center around a much less famous person, a chambermaid named Sallie White, who lived in one of the shacks that lined Commerce Street in the late nineteenth century. On March 28, 1876, after Sallie's husband, Henry, had been particularly abusive during a heated argument, she went to the police station and complained, but the officer in charge told her to go home. Instead, Sallie spent the night at the Menger Hotel. According to one variant of the tale, her irate husband went to the hotel the next morning and killed Sallie there. Another version says that Sallie went home the next morning, and just as she walked through the door, her husband shot her in the stomach. Then, when she turned around, Henry shot her in the back. Amazingly, Sallie lingered on for three days in the local hospital before finally succumbing to her injuries. After she died, the Menger Hotel paid for Sallie's funeral. The receipt from the funeral home is still on display in the lobby. Sallie's ghost is usually identified as a female spirit whom guests on the third floor hear crying in the middle of the night. Guests staying on that floor have also reported that when they woke up in the morning, jewelry and money that they tossed on the nightstand the night before had been arranged in a very orderly fashion. Sallie's apparition has been sighted in the Victorian wing of the hotel. She is usually described as a young woman wearing a long, gray skirt and a bandanna on her head, carrying a load of towels down the hallway.

The specter of an entirely different woman has been witnessed numerous times in the hotel's original lobby. On many occasions, employees have seen an elderly lady wearing a blue dress, spectacles, and a beret sitting in a corner, knitting. One day, a desk clerk walked up to the woman and asked if he could help her. She looked up from her knitting, nodded slightly, and promptly disappeared.

Another ghost is that of a man dressed in a buckskin jacket and gray pants, who appeared to a male guest just as he stepped out of the shower. The apparition seemed to be involved in a heated discussion with another person who was not visible. The guest recalled that the frontiersman asked, "Are you gonna stay or are you gonna go?" three times before dissipating into thin air. The kitchen help have also claimed that their work has been interrupted by a poltergeist-type entity. Kitchen utensils, silverware, and dishes have been known to levitate in the air. Some objects have floated from one part of the kitchen to another by themselves.

Only a small handful of the spirits who are said to haunt the Menger Hotel have been identified. Because of the hotel's close proximity to the Alamo, some of these ghosts are believed to be the spirits of men who died in the battle. The sound of heavy boots stomping up and down the stairs and hallways has led some of the staff to this conclusion. Even though a number of famous people have stayed at the Menger Hotel, its most fascinating guests may be the ones who have never left.

The Alamo

The long and violent history of the Alamo has led to encounters with a number of spirits, and many tales of supernatural phenomena surround the site. In 1718, a group of monks constructed a "mission system" church called Misión San Antonio de Valero. In 1739, a devastating smallpox epidemic took a heavy toll among the monks and the people they served. By 1789, the Alamo resembled a fortress more than a church. A military garrison consisting of 275 men, women, and children was quartered behind the eight-foot walls surrounding the chapel. The Alamo was supplied with water from two aqueducts running along either side of the walls. Spanish soldiers were stationed at the Alamo in 1802 to dissuade French or American forces from invading the territory. After Spain ceded control of Mexico to the people who lived there in 1821, the provisional government of Mexico granted Anglo-Americans permission to settle in what is now known as Texas. Before long, though, the Texans' insistence that they be allowed to govern themselves became a constant source of irritation to Gen. Santa Anna, who proclaimed himself the rightful emperor of Mexico in April 1834. He swore that he would never surrender control of Texas.

In October 1835, the immigrants from the United States defeated Santa Anna's raw recruits in battle. On December 9, the last company of Mexican soldiers surrendered to the Texas Army after the siege of Béjar, which is now San Antonio. The victorious Texans occupied the Alamo and converted it into a fort. They placed the nineteen cannons left behind by the Mexican Army along the walls. By January 1836, only one hundred Texans were occupying the Alamo. Sam Houston sent Col. Jim Bowie and a small company of men to evaluate the situation there. Bowie reported that the Alamo could withstand an attack from the Mexican Army. He also had implicit confidence in the ability of his men to repel such an attack. On February 11, Col. James C. Neill, acting commander of the Alamo, transferred command to Col. William Barrett Travis, who had arrived at the Alamo with thirty men about a week earlier. A few days earlier, Davy Crockett and a small group of reinforcements had also walked through the gates of the Alamo. The number of defenders of the old church had thus increased from 104 men to 150.

On February 23, General Santa Anna and a force of approximately four thousand men took up positions outside the Alamo. When the general raised a red flag, signifying "no quarter," Travis responded by firing the Alamo's largest cannon, an eighteen-pounder that the New Orleans Greys had brought with them. Santa Anna retaliated by pounding the walls of the Alamo with his artillery. On March 1, a small relief force of thirty-eight men arrived. By March 3, some two hundred cannonballs had been fired into and over the walls of the Alamo. Convinced that Sam Houston's "Army of the People" would arrive at any time, the defenders fought back as hard as they could. Davy Crockett's sharpshooters from Tennessee picked off any Mexican soldier who ventured within two hundred yards of the wall. Miraculously, not a single defender had been killed in the bombardment.

At about midnight on March 6, the entire Mexican Army surrounded the Alamo. Around 5 A.M., Mexican soldiers placed their scaling ladders against the walls, but most of them were shot by the defenders before reaching the top. After his soldiers regrouped, Santa Anna launched another assault on the walls, but it was repulsed as well. Despite suffering heavy losses, Santa Anna decided to merge all his soldiers into a massive fighting force. Mexican soldiers immediately began scaling the north wall. After Gen. Juan Amador opened the postern on the north wall, Mexican soldiers began streaming into the Alamo. Texas gunners stationed along the south wall turned their cannons toward the breach in the north wall, thereby leaving the south wall undefended. In just a few minutes, Mexican soldiers killed all the artillery men and took possession of the cannon. Meanwhile, Santa Anna's troops began running from building to building, killing any Texan who opposed them. The remaining defenders took refuge in the chapel and barracks. Bowie, who had taken ill several days before and was confined to his bed in the Long Barracks, was mercilessly bayoneted by Mexican soldiers. Travis was shot in the head and killed near the west wall. Davy Crockett died in the corner near the church.

After ninety minutes, the battle was over. Statistics regarding the death toll are sketchy at best. Between 183 and 188 defenders of the Alamo died that day. Approximately 521 Mexican soldiers died in the three assaults. The bodies of the Texans were stripped and unceremoniously thrown in piles and burned. Only Gregorio Esparza received a proper burial. The survivors included Travis's African American slave, Joe; two Mexican women; and Susanna Dickinson, the wife of Lieutenant Dickinson, and their child.

The seeds of victory were sown in the Texans' defeat at the Alamo. Scores of volunteers poured into Texas, eager to avenge the slaughter of the valiant defenders of the Alamo. "Remember the Alamo" became a battle cry that galvanized the Texan soldiers six weeks later at the battle of San Jacinto. At the end of the battle, which lasted only eighteen minutes, Santa Anna surrendered to Sam Houston. The Mexican general's troops were ordered to leave Texas, and a new republic was formed on Texas soil.

Throughout much of the nineteenth century, the Alamo was taken over by several commercial establishments. In 1883, the Daughters of the Republic of Texas initiated a campaign to raise funds for the purchase of the Alamo. Twenty years later, the Texas legislature appointed the group the permanent caretakers of the Alamo. Now a state shrine, the Alamo has given rise to a number of legends, many of which are ghost stories.

The earliest ghost sighting at the Alamo was reported in 1836, just a few weeks after its fall. Santa Anna had moved fifteen hundred of his troops to San Jacinto, leaving a thousand troops in San Antonio to prevent any rebel uprisings. After being attacked by Sam Houston's forces, Santa Anna sent an urgent dispatch to San Antonio, ordering his soldiers to destroy the Alamo and march with all haste to San Jacinto. According to an account that appeared in the personal diary of the commanding general of the Alamo, Colonel Sanchez, a group of Mexican soldiers holding flaming torches approached the old church with the intent of burning it down. Suddenly six large men, also brandishing flaming torches, materialized before the two front doors. The terrified Mexican troops stood frozen on the spot as they heard a chorus of spectral voices yell, "Do not touch the Alamo! Do not touch these walls!" The Mexicans threw down their torches and fled into the darkness. The men refused to return to the chapel, despite threats of corporal punishment by their superior officers. Afterward, the troops gave varying descriptions of the six "diablos." Some soldiers described them as monks, while others swore that they were the spirits of the defenders of the Alamo.

When General Andrade received word of the failed attempt to destroy the chapel, he dispatched more troops to the Alamo to burn down the Long Barracks. Before the fresh troops could set fire to the building, a tall male apparition appeared on the roof with arms extended, holding a ball of fire in each hand. The soldiers immediately fell to their knees and shielded their eyes. When the spirit disappeared, the soldiers fled, screaming and crying. Convinced that the reports he had heard of ghostly presences at the Alamo were genuine, Andrade and his troops marched off to San Jacinto, leaving the Alamo and its outbuildings intact. The protective ghost is depicted in a monument erected in front of the Alamo in 1939. Legend has it that the energy released from the cremation of the corpses of the defenders of the Alamo manifested in the form of a spirit guardian.

More ghost stories surfaced in the 1890s, when the city of San Antonio decided to use the chapel as police headquarters and the barracks as a jail. Just a few days after the move, prisoners and guards began reporting paranormal activity inside the building. Between 1894 and 1897, a number of these accounts appeared in local newspapers. People said they saw strange, shadowy figures and heard eerie moans emanating from the rooms and hallways. Before long, most of the guards refused to work the night shift. Eventually the city decided to move the prisoners to a different building.

One of the most commonly sighted spirits in the Alamo is the ghost of small, blond boy who usually appears during the first two weeks of February, standing in the left upstairs window of the gift shop. The mournful little spirit has also been seen wandering around the grounds of the Alamo. He is believed to be the ghost of one of the children evacuated from the Alamo shortly before the attack. Some staff members believe that the little specter returns to the place where he last saw his father.

Four other spirits seem to show up on a fairly regular basis. One is the ghost of a man whose head and shoulders have been seen hanging out of the window over the double doors in the back of the chapel. Staff members and visitors have also seen the full-bodied apparition of a cowboy wearing a black duster and cowboy hat. Because he seems to have just come out of the rain, some people believe he is the ghost of one of Colonel Travis's dispatch riders. A tall, bare-chested Indian has been scaring people for years in the basement of the Alamo. Because he reportedly sneaks up behind unsuspecting victims, a large number of employees refuse to go down into the basement. A couple female spirits are also said to haunt the Alamo. Many people have seen the misty torso of a woman standing by a well, usually at night.

At least one ghost has been sighted in the Long Barracks. In the 1990s, a young girl arrived at the Alamo with her family. When she entered the barracks and looked at a case where a replica of a Mexican soldier's uniform was displayed, she was overcome with a chilling sensation. The girl glanced over at a corner of the room and saw the huddled figure of a young Hispanic man. She noticed that he was about thirty years old and was wearing a white sombrero, a white shirt, and a red bandanna, and he had beads of perspiration on his face. When his gaze met hers, his face contorted into a mask of terror. The frightened little girl hid behind her mother and closed her eyes. She did not open them again until she was out of the barracks.

In another incident, a native of San Antonio named Jorge was visiting the Alamo around closing time. As one of the guards was locking up, Jorge looked across the room and saw a man wearing nineteenth-century clothing gazing at a glass case where Jim Bowie's trademark knife was displayed. Jorge's flesh began to crawl when he realized that he could see through the strange figure. At the same instant, the man vanished.

James L. Choron, who has posted his experience online, says that in 1990 he visited the Alamo with his three children, four-year-old Heather, six-year-old Megan, and eight-year-old Eric. As they were leaving the Alamo, Megan turned around and said, "Good-bye, Jamie." Choron turned around to see that no one was standing behind them. He asked her whom she was talking to, and Megan pointed to a spot just in front of the Alamo's doors. When he asked his daughter to describe the person, Megan said that he was a boy of around fifteen or sixteen years old, wearing a white shirt, cotton pants, and a black hat. The child went on to say that the boy had been standing there the entire time they were touring the chapel and had described the battle to her in great detail. He told her that he had been hanging around the Alamo for a very long time.

A few of the Alamo's ghosts have been identified. One of these is the spirit of a Mexican officer who walks across the grounds and around the buildings with his hands clasped behind his back. He appears to be pensive and is usually seen shaking his head, as if he is arguing with someone. Many people who are familiar with the history of the Alamo believe he is the spirit of a regimental commander named Gen. Manuel Fernández Castrillón, who opposed the assault on the Alamo on the grounds that victory would cost too many lives. After the Alamo fell, Castrillón refused to execute six of the defenders of the Alamo who had surrendered.

Some staff members believe that Davy Crockett's ghost also haunts the Alamo. A ghostly figure dressed in buckskins and holding a flintlock rifle has been seen standing guard outside the chapel. Crockett's spirit has been sighted standing at attention at other locations around the chapel as well, often by several witnesses at the same time. According to a park ranger who worked the night shift, Crockett's ghost has also reenacted his own death. The ranger had just entered the Long Barracks when he saw the prostrate figure of a man lying on a bed. Judging from the man's bloodstained shirt, the ranger concluded that he had been shot several times. As the ranger stared at the figure on the bed, a group of Mexican soldiers emerged from the shadows and began stabbing the man with their bayonets. Before the awestruck ranger could react, the figures faded away.

Colonel Travis, who refused to abandon the Alamo when he was alive, might still be at his post after death. One hot spring day, a park ranger noticed a strangely dressed man walking toward the library. The man was wearing high boots, a long overcoat, and a plantation hat, similar to the type that Travis wore during the battle. The figure faded away near the chapel. Goosebumps rose on the ranger's arms when he could find no footprints in the dirt.

Even the spirit of an actor from the twentieth century has been sighted at the Alamo. As director of the 1960 film *The Alamo*, John Wayne made several trips to the site and consulted blueprints of the original buildings in order to make the film as historically accurate as possible. Not long after Wayne's death in 1979, sightings of his ghost began circulating among the Alamo's staff. Stories of Wayne's ghost became so frequent that a psychic was called in to make contact with the spirit. She revealed that Wayne's ghost returned to the Alamo at least once a month, but she could not explain why.

The book *Spirits of the Alamo* includes a number of ghost stories collected by Robert and Anne Powell Wlodarski from staff members at the Alamo. Many years ago, when the Alamo was locked up by a single park ranger, he entered the middle door of the Long Barracks and had just started his inspection of the building when he heard the slamming of a door. He ran back to where he had heard the door slam, but that door was still locked. Assuming that the intruder had exited the building somehow, the ranger left the building and began patrolling the grounds. Nobody else appeared to be on the grounds, so he reentered the building, where he was still unable to find another person.

Another former park ranger told the authors that he had the responsibility of lowering the flags of Texas and the United States every day at 5:30 P.M., folding them up in the standard way, and laying them on his desk. One morning, he walked into his office at 6 A.M. and was preparing to raise the flags when he discovered that they were lying on the floor, still neatly folded.

A female employee reported that she and several other employees had a very unnerving experience in the basement of the gift shop. They were counting souvenirs and books when suddenly they heard the unmistakable weeping of a woman. The wailing lasted for about an hour. The next day, the women heard the same crying sounds. Three historical figures have been suggested as the source of the phantom weeping. One is Susanna Dickinson, whose husband was killed while firing the cannons. Another is Ana Salazar de Esparza, whose husband fired a cannon close the place where his wife was hiding. He too died at the Alamo. The third possibility is Juana Navarro Alsbury. According to Juana's own account, which has been passed down for generations, she was in the Alamo during the entire siege and was protected by two defenders until they were killed by Mexican soldiers, who then stole some of her family's valuables.

Another employee related an equally eerie tale. She was walking through the long barracks, wiping fingerprints from the glass display cases, when she heard the sound of someone coughing in the southern portion of the barracks. Suspecting that a man had broken into the barracks, she continued her walk-through of the building when she heard the coughing sounds once again. The strong smell of whiskey seemed to permeate the entire building. Fearing for her life, she bolted through the door and did not reenter the building for the remainder of the night. The next day, she informed her supervisor of her weird experience the night before. He told her that during the siege of the Alamo, Jim Bowie drank whiskey and coughed in his room inside the long barracks. He also said that other rangers had also reported hearing coughs and smelling whiskey late at night.

Some people visit this historical site to "Remember the Alamo." Others come in hopes of possibly witnessing some of the spirits still said to haunt this place that saw so much bloodshed.

Woman Hollering Creek

Woman Hollering Creek, which is located between San Antonio and Seguin, is nothing more than a trickle most of the time. The "creek" only flows when there is sufficient rainfall to fill its banks. In the early 1980s, Woman Hollering Creek was mistakenly called Woman Hollow Creek on a Highway Department sign. After a couple years, the name on the sign was corrected. The crossing can be found off Interstate 10 just before the FM 755 exit to New Berlin. The creek flows under the interstate and empties into Martinez Creek just northeast of St. Hedwig.

The Hispanic and Anglo cultures have two entirely different explanations for the creek's colorful name. Older residents in the Universal City area tell the tale of a pioneer woman who was walking to the creek one day, either to fill a bucket with water or to wash some clothes in the creek, when she was attacked by a band of Indians. As the Indians tore at her clothes and proceeded to rape her, she screamed for help, but her fellow settlers were miles away. Her mutilated corpse was discovered by a neighboring group of settlers a few days later. It is said that her piercing screams still resonate from the creek on the anniversary of her murder.

Several variants of the Hispanic version of La Llorona, or the Weeping Woman, are told in Texas. In the most common version of the story surrounding Woman Hollering Creek, a beautiful young woman named Maria Gonzalez fell hopelessly in love with a handsome young ranchero. She attracted his attention by ignoring his advances. Not accustomed to girls who played hard to get, the ranchero began wooing her in earnest, even serenading her with his guitar in the evening. After a few months, they became engaged and were married. The couple had two children. Although he had a lovely wife and children, the ranchero found the "wild life" too hard to resist. He began leaving town for months at a time without telling Maria where he was going. Maria's friends told her that he was spending all his money playing cards and courting other women. One day, Maria's husband rode up to the house in a large wagon, a beautiful woman at his side. He greeted his children and gave them bags of candy, but totally ignored his wife. Then he rode off, leaving behind nothing but a cloud of dust.

As Maria watched her unfaithful husband ride off, her fists clenched and her eyes glowed with rage. Knowing that the only thing he really cared about was his children, she led them down to the river and stopped at a steep cliff. With tears streaming down her face, she pushed her children off the cliff and into the river, where they drowned. When she realized what she had done, Maria ran down to the river. She ran along the banks, wailing and screaming the names of her children, but it was too late. They had drowned.

That night, the people in the village were awakened by the sounds of weeping. Several men made their way down to the river and found Maria on her knees, crying uncontrollably. They could tell immediately that she had lost her mind. For the next several months, she lived on the outskirts of town, scavenging for food. Finally, one day, her emaciated body was found dead on the riverbank. She was buried where she was found, not far from the spot where her children had drowned. That night, the villagers heard a woman down by the river. As they approached Maria's grave, they saw a woman dressed in a flowing white dress, crying, "Where are my children?" Night after night, La Llorona kept up her lonely vigil, searching for her lost children.

In another version of the story, La Llorona was a woman who had had several children by her first husband. After he died, she fell in love with another man. One day, he informed her that he did not wish to raise another man's children, so she would have to choose between him and her children. After struggling with her conscience for several days, she took her children down to the creek and drowned them. She continued living with her lover for several months, but eventually he became bored with her and took a mistress. A few weeks later, the woman died of grief. She can still be heard screaming the names of her drowned children as she walks along the creek.

Parents who fear that the spirit of La Llorona might snatch up their children have cautioned them never to go down to the creek without an adult. They say that as punishment for her heinous crime, La Llorona is condemned to look for her drowned children for eternity.

The Old Bexar County Jail

When the two-story Bexar County Jail was built in 1879, it could accommodate eighty-six inmates. It was expanded twice in the early twentieth century but was eventually closed in 1962. It later was renovated and used for records storage. Interestingly, the old jail was remodeled yet again in 2002, this time as a Comfort Inn. Not only did the architect preserve the jail's historic exterior, but he even left bars in some of the windows. The old jail's past is also preserved in the ghost stories that have been circulating since the hotel first opened its doors.

It is said that the hotel's paranormal activity can be traced back to a hanging that took place there. A trail boss named R. F. Gilbreath was driving a herd of cattle from Medina County to Ellsworth, Kansas. On the way back to Texas, he became embroiled in a heated argument with a man named Joe Cordova. In a fit of rage, Cordova pulled his pistol and shot Gilbert. The wheels of justice turned much faster at that time in Texas than they do today. Soon after Gilbreath's murder, Joe Cordova was apprehended, tried, and convicted. He was hanged inside the Bexar County Jail, as were many other people during the years that the building was used as a jail.

In *A Ghost in the Guest Room*, Olyve Hallmark Abbott says that when the old jail was being converted into a hotel, construction workers had difficulty carrying concrete from the second to the third floor. When the men had carried the concrete up thirteen steps, they found that they could go no farther. Some unseen force seemed to be blocking their way.

Once the Comfort Inn opened its doors for business, guests began having weird experiences. People have heard disembodied footsteps walking down the hallways and across their rooms. One guest had a terrifying night while staying in one particular room on the first floor where the bodies of prisoners who were hanged on the second floor dropped through a trapdoor in the ceiling. He was sleeping in the bed with his wife when suddenly he awakened to hear a creaking noise, something that sounded like the slamming of a door, and soft voices. He jerked up in bed, not totally convinced that he had dreamed the incident.

Today, the Holiday Inn Express San Antonio North Riverwalk occupies the Old Bexar County Jail building. The hotel is, in many ways, a typical twenty-first-century hotel. Sometimes, though, guests may get the feeling that the old building has not totally outlived its brutal past.

The Crockett Hotel

The Crockett Hotel is located on the exact spot where Davy Crockett and a band of settlers defended the southeast palisade of the Alamo against Santa Anna's much larger army during the thirteen-day siege of the old mission in 1836. After the fall of the Alamo, the property was used for farming. In 1874, it was purchased by a Frenchman named Auguste Honore Grenet, who built and operated a mercantile on the land. The site subsequently had several other owners, until 1909, when the Odd Fellows built a six-story hotel and fraternal lodge on the property. In 1977, a seven-story addition to the hotel was constructed. The next year, it began operating as a Holiday Inn. After an extensive renovation in 1987, the hotel was listed on the National Register of Historic Places. For years, guests and employees at the hotel have reported seeing and hearing apparitions from San Antonio's historic—and bloody—past.

Much, but not all, of the paranormal activity at the Crockett Hotel seems to have been generated by the fall of the Alamo. The ghosts of Spanish soldiers have been seen in the pool area for many years. People passing by the Crockett Hotel have witnessed the curtains move in the executive offices on nights when nobody was there. In *A Ghost in the Guest Room*, Olyve Hallmark Abbott reports that a number of strange occurrences have taken place at the hotel over the years. Elevator doors open when guests are five feet away. One guest was awakened at midnight by the chanting of monks, but the missions in the area were not open at the time. Another guest heard the clopping of horses' hooves in the middle of the night. A young woman in her twenties was sound asleep in her room when a glimmer of light filtered through the window. When she turned over, she was surprised to see a woman wearing nineteenth-century clothing moving around her room, almost as if she were floating. The apparition seemed to be looking for something. At first the guest thought that someone had wandered into her room by mistake. She asked the spectral woman what she wanted, but instead of answering, the phantom walked through the locked door.

Paranormal investigators say that some of the most haunted sites are those where people died suddenly, such as murder victims or soldiers. It is not surprising, therefore, that many of the buildings surrounding the Alamo, like the Crockett Hotel, are reputed to be haunted.

The St. Anthony Hotel

The St. Anthony Hotel was built in 1909 at 300 East Travis Street. A year later, an eight-story annex was added. The St. Anthony attracted the rich and famous between 1920 and 1941, mostly because of its lavish accommodations and its rooftop nightclub, where guests danced to the music of some of America's most best-known big bands. Among the hotel's most illustrious guests were Eleanor Roosevelt, Presidents Dwight D. Eisenhower and Lyndon Baines Johnson, Princess Grace and Prince Albert of Monaco, Lucille Ball, John Wayne, and George Clooney.

The grand ballroom is said to be the most haunted area in the St. Anthony Hotel. A despondent-looking woman has been spotted wandering aimlessly around the ballroom. People have seen the ghosts of guests dressed in formal wear in the Anacacho Ballroom. These sightings are often accompanied by strange, unidentifiable sounds. The ghost of a former employee known as Anita has been sighted by staff members and guests alike. Women have reported seeing an elderly woman in the restroom.

Reports of spirits have come from other parts of the hotel as well. Guests have heard disembodied voices and footsteps throughout the hotel. Occasionally the ghosts of a gentleman wearing a top hat and a woman in a red dress have been seen in the elevator. As a rule, they seem to appear out of nowhere and then disappear. The ghosts of a married couple are said to return to the room where they spent their honeymoon years ago.

One of the strangest incidents in the St. Anthony occurred in the 2000s. A guest sitting on the balcony of her locked room looked through the window and was shocked to see a man sitting in a chair in the middle of the room. She also noticed that the furnishings were different and a grand piano now stood in the room. When she walked through the sliding doors, the man was gone. Staff members told her that no one had been in her room. They also said that the room was not furnished the way she had described and that there was no piano in the room. When a member of the hotel staff returned to the room with the woman, the room was nearly vacant. The woman was beginning to worry about her sanity, when an employee told her that one of the former owners, Ralph W. Morrison, had used the room as his office in the 1930s. He also had a piano in the room. When the guest noticed a portrait of Mr. Morrison on the wall, she told the employee that this was the man she had seen. This room also has a reputation for staying very cold much of the time, even when the air-conditioning has been turned off. Employees have heard strange noises in the room as well.

A ballroom called the Peraux Room is another place where employees have reported feeling uncomfortable. This lavish room still has the original chandeliers. Like Mr. Morrison's former office, the ballroom also stays cold much of the time, and the doors open and close by themselves. Sometimes a spectral woman in a red dress has been seen floating across the room.

The basement, where the business offices, break room, and employees' locker rooms are located, has been described by employees as a very creepy place, especially the hallways. One female employee was in the laundry room all by herself when she heard the unmistakable sound of a woman crying. Shelly Kneupper Tucker, author of "Ghost Hunting at the Saint Anthony Hotel," was walking through the basement in October 2010 when she heard a strange banging sound. She walked over to the elevator and noticed that the door was opening and closing on its own. Shirley pressed the button, but the door continued to open and close.

A cleaning woman had a terrifying experience in Room 1080. She was cleaning the tub when suddenly her name appeared on the porcelain. Even though she was scared, she finished scouring the tub and left the room. When her supervisor entered the room later that day he found the woman's name written on the tub. Thinking the woman was playing a joke, she asked her to scrub the tub all over again. This time the supervisor stood behind the cleaning woman while she scrubbed the tub. Amazingly, her name appeared once again. The cleaning woman was so frightened that she quit her job on the spot.

Today the St. Anthony Hotel is owned and operated by the Wyndham Hotel chain. The old hotel's luxurious luster still emanates from its guest rooms, and its Sunday brunch attracts both guests and locals. In recent years, however, the St. Anthony's ghosts have proven to be a big draw as well.

South Texas

The Lady in Black

Alice

Tales of star-crossed lovers can be found throughout the world. Texas has a number of romantic ghost stories. For example, the flickering lights that are frequently sighted on the Delores Mountains are said to originate from a fire set every night by a young woman named Delores as a signal to her lover, a shepherd who was murdered by Apache Indians. The San Gabriel River near the little town of San Gabriel is said to be haunted by the spirits of a wealthy young woman and her lover, a ranch hand, who drowned in the river during one of their rendezvous. But the best-known of the tragic love stories set in Texas is the one that took place outside the little town of Alice.

In the 1700s, a wealthy landowner named Raul Ramos lived in a hacienda at Falfurrias. At this time, most of the Rio Grande valley was still part of the old Spanish province of Nuevo Santander. A beautiful woman who lived nearby was certain that Don Ramos would eventually choose her as his bride. But one day, her dream of becoming Doña Ramos was smashed when Don Ramos returned to his ranch with his bride by his side, a lovely young Mexican woman named Leonora. The angry woman clenched her fists and vowed revenge as the happy couple drove by.

Don Ramos and Leonora had been married for only a few weeks when he informed his bride that he had to travel to Spain on business. With tears streaming down her face, she kissed her husband and begged him to come home to her safely. Six months later, Leonora was keeping her daily vigil at one of the windows of the hacienda when she saw her husband ride up the road and through the gate. She ran down the steps, embraced Don Ramos, and informed him that he would soon be a father. He could not contain his joy and lifted Leonora up into the air and spun her around. He then kissed her and told her how happy he was that he would soon have an heir.

Don Ramos told everyone in the area that he and his wife would soon become parents. One of the people who heard the news was the proud beauty who still resented Leonora for taking the man she felt, by rights, should have been her husband. She decided that she would do her best to destroy their happiness. She embarked on a campaign to soil Leonora's reputation by spreading the rumor that she had been unfaithful during her husband's absence and the baby was not his. When Don Ramos learned of his wife's alleged infidelity, he confronted Leonora. She assured him that the rumors were false and begged him to believe her. Instead of considering the possibility that his wife might be innocent, Don Ramos stormed out of the room and summoned two of his ranch hands to his office. Don Ramos instructed them to tell his wife to put on a black dress. They were then to place her on a horse and take her on a twenty-four-hour journey to a crossroads, where they were to hang her.

When the cowboys reached the intersection of two roads, they led Leonora's horse to a tree. One of them threw the end of a rope over an overhanging branch and tied the other end around her neck. When asked if she had any last words, Leonora responded that she had committed no crime. She added that if the men hanged her, she would never let them forget that they had hanged an innocent woman. Meanwhile, Don Ramos was riding south so that he would be unable to stop the hanging if he changed his mind in a moment of weakness. At the same time that the rope broke Leonora's neck, Don Ramos pulled a pistol from his belt and put a bullet through his own head. Thus ironically, the woman who had orchestrated this tragic chain of events never achieved her dream of marrying the richest man in the Rio Grande valley.

It is said that ever since that fateful day more than two centuries ago, the intersection of Highways 281 and 151 is haunted by the ghost of Leonora Ramos. Her specter is usually seen dressed in black, standing near the spot where she was unjustly hanged. In the early 2000s, four men were on their way to their job at an oil refinery early one morning when they saw a woman in a black dress standing in the middle of the road. The driver hit the brakes, but by the time he saw the woman, his truck was on top of her. He pulled over to the side of the road and called the sheriff. When the sheriff arrived a few minutes later, he conducted a thorough sweep of the area in search of the dead woman. No female corpse was ever found. The frequent sightings of the Lady in Black suggest that Leonora's spirit refuses to let this region forget that she was unjustly hanged.

La Posada Hotel

Laredo

Laredo's La Posada Hotel opened in 1961, but its history goes back much farther. The 280-room hotel was built around four historic buildings. The main part of the hotel, which includes the entrance, front desk and lobby, meeting rooms, administrative offices, and restaurants, used to be the old Laredo High School. The ballroom is located in what used to be a convent. The Tack Room restaurant was once the Old Laredo Telephone Exchange. An adjacent museum, which contains artifacts relating to the history of Laredo, is housed in the Capitol of the Republic of the Rio Grande, dating back to the 1830s. Because of the hotel's rich and varied past, it is small wonder that many guests and employees swear that something paranormal is going on there.

A number of strange sightings and sounds have been reported at the La Posada Hotel since it first opened its doors. The ghost of a nun, an apparition of a woman in black, and the spirits of former employees have been seen walking through the hallways, apparently in search of someone or something. Eyewitnesses have described these entities as unfriendly spirits who stared straight ahead, seemingly oblivious to their surroundings. People have encountered cold spots in specific areas of the hotel. Desk clerks have received numerous reports from guests who have heard disembodied footsteps and voices calling their names. Objects have been known to move and fall off desks and tables by themselves.

A few guests have had personal encounters with the hotel's phantom residents. A number of guests have reported being awakened at 1 or 2 A.M. by someone knocking on their door. When they looked through the peephole, they were shocked to find that no one was standing in the hallway. Several guests have had weird experiences in Room 100, where they were awakened by the sound of water running in the bathtub. These guests swore that they had turned off the water before going to bed. A couple who spent the night in this room said that the next morning, they were astounded to find that their blankets had been piled in the middle of the room sometime during the night. One guest said she heard deep breathing in the middle of the night. She was alone in the room at the time. Another guest said that at 9 P.M. her pillow flew off the bed and struck the wall.

Aside from the hotel's historical importance, it also serves the community by hosting weddings, quinceaneras, and the town's annual George Washington's Birthday celebration. One might argue that the ghost stories that have been generated inside the hotel have also contributed to the city's cultural life.

Espantosa Lake

Zavala County

Rumors that Espantosa Lake was haunted began in the early 1800s. Several Mexican families en route to San Antonio camped by the lake one night in what appeared to be a pleasant spot. In the middle of the night, the travelers were awakened by a woman's voice screaming, "My God!" The groggy men got up and stumbled to the edge of the lake, just in time to witness a monstrous alligator drag a woman beneath the surface of the water. Although upset by the horrible death of the unfortunate woman, the families eventually went back to sleep. Just before dawn, they heard the same scream coming from the lake's murky depths. The next morning, the families broke camp and left, but not before giving the lake the name it holds today, which means "Lake of the Ghost."

A few years later, another incident occurred that solidified the lake's reputation for being haunted. A Spanish wagon laden with gold, silver, and jewels had been traveling for several hours from San Saba when the drivers decided it was time to take a break. They camped fairly close to the edge of Lake Espantosa, despite the rumors that had been circulating throughout the area. The men had just drifted off to sleep when they were awakened by tremors from deep underground. Then suddenly the bank on which the men, horses, and wagon were spending the night collapsed into the lake. After that night, the fate of the treasure wagon became the stuff of legend.

Not long after the wagon and the men who drove it had disappeared, a cattleman named Cleary and his hired hand were camping near the lake along the Presidio Road when they were awakened by the rumbling of what Cleary assumed was a freight wagon on its way to a general store just a few miles away. The next morning, Cleary rode into town and asked if the freight wagon had brought the tobacco he had been waiting for. With a puzzled look on his face, the shopkeeper replied that the shipment of goods he was expecting had not yet arrived. Convinced that he and his hired hand had not been imagining things, Cleary returned to the Presidio Road to search for evidence of the wagon he had heard, but he was unable to find any wagon tracks.

A few weeks later, a group of cowboys bunked down at the same spot where Cleary had spent the night also heard the clanking of a wagon rolling by during the night. The next morning, the men concluded that they had heard the passing of the famed "ghost wagon." A skeptical member of the group announced that there was no ghost wagon and he was going to prove it. The next night, as he stood in the middle of the road with pistols drawn, he heard the unmistakable sound of an approaching wagon. The cowboy was baffled because he undoubtedly heard the sound of a freight wagon but could not see it. He ordered it to stop, but the sound continued. Just before he thought the wagon was going to run him over, the sound ceased. A few seconds later, the cowboy heard the sound of a moving wagon again, now behind him. Frustrated by his inability to stop the wagon, the cowboy fired his pistol at the sound, but the ghostly wagon continued to roll down the road. Since this cowboy's fateful encounter, many people have heard the sound of a wagon down by Espantosa Lake.

The fate of Charles Beale and his band of pioneers became a part of the ever-growing body of lore centered around the lake. In 1836, Dr. Beale and his party had just camped by the lakeshore when Gen. Santa Anna's Mexican army decided to stop by the lake on its way to the Alamo. Dr. Beale and his party moved to the chaparral nearby, where they stayed until Santa Anna's army marched off. The group once again set up camp by the lake, but later that evening, they were attacked by a band of Indians. Most of the group perished in the ensuing massacre. Years later, people lured to the lake by tales of the lost treasure wagon claimed to have seen the spirits of Beale and the settlers wandering along the lakeshore.

The most bizarre ghost story connected to Espantosa Lake involves a man named George Dent, who was camped near the lake at the same time that Dr. Beale and his party were staying there. Dent and his wife were camped about half a mile from Dr. Beale's group and therefore escaped their fate. Late one night, Dent's wife informed him that she was having sharp labor pains. George assured his wife that he would find a midwife to assist her with the birth of her child. As lightning flashed across the sky and thunder rumbled over the plains, George rode off. A few miles away, he met up with a group of Mexican goatherders. When he told them where he and his wife were camped, the goatherders refused to accompany him to the accursed lake. George then turned his attention to an elderly woman, who was touched by the desperate man's pleas and agreed to ride back to his camp with him. The pair had not ridden very far when George was struck and killed by a bolt of lightning. After the storm subsided, the goatherders tried to find George's campsite. By the time they made it to the camp, they found George's wife, lying on the ground dead. They could tell that she had just given birth but could find no trace of the baby. The men assumed that the baby had been snatched away by wolves and rode off.

According to the legend, however, this was only the beginning of the story, not the end. In 1851, several cowboys were herding cattle near Espantosa Lake when they saw a naked white girl running with a wolf pack. The girl seemed to be covered with hair. Spurred on by curiosity, the cowboys rode off in pursuit of the wolf girl. They reached a steep draw where she could run no farther, and the cowboys were able to lasso the girl. The only vocal sounds she was able to make were a series of low growls. She was unable to stand or walk upright without assistance. The men locked her in the back room of an abandoned house. Later that night, the wolf girl began howling. A few minutes later, a wolf pack surrounded the house. While the wolves attacked the horses and scratched at the doors of the building, the cowboys heard the shattering of wood from the back room. They ran inside the room and discovered that the girl had pried up the floorboards and escaped by crawling under the house.

Nothing more was heard of the wolf girl until two years later, when cowboys and settlers reported seeing a naked, hair-covered girl running with a pack of wolves. One man said he saw the girl lapping up water from the edge of the lake while a couple wolf cubs with human faces suckled at her breasts. Sightings of the wolf girl and her semi-human wolf cubs continued well into the twentieth century. Their ghosts apparently have joined the company of spirits—the screaming woman, the ghostly treasure wagon, and Dr. Beale and his band of ill-fated pioneers—whose presence occasionally disturbs the tranquility of Espantosa Lake.

Von Minden Hotel

Schulenburg

The Von Minden Hotel is the last of the theater-hotels in Texas. The four-story, forty-room hotel was built in 1927 by Gerhardt Von Minden as a wedding present for his daughter, Leonida, and her husband. In the 1930s, it was reputed to be the temporary home of some of the decade's most notorious outlaws, such as Clyde Barrow and Ma Barker. The hotel was operated for more than forty years by Mr. and Mrs. Speckels (nee Von Minden) until 1977, when it was purchased by Bill and Betty Pettit. For years, Betty was the ticket taker at the hotel's movie theater, while Bill ran the hotel and oversaw the operation of its restaurant. Today the Von Minden Hotel is a favorite "haunt" for ghost hunters. Almost every weekend, paranormal investigators set up their equipment inside the old hotel in a search for the truth.

At least three ghosts are thought to haunt the Von Minden. One of the ghost stories is centered around Room 37, called "Jumper's Room" after a World War II paratrooper who spent the night at the

Von Minden in 1945 while on his way back home to his girlfriend after the end of the war. He was lying on his bed, reading a stack of letters sent by his girlfriend, known as "Miss Polka Dot" by the locals. One of the first letters he opened was a "Dear John" letter, in which Miss Polka Dot confessed that her love for him had died. In another version of the tale, she told him that she had married someone else. Unfortunately, the paratrooper did not read one of her letters written a few weeks later, in which she said that she realized that she really did love him after all. With tears streaming down his face, he jumped out the window. Before his body hit the ground, his neck struck a clothesline and was broken. The next day, Miss Polka Dot arrived at the Von Minden Hotel to welcome her lover home. She was overcome with sorrow and guilt when she discovered that her boyfriend had killed himself. Legend has it that her ghost is still roaming around the hotel, looking for her paratrooper.

The first person to meet up with Miss Polka Dot's ghost was Betty Pettit. One night after closing up the ticket booth, Betty was walking through the darkened auditorium, finding her way up the aisles by touching the seats, when all at once she felt someone touch her hand. Betty's family reportedly got a good laugh from hearing about her otherworldly encounter, but Betty swore that it was no laughing matter. Since Betty's sighting, a number of guests have seen the apparition of a twenty-year-old woman wearing a polka-dot dress, a broad-brimmed straw hat, and white gloves walking down the hallways. She is usually carrying a cardboard suitcase.

Another ghost is said to haunt Room 23, where a railroad worker was staying. The manager became concerned when the man did not leave the room for several days, but he couldn't open the door to check on him because something was obstructing it, so he had a small employee climb into the room through the transom to remove the obstruction from the inside. The employee was shocked to find that the man's corpse was blocking the door. Reportedly, the railroad worker's ghost has never left the room.

The ghosts of Mr. and Mrs. Speckels also appear to have trouble tearing themselves away from the hotel. Their apparitions have made appearances in the theater and are also credited with creating disturbances within the hotel. When doors open and close on their own or air-conditioners turn off and on, the former owners are usually suspected of being active in the hotel.

Ghost hunters have been lured here by the testimonies of guests who have made the acquaintance of the hotel's spirits. One guest reported being punched in the stomach when he opened the door to his room. Another guest was taking a shower when she heard someone moving around outside her shower curtain, but when she opened it, no one was there. When she walked into the bedroom, she was surprised to find that the clothes she had carelessly tossed on the floor were neatly stacked on the bed. During the night, she was rudely awakened by someone shaking her bed. When she turned on the light and saw that she was all alone in the room, she found it difficult to get back to sleep.

The hordes of paranormal investigators who have visited the Von Minden Hotel have collected quite a bit of evidence over the years. Orbs frequently appear in photographs taken in Room 23 and in the lobby. Investigators using EMF detectors have experienced a number of spikes in the electromagnetic field throughout the hotel. The Von Minden has even been the setting for a paranormal conference hosted by the Spring Texas Spirit Seekers.

The Lechuza

Batesville

In Greek mythology, harpies are winged creatures with the heads of elderly women and the bodies of eagles or hawks, equipped with deadly talons. Harpies were used by the gods as instruments of vengeance, either to inflict punishment on evildoers or to transport them to the underworld. Zeus used harpies to torment Phineas, a king whose prophecies revealed too much, by snatching away his food before he had a chance to eat it. Interesting enough, people living in South Texas and Mexico have told stories for years of a similar creature that is said to be a hybrid of an evil spirit and a bird: the lechuza.

Tales of the lechuza date back to the Spanish colonial period, when parents and grandparents told children about witches who transformed themselves into large, black birds. In most versions of these tales, the lechuza are owls with the faces of old women. According to Ed Syers in *Ghost Stories of Texas*, brujas who possess the ability to transform themselves into their own familiars often change into birds, such as owls. Some people believe that the lechuza are the spirits of women that take the form of birds and terrorize their unfaithful husbands. Lechuza are usually seen at night. They are said to visit people who are experiencing problems at home. Some say that lechuza feed on the anger generated by family arguments, and some people who have been involved in family squabbles reportedly found scratches outside their windows the next morning. Lechuza are also said to appear just before a death in the family.

Stories of what are said to be genuine attacks by the lechuza abound in Texas border towns. One well-known story involves a man who heard a lechuza hooting outside his house late one night. He picked up his shotgun and walked toward the tree where he had heard the noise. He shot the bird and returned the bed. The next morning, the man and his wife walked outside and found a naked crone lying across the branch of the tree where he had killed the bird the night before. In some variants of the tale, the corpse of the old woman was taken away by other lechuza.

In some of the first-person accounts of encounters with the lechuza, the demon seems to possess poltergeist-like powers, such as the ability to turn electrical devices on and off. Writer Mike Cox tells the story of three women from Zavala County who were driving down Highway 57 just outside Batesville late one night when a large, black bird swooped in front of their car. The bird flew ahead of them for several miles, zigzagging back and forth across the road. At the very moment the driver stepped on the accelerator, the engine stopped and the lights went off. The frantic women locked the car doors and remained stranded in the middle of the highway until they were rescued by a passing driver.

Newspaper columnist Richard G. Santos tells a similar tale of a young couple who were driving on State Highway 1919 in the direction of Eagle Pass just after dark. Suddenly the car's windshield wipers came on. Right after the man turned off the wipers, he and his companion saw a large, black bird sitting on top of a telephone pole. After the couple returned home, they told their friends and neighbors that they had been visited by a lechuza on the highway the night before.

The legends of the lechuza are such an integral part of Texas folklore that many people living along the border truly believe in their existence. It is important to note, however, that many of the people who claim to have seen the lechuza were drinking at the time.

El Muerto

In an excised chapter from Bram Stoker's *Dracula*, called "Dracula's Guest," it is said that an inscription on a tomb reads, "The Dead Travel Fast." In the nineteenth century, the fastest way a person could travel on land, other than by train, was on horseback. The most famous American headless horseman is undoubtedly the decapitated Hessian in Washington Irving's classic short tale, "The Legend of Sleepy Hollow." In South Texas, the best-known mounted specter is El Muerto.

The tale begins only five years after Texas achieved statehood in 1845. Texas encompassed so much territory that in the mid-nineteenth century, lawlessness prevailed, especially in the wild, arid stretches of the state. To combat the constant threat from Indians and bandits, Texas had officially established a posse of gunmen called the Texas Rangers in 1835 when it was still a Spanish province. In South Texas, two of the most prominent of these courageous men were Creed Taylor and William Alexander Anderson "Bigfoot" Wallace. Taylor owned a ranch west of San Antonio, near the headwaters of the Nueces River. This area was reputed to be a hotbed of bandits, the most vicious of whom was a former lieutenant in the Mexican Army known only as Vidal. In the summer of 1850, Vidal and three of his cohorts profited from a rise in the number of raids by bands of Comanche Indians. While the ranchers rode northward in search of the Comanches, Vidal and his band of outlaws preyed on the undefended settlements.

But then Vidal and his men made a fatal mistake by making off with a number of Creed Taylor's mustangs. Unknown to Vidal, Taylor had elected to stay home instead of pursuing the Comanches. Taylor and one of his Mexican cowhands joined forces with "Bigfoot" Wallace at a spot where the river bends below Uvalde. The three men picked up the trail of the desperadoes and followed them all day. They decided that the safest course of action would be to track Vidal and his men to their camp and attack them at night. After Vidal made camp, the small posse waited in the bushes until the four men were asleep. Then they jumped up and began firing at the prostrate bodies. When Wallace was certain that Vidal was dead, he decided to make an object lesson of the bandit. He and his companions severed the bandit's head from his body, then lifted his corpse onto the back of a black mustang and forced it to sit upright by means of a makeshift brace. Wallace tied Vidal's hands to the pommel of the saddle and attached his head and sombrero to the saddle horn with a long strip of rawhide that Wallace had worked through the dead man's jaws.

When Wallace was satisfied with the horrific appearance of the horse's grisly burden, he slapped the mustang's rump. The terrified animal ran off through the desert sage and into Texas folklore. For the next few years, settlers claimed to have seen a headless horseman, wearing a buckskin jacket, rawhide leggings, and a billowing serape, thundering through the desert on a black horse that spouted fire through its nostrils. Sparks flew from its hooves as the horse galloped over the rocky terrain. The rider's head, tied to the saddle, glared at the witness through his red eyes. People said that misfortune followed those who were unfortunate enough to see the apparition. Skeptics assumed that the headless horseman was nothing more than the fanciful imaginings of a few overly excited observers, until a band of cowboys caught up with the "ghost horse," drinking water at a pond near Ben Bolt. They immediately noticed that "headless horseman" was actually a mummified, decapitated corpse that had been lashed to the mustang. The rider's body was riddled with spears, arrows, and bullets. Once the men were able to subdue the animal, they removed its gruesome cargo and buried the body in an unmarked grave in a small cemetery near Ben Bolt.

The cowboys assumed that the burial of the desiccated corpse would mark the end of the legend of El Muerto, the "Dead One," but this was not the case. Not long after Vidal was laid to rest, soldiers at Fort Inge, near present-day Uvalde, reported seeing the headless horseman. The ghost was also seen by scores of people traveling through an area known as No-Man's Land. Around the turn of the nineteenth century, a headless horseman was said to have run right through the traces of a wagon team in old San Patricio. The specter was seen so frequently at a certain spot in this area that it came to be known as Headless Horseman Hill.

In 1969, members of a mounted posse followed a headless rider through the brush near Freer. They gave up the search when they realized that they could find no sign of their quarry anywhere. To this day, residents of the little town of San Diego in Duval County claim to have encountered a headless horseman who rides in the direction of Dead Man's Lake, which has been dried up for many years.

Fort Clark

Brackettville

In the mid-nineteenth century, the brush country of South Texas was as inhospitable as any other region in the state. At this time, U.S. Army outposts were used as staging points for military expeditions. Fort Clark was established in 1852 to protect people traveling along the lower road from San Antonio to El Paso and settlements along the Nueces Strip. The new fort was manned by two companies of the 1st Infantry and the advance and rear guard of the U.S. Mounted Rifles, under the command of Capt. W. E. Prince. The fort had barracks for the soldiers, three grass-covered officers' quarters, a stone hospital, and a two-story storehouse. After Texas seceded from the Union in 1861, the Federal soldiers evacuated the fort and did not return until 1866. In the interim, Fort Clark was taken over by the 2nd Texas Mounted Rifles. The Confederate army also used the fort as a hospital for Confederate soldiers and civilians. In 1872, the Seminole-Negro Indian Scouts were stationed at Fort Clark after having spent twenty years protecting Mexico's northern state of Coahuila from hostile Indians for the Mexican Army. Between 1873 and 1881, the scouts were under the command of Lt. John L. Bullis, and they continued serving at Fort Clark until 1914.

A number of infantry and cavalry units, including two regiments of "Buffalo Soldiers" and Col. Ranald S. Mackenzie's Raiders, were stationed at Fort Clark from time to time. For the most part, the cavalry's role here in the late nineteenth century was to pursue the Apaches, Comanches, and Kickapoos into Mexico. The army's last horse-mounted unit, the 2nd Cavalry Division, was activated at Fort Clark on February 25, 1943. Fort Clark was finally closed in June 1944 and officially deactivated in 1946. For a time, the old horse cavalry post was used as a salvage yard and as a guest ranch. In 1971, Fort Clark was converted into a gated residential community and resort called Fort Clark Springs. Today, eighty of the historic buildings remain standing and are privately owned. Some of the people who live and work here claim to have mingled with the spirits of earlier occupants of the old fort.

Most of what used to be the old barracks are now two-story family dwellings. In *Phantoms of the Plains*, Docia Schultz Williams reports on interviews with several occupants of the old quarters. Barbara Niemann, who lived in number 11, said that she was frequently awakened by the smell of frying bacon and hot coffee. She also heard a deep sigh one evening when she was all alone. Georgia and Pete Cook, who lived in numbers 8-9, said that Pete's cousin was awakened one night by the sounds of a baby and a woman crying. Not long after the Cooks moved in, Georgia was lying on the bedroom floor, shoving some boxes under the bed, when she felt someone grab her leg. At first, she thought her husband was trying to scare her, but when she got up, she found that she was all alone. The Cooks also have woken up to the smell of brewing coffee and sizzling bacon, as have their neighbors in number 10, Joy and Russell Williams, who said that they usually smelled the aromas at 4 A.M. The Williamses also reported seeing a metal candleholder fly off the kitchen wall. It appeared as if someone had pulled the candleholder off the wall and dropped it on the floor. Several nights when her husband was out of town, Joy's dog growled late at night in their bedroom, as if an unwelcome presence were standing there.

A number of famous people have lived at Fort Clark over the years, including Generals George C. Marshall and George S. Patton. However, since becoming a recreational community in 1971, Fort Clark's best-known former residents are the ones who have taken spirit form. The ghosts of Fort Clark seem to be intelligent spirits who enjoy interacting with the new occupants of their fort.

The Black Hope Horror

Crosby

The first indication that something was terribly wrong in Newport Subdivision in Crosby came in 1980, when Sam and Judith Haney moved into their new home. They were in the process of digging a swimming pool in their backyard with a backhoe when an old man showed up at their doorstep to inform them that two bodies were buried in their yard. He led Sam around the house to the spot where he claimed a black man and woman were buried. Sam was not convinced that the mysterious stranger was telling the truth, so he decided to test the validity of what he had said by digging in the exact place the old man had pointed to. Within a few minutes, Sam uncovered an old wooden coffin. He contacted the sheriff and country coroner, who found a second coffin. The skeleton inside this coffin had a wedding ring on its ring finger.

Eager to discover the identities of the two skeletons, the Haneys contacted Jasper Norton, who had worked as a gravedigger in the area as a young man. Norton told the Haneys that the entire subdivision had been built on top of an old graveyard called Black Hope, where a number of former slaves had been buried up until 1939. He identified the two skeletons in their backyard as the remains of Betty and Charlie Thomas, two ex-slaves who had died in the 1930s. The Haneys decided that the decent thing to do would be to rebury the couple in the same place where they had originally been interred.

A few days later, Judith was walking around outside when she heard the sliding door open and a voice call out, "What you doing?" At first she thought her husband was calling for her. She became concerned when she walked back into the house and found that she was all alone. On another occasion, Judith was looking in her closet for a pair of red shoes. She had just about given up her search when she happened to look outside. There, perched on top of Betty Thomas's grave, were her two red shoes. Judith's uneasy feeling intensified when she realized that it happened to be Betty's birthday.

This, it turned out, was only the beginning of the strange story of the Newport Subdivision. Ben and Jean Williams, who moved across the street from the Haneys in the 1980s, noticed right away that their house seemed unusually cold. Before long, lights and televisions began turning on by themselves. Toilets flushed when the bathroom was empty. Armies of ants crawled out of their dishwasher. A black substance oozed from the walls of their bedroom. They began hearing disembodied voices and footsteps late at night. Soon, snakes began appearing out of nowhere. Several of their pets died for no apparent reason. Storms brewed up and centered primarily on Ben and Jean's house. The couple tried to plant a garden, but nothing would grow, despite the amount of fertilizer they used. Sinkholes began appearing in the shapes of coffins. One night, Ben returned late from work and found two apparitions standing in the kitchen. The ghostly figures slowly moved backward into the den and down the hall to the bedroom. Ben flung open the door and saw a dark form standing at the foot of the bed where his wife was sleeping. As he walked through the ghost to sit by his wife's side, he felt what he described as a "sticky, cold sensation." After this incident, the couple began seeing random shadows sliding along the walls. One afternoon, Jean and her granddaughter Carli were awakened from an afternoon nap by the sound of phantom footsteps.

Not only was the neighbors' peace of mind shattered by the bizarre occurrences, but so was their health. Sam and Judith Haney became afflicted with a number of health problems. Six members of the Williamses' extended family contracted cancer; three of them succumbed to the disease within a year. Convinced that they were being tormented because they were living on top of the dead, the Haneys sued the contractor for not telling them that their home was built over a cemetery. A jury awarded the couple $142,000, but the decision was reversed on the grounds that the developer was not liable. When the couple was ordered to pay $50,000 in court costs, they were forced to declare bankruptcy.

Ben and Jean Williams considered suing the developer, but they were told that they had to have concrete evidence before they could proceed in court. One day, Jean began digging in one of the sinkholes. When she was too tired to continue digging, her daughter Tina took the shovel. After digging for thirty minutes, Tina clutched her chest and fell to the ground. Two days later, she died of a massive heart attack at only thirty-two years old. Certain that the spirits had taken their daughter's life because of the attempted desecration of the graves, Jean and Ben left their house and moved to Montana. A few years later, they moved to another neighborhood in Texas. All reports indicate that Ben and Jean's quality of life improved immensely after they moved away from the Black Hope Horror.

Presidio La Bahia

Goliad

The Presidio La Bahia ("Fort on the Bay") was built in 1721 on the site of LaSalle's Fort St. Louis. However, because of hostile relations with the Karankawa Indians, the fort was relocated twenty-six miles away along the Guadalupe River, near the site of present-day Victoria. In 1749, the fort and mission were moved one more time to their present location near Goliad. Even though the Presidio was an inland fort, it was responsible for the defense of the entire coastal area and eastern province of Texas. The Presidio assisted the Spanish Army in fighting the British along the Gulf Coast. Consequently, the town of La Bahia became one of the only communities west of the Mississippi River to have participated in the American Revolution. In 1810, military barracks were constructed at La Bahia. By this time, the town had become the second-largest populated settlement in Spanish Texas. On October 9, 1835, a group of Texas patriots, led by Capt. George Collingsworth, stormed the Mexican garrison and took control of the fort. Before the end of the year, the signing of the first Texas Declaration of Independence took place at Our Lady of Loreto chapel. A few months later, Presidio La Bahia became the site of one of the most notorious incidents in the history of Texas.

Col. James Walker Fannin took command of the Goliad fort in January 1836. His forces were defeated at the battle of Coleto on March 20 and marched back to the Presidio, where they were imprisoned.

The Mexican commander, a Colonel Portilla, received orders from Gen. Santa Anna to execute the prisoners. Shortly thereafter, however, he received an order from Gen. José de Urrea to "treat the prisoners with consideration." The following morning, Colonel Fannin's remaining troops were divided into three groups and marched out of the Presidio on separate roads: the San Antonio road, the Victoria road, and the Copano road. When the three groups of prisoners had marched about three-quarters of a mile from the fort, the officer in charge ordered them to stop. The guards then gathered on one side of each group and opened fire with their rifles. The prisoners who were able to run away were chased down by the cavalry.

After completing their grisly task, the soldiers returned to the Presidio and had the wounded prisoners evacuated from the chapel and laid out in front of the doors. The soldiers then shot all forty men as they were lying on the ground. The last prisoner to be executed was Colonel Fannin himself. He was led out of the chapel to a spot called the Watergate, where he was blindfolded and told to sit down in a chair. Fannin was shot in the face, despite his request that he be shot in the chest. His corpse was burned along with the bodies of the other 342 men who died in the Goliad Massacre. Almost twice as many men died at Goliad than perished at the Alamo.

After the Texas Revolution, La Bahia fell into ruin. In 1960, it was carefully reconstructed from cypress timbers and locally quarried limestone. The architect used a map drawn in the 1830s as a guide. The only original building remaining is the chapel, which is used for weddings and for one service a week. It seems that the builders did such a good job rebuilding the Presidio that the spirits of some of the original residents have returned.

For many years, visitors and staff at the Presidio La Bahia have reported hearing strange noises. People claim to have heard bells chiming from the chapel on days when the chapel was empty. Some have heard phantom footsteps, the cries of babies, and even cannon fire. Several apparitions have been sighted in the Presidio, including an evil entity that watches over the quadrangle, a woman in black who cries in the chapel, and a woman who floats above the ground across the quadrangle and over the back wall to the cemetery by Fannin's Memorial.

Several ghost-hunting groups have conducted investigations at the Presidio. On January 1, 2000, Lone Star Spirits had just set up their equipment when they recorded a voice saying, "It doesn't fit." At 11:30 P.M., a member named Pete saw the ghostly shapes of several decaying corpses in the quadrangle. At 1 A.M., the members' sleep was interrupted by the sounds of horses' hooves and someone banging on their door. After Pete finally got to sleep, he said he felt his bed rising up underneath him. Texas Paranormal Spook Central investigated the building twice: on May 12, 2006, and May 18, 2007. The members recorded some very unsettling EVPs, including "Close the door!" "Help me!" "Who built this building?" and "We're all dead."

On October 8, 2007, the G.H.U.R.U. Group spent the night there, fully equipped with digital voice recorders, digital cameras, and motion detectors. One of the cameras the members set up began shaking uncontrollably before turning itself off. Later that evening, a camera was rolling while one member demanded that the spirits show themselves. Suddenly the members heard a loud scraping sound, as if something heavy were being shoved across the floor in another room. The members ran into the room where the strange sound came from but found nothing unusual. However, while they were there, the sound on their handheld camera became very fuzzy. By the time the group left the next morning, they had recorded several sounds: loud banging from the office area, a man clearing his throat, and horses galloping. They also detected the strong smell of rotting meat.

The Presidio La Bahia has acquired a dark reputation because of the massacre of Colonel Fannin's men. Ironically, though, the same place that was a scene of horror for Fannin's men was also home for the women and children who lived there—and who may live there still.

Southeast Texas

Weinert House Bed and Breakfast

Seguin

This beautiful example of Queen Anne architecture was built in 1895. F. C. Weinert, a Texas politician, lived in the home with his wife, Clara Bading Weinert, and their seven children. He served as a state representative three times between 1892 and 1910 and as a state senator in 1912. Weinert also served as Texas secretary of state in 1913 and once again as a state representative between 1930 and 1934. Weinert's granddaughter and her husband, Mr. and Mrs. Thomas Lovett, lived in the house for many years after the death of her father. The house remained in the Weinert family for almost a century until it was sold in 1990 to Lenna Thomas, who converted it into a bed-and-breakfast. In 2005, Christina and Robert Kibel bought the old house, and members of the Weinert family also sold them the adjoining rear lot. The Kibels then embarked on an extensive renovation project, which included transforming the former carriage house into a guest house. All the owners did such a good job preserving the historical integrity of the old house that the spirits of several members of the Weinert family seem to be reluctant to leave.

In *A Texas Guide to Haunted Restaurants, Taverns and Inns*, Robert and Anne Powell Wlodarski write that the Weinert House is haunted by the mischievous ghosts of Clara Weinert and a spinster sister named Miss Ella. Most of the sightings of these ladies have come from families staying at the bed-and-breakfast. Clara and Ella seem to enjoy putting on impromptu recitals for guests, who marvel at the piano that plays by itself when no one else is near. Even the boom of a timpani echoes through the house on occasion.

Clara Weinert's full-bodied apparition has appeared to a small number of guests. A female guest was awakened one morning when an attractive young lady in a white dress entered her room holding a breakfast tray. The startled woman turned over to wake her husband, but when she looked back at the doorway, the beautiful intruder was gone. The woman reported her strange visitation to Lenna Thomas, who showed her a picture of Clara Weinert. The woman's eyes grew wide as she replied, "That's her. That's the woman I saw in my bedroom." That same year, a male guest standing at the foot of the staircase happened to glance up to see a pretty lady in an old-fashioned dress on the landing. The man said the woman smiled at him and then disappeared. Poltergeist-like activity also occurs in the Weinert House on a fairly regular basis. Objects like clocks and vases are frequently moved to different places.

Not all of the paranormal activity in the Weinert House is scary. A few guests have reported being tucked in at night by invisible hands. Clara and Ella, it seems, are trying to balance their sometimes frightening sightings by showing their nurturing side.

Prince Solms Inn

New Braunfels

In 1898, Emilie Eggeling had the Comal Hotel built at New Braunfels, which was a small town of only two thousand at the time. The enterprising woman was confident that in the future, visitors to the growing city would need a nice place to stay. Two years later, Emilie left New Braunfels to care for relatives in Galveston who had been injured during the hurricane. Emilie's family members took over the hotel in her absence and continued running it for many years. Today the Prince Solms Inn is the oldest—as well as the most haunted—operational hotel in New Braunfels.

The bed-and-breakfast's ghost story begins in the 1900s, when a young woman and her family booked rooms at the hotel a few days before her wedding. On the day of the wedding, the young woman stood inside the church, eagerly awaiting the arrival of her fiancé. Thirty minutes after the young man was due to arrive, his jilted bride began to weep uncontrollably. Her two overly protective brothers mounted their horses and rode off in search of the errant groom.

When they returned, they informed their sister that her fiancé was nowhere to be found. Her family urged her to return home with them, but she refused because she was certain that the love of her life would eventually show up. A few days later, when it became clear to the hotel owners that her fiancé would never arrive, they offered the distraught young woman a job to pay for her room and board. Eventually she worked her way up to manager of the hotel.

The story goes that the unfortunate woman remained at the hotel for the rest of life, finally dying there in the 1920s or early 1930s. Then, in 1935, the new innkeeper saw a young man walk into the hotel and proceed down the hallway to the staircase. When she asked if he needed any help, the young man responded that he had come to the hotel to meet someone and continued ascending the stairs. Her curiosity piqued, the innkeeper watched the mysterious stranger climb the stairs. At the top of the staircase, a beautiful young woman in a wedding dress ran over to the young man and fell into his open embrace. As the couple kissed, they slowly faded away.

The innkeeper was so flabbergasted by what she had just witnessed that she ran to the front of the hotel to find out if anyone else had seen the young man. Three men sitting on the porch confirmed that a young man had indeed entered the hotel. One of them pointed to a horse tied to a hitching post and said it was the young man's horse. The men did not believe the innkeeper's story, so they walked through the entire hotel, including the attic and basement, but could not find a trace of the young man.

The ghost of the jilted bride has been seen a number of times since then. One guest walked into his room and was shocked to find a woman in a wedding dress lying on his bed. Her smiling ghost has also been seen walking down the hallway on the second floor. In 1960, an employee at the hotel saw the spectral bride in the cellar.

Today, the period antiques and stunning paintings and prints in the Prince Solms Inn bed-and-breakfast transport guests back to a more genteel era. And so, apparently, does the faithful spirit of the young bride who continues her lonely vigil in her room.

La Lomita Chapel

La Lomita

The grounds on which La Lomita Chapel is located were awarded as two Spanish land grants in 1767. The land passed through several hands until 1861, when it was left to the Oblate priests who had been using La Lomita as a meeting place since they began ministering to the Catholics of the Rio Grande valley in 1849. The order did not have a real chapel until 1889, when La Lomita Chapel was built from sandstone taken from the nearby hill. In 1907, the Oblate priests sold most of their property to fund the development of schools and churches along the railroad, but they retained possession of the chapel as well as some acreage along the river and in town. For many years, mentally disabled people received assistance here. After the Oblates relocated elsewhere, La Lomita Chapel began to fall into disrepair. The old chapel was renovated in 1928 and again in 1939 after suffering tornado damage. La Lomita Chapel was added to the National Register of Historic Places in 1975. Today it is known throughout Texas for its historic and religious importance—as well as its ghosts.

Most of the haunted activity inside La Lomita Chapel is attributed to the spirit of a nun who died there. For many years, visitors have seen the apparitions of a praying nun suspended in the air. In 2003, when a man and his wife arrived at the chapel, the gates were locked, so they drove around the exterior of the building. When they glanced up at the top of the chapel, they saw a man standing on the balcony with his arms spread apart. Just before they drove away, a bright glow was emanating from the balcony. In 2005, a tourist videotaped the chapel through an opening in the fence. When she viewed the tape later, she was surprised to see the figure of a woman standing in the doorway, facing a corner of the chapel.

Other ghostly tales have made La Lomita Chapel a popular destination spot for curiosity seekers. Visitors claim that they have encountered cold spots in the basement. Disembodied footsteps and voices are said to echo through the old chapel late at night. Some say that at twilight, the stains on the weather-beaten exterior walls take the form of human figures, which seem to float in midair. Many people are certain that La Lomita Chapel is still the spiritual home of the unfortunate nun.

Bailey's Light

Bailey's Prairie

Bailey's Prairie is a small village in Brazoria County that was named for Texas pioneer James Briton Bailey. Bailey built his home here in the early 1800s on land he bought from the Spanish government. The Mexican government later tried to evict him from his property, but Bailey was a contentious, cantankerous man and refused to leave. He always seemed to be involved in some sort of altercation with his neighbors, although his innate aggressiveness may have become an asset when he was commissioned captain of the local militia. Apparently he continued his ornery ways even after his death in 1832, according to those who reported sightings of his ghost.

As the story goes, Bailey had specified that when he died, he did not want to lie in a grave. Instead, he was to be buried standing up and facing the west, along with his rifle and a jug of whiskey. Some say that the slaves who buried Bailey helped themselves to the old man's whiskey. Others say that his wife, who disapproved of her husband's drinking, disposed of his favorite beverage just before his burial. Regardless of whatever really happened to his whiskey, it seems that Bailey's ghost was none too happy to find that it was gone.

Soon after his burial, sightings of Bailey's ghost were reported. Johan and Ann Thomas, who purchased the Bailey home a few years after his death, swore that the old soldier never really turned over his home to the new owners. Ann awoke from her sleep one night to see a shadowy figure standing at the foot of her bed. When the apparition moved a few steps closer and reached out to touch her, she covered her eyes with her blanket and screamed. A few minutes later, she lowered the blanket to find that the entity was standing by the door, but then it floated back toward the middle of the room. The specter continued to torment Ann all night long. She would scream and the figure would vanish, only to reappear at the door a few minutes later. After three experiences with manifestations of Bailey's ghost, the Thomas family moved out of the house.

Reports of sightings of Bailey's ghost continue to this day, but in a much different form. A strange ball of light is occasionally seen within the town limits, and people have claimed that it chased their vehicles as they drove down the road. It is said that the light emanates from a lantern carried by Bailey's ghost, searching in vain for his missing whiskey.

Bragg Road Ghost Lights

Saratoga

Saratoga is located between Beaumont and Livingston. The dirt road that has come to be called Bragg Road was named after a town that once existed near Saratoga, Bragg Station. The road was originally the bed for railroad tracks that were laid in 1902 as part of the Santa Fe Railroad's survey line from Bragg to Saratoga. Trains hauled people, cattle, oil, and logs through the Big Thicket forest. After the supplies of virgin pine and oil were depleted, railroad crews pulled up the tracks. The county then purchased the old railroad line and created the county road known as Bragg Road. In the 1940s through the 1960s, sightings of ghost lights gave the old road a new name: the "Ghost Road."

Not long after the railroad tracks were removed, hunters walking and driving down the dirt road began talking about a ball of light that hovered over it. One old man said that one night while driving down Bragg Road, a ball of light sailed between the horses pulling his wagon, causing it to overturn in a ditch. Some people described red, white, blue, and green ghost lights that flitted through the woods. In *Tales from the Big Thicket*, Francis Edward Abernethy says that in the 1940s and 1950s, hundreds of people drove down Bragg Road in hopes of catching a glimpse of the mysterious lights. Some people chased the elusive lights, and others fired their guns at them. A preacher is said to have climbed onto the top of his car and warned that the light was a sign of the end of the world. In the 1960s, people claimed that not only did the light chase them and stop their engines, but it even burned their hands as it passed through them.

Folklore offers a number of different explanations for the ghost lights of Bragg Road. The oldest legend chronicles the efforts of ghostly conquistadores to find the golden treasure that they hid in the area. Other people say that the ghost lights are remnants of the Kaiser Burnout. In the spring of 1865, Confederate captain James Kaiser set fire to the Big Thicket in an attempt to flush out a group of Union partisans. In a variant of this legend, the ghost light is the spirit of a man killed during the Kaiser Burnout. But the most commonly told story is that of a railroad worker who was decapitated while walking down the tracks. To this day, he still wanders up and down the old railroad bed with a lantern in his hand, searching for his head. Less fanciful explanations for the strange lights include swamp gas and the headlights of automobiles.

The enduring popularity of the Bragg Road ghost lights might provide an economic boon to the region. Hardin County commissioner Ken Pelt has been trying to promote Bragg Road as a tourist attraction. Most of the area's appeal lies in the bizarre lights that can be seen on certain occasions at night, but the creepy canopy of branches formed by the trees growing along the road also contributes to its haunted reputation.

San Bernard River's Music Bend

Brazoria County

The San Bernard River flows 120 miles southeast from southwestern Austin County, cutting across southern Brazoria County and the Gulf Intracoastal Waterway before feeding into the Gulf of Mexico. In the late nineteenth century, residents of Brazoria County began talking about ethereal-sounding music that emanated from the river at a point that has come to be known as "Music Bend." Some people have likened the sound to violin music; others believe the music is produced by a flute or a human voice. Most witnesses have heard the music at the night during a full moon. People who have heard it from a boat say the music originates underwater and then moves to the seats before enveloping the entire boat.

Most of the people who have heard the music did not enjoy the experience. An elderly man who was rowing his boat through Music Bend said that all of a sudden he began trembling. Then the most beautiful music he had ever heard wafted through the air, but he said he never wanted to hear the music again. In 1920, searchers found the bodies of two girls who had drowned in the river. As they retrieved the corpses from their watery grave, they heard the lilting tones of funeral music. Even though the music was lovely, they also hoped that they never heard it again.

A number of legends explain the origin of the music. Some people say that a hermit who loved to fiddle away the hours was murdered by pirates who sought refuge in his cabin by the river during a storm. In an African American version of the tale, two sailors docked their boat along the banks of the San Bernard River during a storm. When the wind picked up, one of the sailors, who was a fiddler, picked up his violin and started to play. He inadvertently woke up the other sailor from a deep sleep, and a fierce fight ensued. The fiddler lost his balance and fell into the river. When his body failed to rise to the surface, the other sailor threw his violin and bow into the river and went back to bed. He had not been asleep for long before he was awakened by the sound of fiddle music. The fiddler's ghost is said to play this same tune over and over again.

Several of the legends have a romantic basis. According to one story, a young girl went to the San Bernard River every evening to get a bucket of water and enjoy a secret rendezvous with her lover, who announced his presence by playing his fiddle. One evening, she was struck by an Indian's arrow and died a few minutes later. Her lover was so despondent afterward that he flung himself and his violin into the river. In a variant of the story, a young woman living along the river became engaged to a violinist. A few hours before her wedding, she was walking down to the San Bernard River, where a number of water lilies grew close to the bank. She went to the edge of the river and plucked one of the flowers to wear in her hair during her wedding. Suddenly a poisonous snake lunged at her neck and bit her. She died almost instantly. When her fiancé found her body lying in the waist-high ferns, he threw himself and his violin into the river.

No one has ever come up with a definite explanation for the mysterious music of Music Bend. Skeptics propose that the sounds are caused by escaping gas. However, as long as people believe they've really heard music at Music Bend, they will continue to turn to folklore for the answer.

Liendo Plantation

Hempstead

Liendo Plantation is located on sixty-seven thousand acres of land purchased by Jose Justo Liendo from the Mexican government in 1830. Leonard Waller Groce, a Texas hero who ferried Sam Houston's army across the Brazos on the way to San Jacinto, purchased the property and built a lavish home for himself and his family in the mid 1800s. Groce named the plantation Liendo in honor of its former owner. Once the plantation house was completed, Groce built a school for his own children and those from neighboring plantations. For almost a decade, the plantation served as the social center of Texas, receiving the state's early dignitaries such as Sam Houston. Between 1861 and 1865, Liendo Plantation served as both a recruiting station for the Confederate army and a prisoner-of-war camp. During Reconstruction, Gen. George Armstrong Custer and his wife stayed at the plantation for three months. They were so impressed by their hosts' hospitality and the beauty of the plantation that they made sure it was not damaged by his soldiers.

Liendo Plantation fell on hard times after the Civil War. Unable to pay people to work his land, Groce declared bankruptcy in 1868 and sold 1,100 acres to Elisabet Ney and Dr. Edmund D. Montgomery for $10,000. Elisabet was an artist who had earned a reputation in Europe for her busts of politicians, artists, and musicians. Dr. Montgomery had tried raising cotton in Georgia but soon discovered that he was better suited as a scientist than as a farmer. He devoted most of his time to writing scientific papers and a book titled *Philosophical Prob-*

lems in the Light of Vital Organization. He died in 1911, four years after Elizabet passed away.

Not only was Liendo known for its lavish parties in the midcentury, but it also achieved notoriety for its ghosts. Rumors of haunted activity inside the plantation house began soon after Elisabet and Edmund's infant son died of diphtheria. Some people say that to prevent the spread of the disease, Dr. Montgomery cremated his son in the drawing room fireplace. The couple then placed the urn containing their son's ashes on the fireplace mantel. Soon thereafter, people began hearing the gasping cries of a baby coming from the white guest house, a lodging for male guests, where the child had been quarantined until he finally died. Guests also claimed to have seen the child's lonely ghost lying on the bed, struggling to breathe.

Other spirits are said to haunt Liendo Plantation as well. Michele Janczak, who has worked at the Plantation for several years, said that a few people have told her they heard weird noises in the house during the night. She had her own encounter one day when she saw a man sitting on the back porch who bore a strong resemblance to Sam Houston. Guests spending the night in the Sam Houston Room reported to their hosts the next morning that a very considerate woman standing at the foot of the bed asked them if everything was all right. The spirit of Elisabet Ney is credited with tugging on the blankets on some guests in the house. Years ago, a guest was staying at Liendo Plantation during a heat wave when suddenly her uncomfortably hot room became frigid. She then felt someone climb in bed with her. She assumed that this was her friend, who was staying in another room. The next morning, however, she was shocked to find out that her friend had stayed in her own room all night long.

In 2010, the Bastrop Paranormal Research Group investigated Liendo Plantation from 10 P.M. until 2 A.M. A ghost hunter who was doing EVP work in one of the rooms asked, "Do you feel trapped in the house?" At the same time, the door slammed shut. When the investigators moved to Dr. Montgomery's room, they immediately detected the odor of cigar smoke. When they scanned the room with their EMF detectors, their meters spiked when they walked past Dr. Montgomery's books and when they asked him about his wife and son.

Although a number of people have reported having paranormal experiences inside Liendo Plantation, not many have been willing to give the details to visitors, possibly because they feel they are too fantastic to be believed. Michele Janczak insists that working in a haunted house is not really a scary job. "No one has ever been scared out of here," she says. "There has never been anything menacing about any of the experiences."

The Headless Soldier of Sabine Pass

Sabine Pass

Sabine Pass is a neighborhood in Port Arthur just west of the Louisiana state line on the Gulf Coast. During the Civil War, Union forces attempted to take control of the mouth of the Sabine River to open up East Texas to occupation by the Union army. The Sabine Pass was guarded by a single Confederate fort, Fort Griffin, manned by approximately fifty soldiers. They were members of Company F, the "Jefferson Davis Guards," under the command of twenty-five-year-old Lt. Richard Dowling. Fort Griffin's artillery included four cannons and two howitzers. In early September 1863, a Union flotilla under the command of Capt. Frederick Crocker approached the fort. While the gunboats lobbed shells toward the fort, Dowling and his men were hiding inside bomb-proof shelters. For a few minutes, Captain Crocker wondered if the fort was occupied at all. In reality, the Union flotilla was entering a trap. As soon as the boats passed a row of stakes that the Confederate artillery had sighted on during target practice, the fort's defenders opened fire. The Union forces hastily retreated, leaving behind two sunken gunboats and two hundred sailors, who were captured by the Confederates. None of the defenders of Fort Griffith were killed. Desperate to find a battle to celebrate about after suffering catastrophic losses at Vicksburg and Gettysburg, Confederate president Jefferson Davis declared the outcome of the battle of Sabine Pass a great victory. In reality, however, this battle had little effect on the outcome of the war.

According to writer W. T. Block, the day after the battle, the Confederate soldiers at Fort Griffin set about the grisly task of burying the Union dead in a mass grave at Mesquite Point. One of the victims was the starboard gunner of the Union gunboat *Clifton*. As the burial detail lifted the body of the dead sailor, they gasped when they realized that his head had been removed by a cannonball bouncing across the deck and apparently had fallen into the Sabine River. The name of the unfortunate Union sailor has never been discovered. Legend has it that when the Confederate soldiers retrieved the body of an African American sailor floating down the river, they found the head of the decapitated man tucked under his jacket. After all the bodies had been buried, one of the soldiers threw the head back into the river.

Brock says that in the late 1860s and early 1870s, when the moon was full, Confederate veterans reported seeing the apparition of the headless Union gunner staggering along the banks of the Sabine River, looking for his head. They claimed that the specter emitted low, grunting sounds, even though he had no vocal cords. Most of the sightings of the apparition seem to have occurred before World War I. Could it be that the phantom gunner finally found his missing head?

The Ghosts of Old Waverly

Old Waverly

The first white settler in the area now known as Old Waverly was James W. Winters, a native of Alabama who moved to Texas in 1835. For the next twenty years, more Alabamians also moved to East Texas, where they set up cotton plantations. The town of Waverly, which was incorporated before the Civil War, was named after one of the towns in the works of Sir Walter Scott. After the Civil War, the planters in Waverly offered former slaves shares of the crops they raised in lieu of payment. Not enough freed slaves were willing to work as sharecroppers, so the planters planned to have 150 peasant farmers immigrate to Texas from Poland. However, the number of Polish farmers willing to move to Texas in the late nineteenth century was far smaller than the farmers had anticipated. Waverly experienced another setback when the Houston and Great Northern Railroad moved its tracks eight miles west of town in the 1870s, primarily because the town leaders feared that the railroad would bring in unsavory elements. A new town called New Waverly sprang up around the railroad tracks and siphoned off a number of families from the original town, which came to be known as Old Waverly. Between 1896 and 1925, the population of Old Waverly declined by about half. In the late 1940s, a subdivision was built on the west side of Old Waverly. Today, however, nothing remains of Old Waverly except its handsome Presbyterian church and a nineteenth-century cemetery—and perhaps one or two ghosts.

In *Ghosts of Texas*, Ed Syers writes of a haunted cabin on a small hill in the woods near Old Waverly. During the Civil War, a young girl was reportedly murdered there, and three Union soldiers were accused of the crime by her friends and relatives. The three soldiers were murdered and buried under the cabin floor. Not long thereafter, people passing by the old cabin said they heard the piercing screams of a young girl and fiddle music coming from the cabin. Dogs and cats refused to enter the door of the cabin. As the story goes, in the 1970s, a newspaper reporter tried to spend the night in the cabin, but she left when she saw a misty shape floating outside the premises. Locals refer to the location of the cabin as Soldier's Hill.

Another haunted hill around Old Waverly is known as Sentry Hill. This knoll is said to be haunted by the ghost of either a Union sentry or a sawmill operator who was accidentally beheaded in the mill. Screams and disembodied voices have been heard coming from a cabin on the hill, usually at night. Syers tells the story of two men who drove out to Sentry Hill late one night to investigate the reports they had heard of paranormal activity. They were walking around the hill, when suddenly they heard someone running toward them. One of the men said that if they were really being chased by a ghost, it could prevent the car's engine from starting. Sure enough, nothing happened when they turned the key in the ignition. They had to get a jump start before they could leave Sentry Hill. They were totally convinced—as have been so many other visitors to the two haunted hills—that the only residents of Old Waverly are of the spectral kind.

The Old Fayette County Jail

LaGrange

The residents of Fayette County felt the need for a jail soon after the county was organized in December 1837. The jail was completed the following summer. After the jail fell into disrepair and could no longer be used, prisoners were incarcerated in private homes for a year, with the amateur "jail keepers" paid $3 per day. In the early 1880s, the county constructed a new jail. In the early years, the jail's employees consisted of the county sheriff and one prison guard. The most famous sheriff who worked out of the Fayette County Jail was Jim Flournoy, who was instrumental in closing the Chicken Ranch, a brothel that operated in Fayette County from 1905 until 1973. The best known "guests" of the Fayette County Jail were two members of Bonnie and Clyde's gang, Raymond Hamilton and Gene O'Dare, who had robbed Carmine Bank. The old jail closed in 1985 when it was replaced by a modern justice center. It stood vacant until 1995, when it was extensively renovated before becoming the home of the La Grange Area Chamber of Commerce.

Today the Old Fayette County Jail is said to be haunted by the spirits of people who were imprisoned there. One of these criminals was the Widow Dach, who murdered a hired hand and then starved herself to death during her imprisonment. Another legend has it that several prisoners were chained to the walls of the jail when floodwaters from the swollen Colorado River swept over the county. Because the sheriff was unable to release the prisoners in time, they perished under sand and silt.

In April 2009, members of the TFC Paranormal Research Team conducted an all-night investigation of the Old Fayette County Jail. The investigators had a number of startling personal experiences. During the night, one member of the team was touched by an unseen hand. Several members heard whispering and disembodied footsteps inside the jail. Sometime in the middle of the night, shackles hanging from the wall rattled, as if being shaken by an invisible force. Although the team's audio equipment captured the bizarre sounds, the volume was too low to be entered as evidence.

Visitors to the Old Fayette County Jail can get a taste of what life was like for prisoners and law-enforcement personnel in the nine-teenth and twentieth centuries. Glass cases contain such relics from the past as badges, holsters, uniforms, belt buckles, knives and forks, guns, and locks. Less visible are the spirits of the prisoners whom death apparently did not grant release from their imprisonment.

USS *Lexington*

Corpus Christi

The USS *Lexington* was one of twenty-four Essex-class aircraft carri-ers built for the U.S. Navy during World War II. Launched in 1942, she was named for the Revolutionary War battle. After arriving in Pearl Harbor in August 1943, she raided Tarawa in late September and Wake Island in October. The *Lexington*'s gunners took a heavy toll, downing twenty-nine Japanese planes on November 23–24. During a raid on Kwajalein on December 4, the *Lexington* inflicted extensive damage on two Japanese cruisers and shot down thirty planes but was struck by a torpedo on the starboard side, which killed nine sailors. With the aid of a hand-operated steering unit, the ship made her way back to Pearl Harbor for emergency repairs. Japan's queen of radio propaganda, Tokyo Rose, erroneously reported the *Lexington* sunk, earning the carrier the nickname it would bear for the remain-der of the war: "The Blue Ghost."

The *Lexington* returned to action the following spring. On April 28, 1944, she emerged virtually untouched from a Japanese counterattack at Truk Island. Once again, however, Tokyo Rose announced the sink-ing of the carrier. In the Battle of Leyte Gulf, the *Lexington* was hit by a kamikaze plane. Despite the destruction of most of the carrier's island structure, her planes continued normal flight actions. When the *Lexington* sailed into the port of Ulithi for repairs, her crew learned that once again the Japanese propaganda machine had reported her sunk. The *Lexington* returned to action in the China Sea on May 22. For the next two months, until the surrender of the Japanese fleet, she went after the remainder of the Japanese fleet at the Yolosuka and Kure naval bases.

In 1947, the *Lexington* was decommissioned and made a part of the Reserve Fleet. After being recommissioned in 1955, the ship was deployed in ports of call all over the world. She reinforced the 7th Fleet off Taiwan during the 1958 Lebanon crisis. During the Cuban Missile Crisis, she was reactivated as an aircraft carrier. In 1969, she began service as a training carrier in Pensacola, Corpus Christi, and New Orleans. On October 29, 1989, a student pilot crashed his T-2 training aircraft on the *Lexington*'s flight deck, killing five crew members. After training pilots for twenty-two years, the proud old aircraft carrier was decommissioned in 1991 and opened as a museum the following year along North Shoreline Boulevard in Corpus Christi. The *Lexington* has been featured in a number of films, including the 2001 movie *Pearl Harbor*, as well as the television miniseries *War and Remembrance*.

The USS *Lexington*'s haunted reputation began soon after the ship museum was opened to tourists. Because of the large number of reports of otherworldly phenomena, her designation as "The Blue Ghost" has taken on an entirely different dimension. Staff and visitors alike have reported hearing strange sounds, such as disembodied voices, the clanking of heavy chains, and elevators moving up and down. One of the most active parts of the ship is one of the showering areas below deck, where people claim to have heard crying and yelling. This is where the sailors died when the ship was struck by a Japanese torpedo in 1943. Staff and tourists walking through the switch room have reported becoming overcome by what can best be described as an uncomfortable feeling. A paint crew aboard the ship who had taken a break returned to the room they were restoring and discovered that someone—or something—had finished their work for them.

Full-bodied apparitions are said to make an occasional appearance as well. One of the ship's phantoms is said to be the "lost soul" of a Japanese aviator who is still searching for his lost plane. In 2008, a girl standing in the picture gallery claimed to have seen a man wearing a blue shirt and khaki pants looking at her. M. Charles Reustle, the museum's director of operations, said he was walking out of his office one day when he heard the rustling of a starched uniform and the sound of footsteps right behind him. He turned around, but no one was there. Reustle said he encountered the invisible sailor several times thereafter.

The best-known member of the USS *Lexington*'s phantom crew is a ghost that is usually described as a handsome, blond-haired, blue-eyed lad with a piercing gaze. Many believe he is the spirit of 1939 Heisman Trophy winner Nile Kinnick, who became one of the *Lexington*'s first casualties when, during a training flight, his F4F Wildcat developed a serious oil leak that forced him to ditch. Others say that this is the ghost of a sailor who was killed when a kamikaze pilot crashed his plane into the *Lexington* in 1944.

Another ghost, nicknamed "Charley," has been seen more than two hundred times. Many visitors, and even a few tour guides, have reported that while they were walking through the aft engine room, a very polite young man walked up to them and began sharing his in-depth knowledge of the engines, such as how they utilized steam and how much horsepower they generated. In the early 2000s, a tour group followed their handsome male tour guide to the bowels of the ship. They were walking around, looking at the machinery, when they realized that they were all alone. The tourists made their way back to the upper deck and informed the manager that their particularly knowledgeable tour guide had abandoned them. The manager listened patiently to their description of the bright young man and then replied that no one like that worked on the ship—at least, not in bodily form.

The USS *Lexington* is known today as the longest-serving aircraft carrier in the U.S. fleet. She participated in twenty-one of the twenty-four operations in the Pacific and also gained distinction as having set more records than any other aircraft carrier in naval history, thanks in large part to the crew members who served on her over her years of service. But she is also known for the ghosts said to be walking her decks along with the tourists and staff ever since she opened as a museum in 1991.

The Headless Ghost of Milan Street

Seguin

Riverside Cemetery, which dates back to the late 1800s, is said to be the most haunted burial ground in Seguin. The more than two thousand burials in the cemetery included pioneers, slaves, elected officials, and clergy. Perhaps the headless ghost that haunts Milan Street is the spirit of one Civil War soldier.

For many years, people have reported seeing the headless ghost of a Confederate soldier walking down Milan Street, away from Riverside Cemetery. Some say that a cannonball removed the soldier's head during a battle in the East. Others say the soldier was decapitated by a sword or bayonet and that his corpse was transported to Seguin, minus his head, by railroad. Writer C. F. Eckhardt points out a serious "hole" in this part of the legend, however: the railroad did not come to Seguin until 1877, twelve years after the end of the Civil War.

Witnesses say the soldier's headless ghost always walks north toward the railroad tracks. He inevitably misses a jog in Milan Street and walks past the west wall of the same house. People sitting on a sofa on this side of the house have sensed the presence of the ghost when he walked by. The ghost always dissolves in a silvery mist when he reaches the railroad tracks.

Olivia Hallmark Abbott, author of *Ghosts in the Graveyard*, has speculated on an entirely different identity for the headless ghost. She says that because of his apparent affinity for the railroad, he likely was a railroad worker who fell on the tracks into the path of an oncoming train and was decapitated. Like so many other railroad ghosts, the unfortunate man's spirit wanders the tracks, looking for his lost head.

West Texas

Buie Park

Stamford

Stamford is a small town in Haskell County. In 1900, the president of the Texas Central Railroad, H. McHarg, named the town after his hometown in Connecticut. Ten years later, Buie Park was opened five miles south of Stamford on Farm to Market Road 1226 and remained open until the late 1960s. Today Buie Park is nothing more than an overgrown patch of woods. In fact, were it not for a cement pillar bearing the name of the park, the casual passerby would not even recognize it as a place where once families picnicked, children played, and lovers spooned. The old park is now remembered primarily for its ghosts.

One of these specters is that of the forlorn mother of a ten-year-old girl named May. As the story goes, around the time of World War I, May and her mother went to the park to take advantage of the beautiful weather. May was playing along the river while her mother watched from a short distance away. Suddenly May disappeared from view. Her mother frantically ran to the riverbank and called her daughter's name. People standing nearby joined her in the search, but the child was never found. The authorities assumed that May had fallen into the river and drowned. Her distraught mother was driven mad by grief. For years, people walking along the river reported hearing a disembodied female voice crying, "May! May!"

Buie Park's best-known ghost is a spirit known only as the Hatchet Lady. Legend has it that a beautiful young woman was brought to the park one sunny day by her fiancé. They walked to an isolated spot, and the young man told the girl to sit down. She assumed that he had some sort of romantic interlude in mind. Instead, he sat next to her and, taking her hands in his, told her that he was breaking off their engagement. Instead of bursting into tears, as the young man expected, she flew into a rage. She grabbed a hatchet and buried its blade in his brain. Her vindictive spirit subsequently tormented young couples who went out to the park to make out.

The legend does not explain how the young woman found a hatchet so quickly after her fiancé broke the news to her. No newspaper accounts of either tragedy have ever been found. The names of May's mother and the engaged couple remain shrouded in mystery and likely always will.

Fort Brown

Fort Brown was originally an earthen fortification built by Gen. Zachary Taylor's troops in 1846. The stage was set for the first battle of the Mexican War in May of that year when Taylor left Fort Texas, as it was known back then, in the charge of Maj. Jacob Brown. Taylor was procuring supplies from Port Isabel when he heard the report of cannon fire. He mustered his troops and hurried back to Fort Texas, where he engaged Gen. Mariano Arista's troops in battle. Despite their smaller numbers, Taylor's troops won the day, thanks in large part to Maj. Samuel Ringgold, who quickly moved his light artillery from one location to the next. The fort was renamed Fort Brown in honor of the major, who was killed while defending the fort. Col. John "Rip" Ford's Confederate troops took possession of Fort Brown during the Civil War but were driven out in 1863 by a Union army under the command of Gen. Nathaniel P. Banks. However, the next year, the Confederate army regained the fort and held it until the end of the Civil War.

Capt. William A. Wainwright constructed a permanent fortification at Fort Brown in 1878. In 1906, a group of African American soldiers stationed at the fort were accused of instigating the Brownsville Riot and dishonorably discharged. Nearly a decade later, the first American plane to be attacked by hostile enemy gunfire took off from Fort Brown. On April 20, 1915, the pilots, Byron Q. Jones and Thomas Millings, were fired upon while searching for Francisco "Pancho" Villa's troops. Fort Brown remained an active military post until it was decommissioned in 1944. The city of Brownsville took possession of the land in 1948, and the buildings making up the fort were turned over to schools and organizations in the area. A number of these post–Civil War structures were acquired by the University of Texas at Brownsville, and sections of the old earthen fort are still visible on the campus grounds. According to students, faculty, and staff at the university, the buildings and earthworks are not the only vestiges of the state's frontier past that can be seen—and heard—throughout the campus.

One of these haunted sites is the Gorgas Building. Now used for administrative offices, the building was originally a hospital. It was named after Dr. William Gorgas, one of the first American doctors to search for a cure for yellow fever. Hundreds of patients suffering from yellow fever, tuberculosis, and cholera were treated by Dr. Gorgas and his staff in the old hospital. People who work in the Gorgas Building claim to have seen the spirits of doctors and nurses in old-fashioned attire walking briskly through the hallways, just as they did in the nineteenth century. Students and faculty have also reported seeing the apparition of a weeping woman dressed in black. Some say she is still searching for her son, who was a patient at the hospital many years ago. On one occasion, a student claimed to have heard a strange hissing sound inside the building. A housekeeper reported that one evening, she was cleaning inside one of the rooms when several objects sitting on a desktop began sliding across the surface on their own. Another night, a janitor was approached by a strange woman who asked where her son was being treated. After the janitor gave the distraught mother directions to the local hospital, her form gradually faded away.

In 2004, a local news crew investigated the Gorgas Building, along with paranormal investigator Victor Perez. During the night, the group captured a number of orbs with their digital cameras. They also recorded a number of EVPs at 3 A.M. One of the recorded disembodied voices responded with a clear "yes" after one of the investigators asked if the spirit needed assistance.

Dr. Gorgas also had a close connection to another haunted building on campus: the old morgue. Legend has it that Dr. Gorgas was arrested for going to the morgue and dissecting the corpses of yellow fever victims in an effort to find a cure for the disease. He was later released, but the doctor's ghost—or some other troubled spirit—seems intent on making its presence known inside the old morgue.

Not only have students and employees sensed that someone was watching them, but one young woman claims that something yanked on her hair one evening. Some people say they have seen objects fly into the air when all the doors and windows in the building were closed. Ghost hunters have captured a large number of orbs inside the building.

The small building now known as the Regimental House was originally called the Little Chapel. After the building was renovated, university employees soon realized that they were sharing the old church with an unseen entity. They heard the sound of disembodied footsteps in empty hallways and saw "shadow people" flitting around corners and into darkened rooms. A photograph taken by paranormal investigator Ken Fairchild shows fingerlike shapes on the blinds in one of the windows.

Over the years, a large number of students have had uncanny experiences in the art building, which was originally the commissary and guardhouse. Built in 1906, the building retains remnants of its dark past, such as the metal-grated cells that can still be seen in the basement. It seems that a few of the original occupants of the building make an occasional appearance as well. Students have left their art projects overnight, only to find that they were moved or mutilated sometime during the night. Students working alone in the building have felt extremely uncomfortable, as if they were being watched by an invisible presence. People have also heard metallic scraping sounds and disembodied voices.

One of the most modern buildings on campus also has spirit activity, apparently because of the site on which it was constructed. In the second half of the nineteenth century, a small island in the middle of an oxbow lake near the fort and on the site of the present-day campus served as a cemetery. In the late 1860s, the quartermaster, Col. William Alonso Wainwright, set up cannons in the cemetery as a monument. In the early 1900s, nearly four thousand corpses were exhumed and moved to a cemetery in Alexandria, Louisiana. However, many locals believe that not all of the corpses were disinterred, because when the Rio Grande flooded in 1933, a number of coffins floated to the surface. Many people believe that the dormitories, which are part of a former hotel built on the island years ago, are haunted because they were built on top of the old military cemetery. A student at the university claimed that she was visited many times in her dorm room by the mischievous spirit of a three-year-old boy, who delighted in pulling the covers off her bed in the middle of the night. Some students say that the ghost boy asked them, in both Spanish and English, to let his mother know that he is doing fine—in the afterlife, one assumes.

Plaza Theatre

El Paso

El Paso's Plaza Theatre opened in 1930 and was a huge hit, not just because of its beautiful artwork and Wurlitzer organ, but also because it was the first public theater in the United States with air-conditioning. A number of well-known entertainers appeared at the Plaza Theatre during its heyday, including John Wayne, Ethel Barrymore, Mae West, the Marx Brothers, Henry Fonda, Tom Mix, James Stewart, Sarah Bernhardt, Roy Rogers, and Tallulah Bankhead. In the 1950s, the popularity of the theater declined as a result of the advent of television and drive-in movie theaters, as well as the exodus to the suburbs. By the 1970s, the theater was closed and all its lavish furnishings had been sold. It reopened for a short time but finally closed again in 1989. The grand old theater was saved from demolition and donated to the city of El Paso, and it was eventually restored to its original splendor and reopened in 2006.

The Plaza Theatre is said to be haunted by the ghost of a man who died there in the 1940s. The man, whose identity is unknown, was watching a movie when he suddenly became very ill. He decided to walk into the lobby and get a drink at the water fountain. After taking several gulps of water, the man stood by the water fountain and began smoking a cigarette. He had just taken a deep drag from his cigarette when he collapsed on the floor. The coroner determined that the man had had a massive heart attack.

For years, employees and customers have reported seeing and smelling the unfortunate moviegoer and his ever-present cigarette.

Many people claim to have seen a man walking toward the water fountain in a great hurry. He vanishes while he is taking a drink. When the theater was planning its grand reopening party in 2006, a cook for a local caterer, Miguel Castro, was standing in the men's restroom when he heard someone rapping on the door. Suddenly the strong aroma of cigarette smoke began wafting through the air. He became uneasy because he knew he was the only one inside the bathroom at the time. He opened the door and was amazed to see a cigarette floating in the air. Miguel was so frightened that he hurried back to his cooking station and tried to forget what he had seen. He asked the other cooks if they had been smoking in the men's room, but they swore that they had not.

It is said that the ghost that haunts the Plaza Theatre can be summoned with the use of chanting or a Ouija board. People also say that if you light up a cigarette inside the theater, you will see a man smoking a cigarette in the balcony. However, because El Paso has banned smoking in public buildings, it is unlikely that anyone will be able to conjure up the apparition of the smoking ghost using this method.

Loretto Academy

El Paso

The beginnings of the present-day Loretto Academy extend all the way to Kentucky in the early 1800s. Pioneering priest Father Charles Nerinckx had been working among the hill people of Kentucky for many years before deciding that the area would benefit from the establishment of a school. Mary Rhodes, Nancy Havern, and Christina Stewart "answered the call" and set up a school in an abandoned log cabin. In April 1812, the three women founded the first truly American religious order with no ties to any specific church.

Soon the nuns' ministry spread throughout the Midwest. In June 1852, six nuns accepted the invitation of Bishop John Baptist Lamy to serve the people of Texas. The sisters braved a cholera epidemic aboard a steamboat at Independence, Missouri, and a rugged trip to Texas via covered wagons before finally arriving in Santa Fe on September 26. In 1892, Mother Magdalen Deitz, along with several nuns, moved to El Paso and took over a school that had been abandoned by the Irish Sisters of Mercy. In 1915, Mother Praxedes Cary oversaw the construction of a new building at Trowbridge.

The first students entered the doors of Loretto Academy in September 1923. All three units of the academy were finally completed fifteen years later. At one time, about a hundred of the sisters who taught in the parochial schools in El Paso lived at Loretto Academy. In 1975, the boarding school closed; the next year, the old academy was converted into a middle school. In recent years, Loretto Academy has expanded its mission to include teaching English as a second language, providing ministry to the deaf, and serving as a retreat center. In spite of the changes that have been made to Loretto Academy, it seems that one tragic episode from the school's past refuses to go away.

Loretto Academy's signature ghost is the apparition of a nun who has been sighted walking around the illuminated bell tower. According to legend, the nun had an affair with a priest not long after the academy was founded. When she discovered that she was pregnant, she took her own life by jumping off the bell tower. In another variant, the nun was locked away in the tower to hide her shameful condition. After a few weeks, she died of starvation. Students and staff who have seen her say that her nun's habit is clearly visible. Another explanation for the spirit is that she is a beloved nun who taught at Loretto Academy for many years before finally succumbing to an illness. Her ghost remains in the school because it is the only place to which she ever really felt a deep connection. In yet another variant, the ghost is the spirit of a female student who jumped from the tower after she became pregnant. Halloween is said to be the best time to see the ghost on the bell tower. Some people say that she floats through the tower on nights when the moon is full. Folklorists say that the nun may still haunt the tower either to protest her mistreatment at the hands of the sisters or to serve penance for her sinful behavior.

Loretto Academy's chapel is supposed to be haunted as well. Some students claim to have heard someone playing the organ at night—even though the organ has been broken for many years. Others say a statue of Mary and Jesus inside the chapel behaves strangely. It is said that students who have read the plaque on the statue aloud heard three knocking sounds that seemed to come from the statue itself.

Concordia Cemetery

El Paso

In 1840, a trader from Chihuahua named Hugh Stephenson started a ranch three miles from El Paso. Sixteen years later, he buried his wife, Juana Maria Ascarte, on a part of the ranch that is now Concordia Cemetery. In the 1880s, the cemetery became a popular burial ground for the residents of El Paso. By 1890, different groups had purchased portions of the cemetery, which was divided into various sections: Jesuit, city, county, military, Chinese, Catholic, Masonic, Jewish, and black. To date, more than sixty thousand people have been laid to rest at Concordia Cemetery, including a number of Texas Rangers, Buffalo Soldiers, and early Mormon pioneers, as well as the outlaw gunslinger John Wesley Hardin and the man who shot him, crooked lawman and outlaw himself, John Selman. The old graveyard is popular with history buffs as well as ghost hunters.

Concordia Cemetery has been known as a hotbed of paranormal activity for many years. Visitors to the cemetery have reported seeing flickering lights flitting among the tombstones. The unmistakable sound of giggling has been heard in the Children's Section, where more than a hundred young victims of a smallpox epidemic were buried in the nineteenth century. A lady in white has been sighted walking through the cemetery. The clip-clop of horses' hooves and the ghostly voices of long-dead cavalry soldiers have also been heard in and around the grounds, and people passing through the cemetery have heard spectral voices. The past, it seems, is not completely buried at Concordia Cemetery.

Camino Real Hotel

El Paso

The Camino Real Hotel was born in the mind of Zach T. White in 1892, when he watched El Paso's Grand Central Hotel burn to the ground. In 1906, White consulted an architectural firm to find out why a few buildings had managed to survive the catastrophic San Francisco Earthquake. The men began planning a brick, steel, and terra cotta structure with a fireproof interior of gypsum. The Hotel Paso del Norte finally opened its doors on Thanksgiving Day 1912. Cattlemen and ranchers from all over Texas bought and sold cattle in the lobby of this luxurious hotel. The old hotel was completely renovated in 1986, when the seventeen-story tower was added. Some of its illustrious guests included Enrico Caruso, Amelia Earhart, Eleanor Roosevelt, Gen. John J. "Black Jack" Pershing, Will Rogers, and Richard Nixon. Apparently not all of the hotel's guests have checked out.

In *A Texas Guide to Haunted Restaurants, Taverns and Inns*, Robert and Anne Powell Wlodarski say that the most frequently reported ghost at the hotel is the spirit of a woman in a white dress who makes fairly frequent appearances in the basement. She is said to be the ghost of a pregnant bride who leaped from a nineteenth-floor window when the groom jilted her. On the mezzanine level of the hotel, housekeeping staff have seen a door suddenly appear in a wall in the older part of the hotel. A group of flight attendants who were staying in adjoining rooms on the fifth floor were standing in the hallway when a woman in a white bathrobe walked in their direction and passed right through them. By the time the manager arrived, the door had vanished. Probably the most bizarre sighting occurred in the Dome Bar, built during the renovations. Late one night in the 1990s, the manager had walked behind the bar and was counting the day's receipts when he saw the figure of a woman step out of the mural on the opposite wall. She stood in front of the wall for a few seconds, with a confused look on her face. Then she stepped backward and faded back into the mural.

The Camino Real Hotel has been listed on the National Register of Historic Places. The owners say that the hotel's grand staircase is the most photographed staircase in the world. From the perspective of those interested in the paranormal, however, the ghost of the white lady is a much more desirable photographic subject.

The Spirits of Thunder Road

Wink

The town of Wink came into being a year after oil was discovered at the Endrick oilfield in Winkler County in 1926. Initially nothing more than a collection of tents and shacks, the town was originally called Winkler, but the citizens shortened the name to Wink when the U.S. Postal Service informed them that there was already a Winkler, Texas. In the late 1920s, Wink was known as a haven for prostitutes, gambling, gangsters, and bootleggers. After the oil was depleted in the early 1930s, Wink's reputation as a wild town was also diminished, and it became legally incorporated as a real town in 1933. Wink's signature ghost story harks back to its early years, when hundreds of adventurous young men descended on the little town in the hopes of striking it rich.

In the late 1920s, a young man whose name has been lost to history settled down and moved his family into a little white frame house he built on the outskirts of Wink, just off Highway 115, also known as Thunder Road. In the beginning, the young man and his father had a streak of luck and made a small fortune in the oil business. Their happiness was short-lived, however, when the pair lost all their money in the stock market crash of 1929. As soon as he heard about the crash, the young man sank into a deep depression, devastated by the sudden end of his dream. As he drove home down the lonely two-lane road, he wondered how he was going to break the news to his family. He felt that he would not be able to look into the sad faces of his wife and daughter and listen to their cries.

By the time the young man's car pulled into the drive, his mind had snapped. He strode past the big tree and the rope swing hanging from one of its limbs. He picked up an ax lying next to a pile of firewood he had been chopping and marched into the house. The next day, the sheriff found the young man's body hanging from the rope swing he had made for his little girl. The grisly murder scene inside the house was seared into his memory forever. Apparently the young man had dismembered his wife and daughter and hanged himself afterward.

Not much remains of the little white house, but the tree from which the man hanged himself is still there. People say that sometimes one can see three owls sitting on the limb under which the little girl spent many happy hours swinging. Some believe that the owls are the earthly forms of the spirits of the three former occupants of the house. Wink would prefer that people think of the town as the boyhood home of Roy Orbison. However, the tragic tale of the ax murder that happened so many years ago still casts a pall on Wink, Texas.

Fort Phantom Hill

Jones County

In 1849, the federal government decided to construct a line of forts to protect settlers and prospectors heading west intent on striking it rich in the California gold rush. Two years later, Lt. Col. John Joseph Abercrombie brought five companies of the 5th Infantry to begin building a fort, which came to be known as Fort Phantom Hill, on the Clear Fork of the Brazos River. Because of a shortage of timber in the area, the jail, powder magazine, and storehouse were constructed of stone quarried along Elm Creek two miles south. Timber for the remainder of the fort had to be carried in from forty miles away.

Fort Phantom Hill was never officially named while it was in operation. It was referred to simply as the post on the Clear Fork of the Brazos. Some people say that the fort derived its nickname from an incident that occurred shortly after it was constructed. A young sentry was on patrol one evening when he fired his rifle at what he thought was an Indian. Because no trace of an Indian was ever found, one of the young man's friends whimsically concluded that he had shot his gun at a ghost. Another possible explanation for the nickname of the fort owes its source to an optical illusion: the fort, which is clearly visible from a distance, seems to disappear as one approaches it.

Life at the fort was difficult at best, primarily because of a shortage of water. The water from the creek was undrinkable, so an eighty-foot well had to be dug. Drawing water from the well proved to be difficult, so fresh water had to be hauled in from Elm Creek several miles away. However, the soldiers sent to fetch the water often found that the creek was dry.

Without any cavalry, the fort simply occupied the site. The soldiers were not involved in any violent engagement with hostile tribes. In fact, the only Indians who came to the fort were from peaceful tribes, such as the Delaware, Kickapoo, Kiowa, Wichita, and Lipan. Four of the five companies that Abercombie had brought to the fort in 1851 were replaced two years later by a single company of the 2nd Dragoons. Permission to close the fort was given in November 1853, primarily because of the absence of Indian attacks in the region. Shortly after all the soldiers marched out of the fort the following spring, most of buildings—constructed of log walls and thatch roofs—caught fire and burned.

The remains of the fort were put to a variety of uses over the next three decades. In 1858, the stone buildings were transformed into a way station on the Southern Overland Mail route. They also served as a stop for the Butterfield Stagecoach. During the Civil War, the fort once again became a military installation, this time for the Confederate army. In 1871, the U.S. Army reoccupied the fort when it became a subpost of Fort Griffin near Albany. When a town grew up around the old fort several years later, it was used as a center for the buying and shipping of buffalo hides. According to the 1880 census, 545 people were residing at the fort. For a brief time, Fort Phantom Hill served as the Jones County seat. By 1890, however, Fort Phantom Hill was completely abandoned. The family of John Guitar of Abilene bought the old fort in 1928. Four decades later, Guitar's grandson deeded the property to the Fort Phantom Foundation. Today the twenty-two-acre historic site is open daily free of charge. In recent years, visitors and staff at Fort Phantom Hill claim that the ruins have lived up to their name.

A number of phantoms are said to remain at their posts at Fort Phantom Hill. One is thought to be the spirit of a man who was wrongly hanged here; afterward, everyone who testified against him died in accidents. Some employees of the fort claim to have seen apparitions of Indians stalking the fort during the night. According to Docia Schultz Williams in *Phantoms of the Plains*, a high school student named Sam Nesmith was walking through the old officers' quarters at 5 P.M. when his surroundings were transformed into their mid-nineteenth-century appearance. A few seconds later, he found himself in the presence of two soldiers. Once the soldiers noticed him standing there, they vanished, along with the antiquated features of the officers' quarters. When he returned home, he became violently ill and was taken to the hospital that evening. The young man was certain that his brush with the paranormal had caused his illness.

A number of theories have been proposed to explain why ghosts return from the dead. The spirits of the dead may return to warn or reward the living, protest their ill treatment while alive, reassure their loved ones that everything is all right, or wreak vengeance on their oppressors. Or perhaps in this case, the spirits of Fort Phantom Hill simply are finding the place more hospitable after the creation of the nearby reservoir, Lake Fort Phantom Hill, in 1937.

The Lady of Lake Fort Phantom Hill

Abilene

Lack of water has always been a serious of problem for Abilene. To ensure a municipal water supply, Abilene dug three lakes in the late nineteenth and early twentieth centuries. In 1937, construction began on a fourth lake, Lake Fort Phantom Hill. To create the reservoir, workmen built a dam at the southeast corner of the county. Today Lake Fort Phantom Hill is known for its fine fishing. It is well stocked with bass, catfish, and other species. The lake is also known for its signature ghost, known by locals as the Lady of the Lake.

The legend of the Lady of the Lake exists in three versions. The earliest variant takes place in the late 1870s, about sixty years before the lake was created. An intrepid young couple built a cabin on the plains, despite the fact that they were surrounded by Comanche Indians. To protect his wife from intruders while he was off hunting, the young man told her never to open the door to the cabin unless he called her name. Some people say that the couple had devised a secret password. The man told his wife to shoot anyone who tried to enter the cabin without first calling her name or using the password.

One day, he was hunting a short distance from his cabin when a band of Comanches appeared on the horizon. He immediately took off running as fast as he could in the direction of the cabin. When he finally made it home, the Indians were right behind him. Without thinking, he threw open the door. At that instant, his wife shot him with her rifle, killing him instantly. As punishment for her crime, the woman, dressed in white, is condemned to walk the shores of the lake for eternity.

A second version of the tale takes place in the 1940s. A young couple was to be married in a local church. The young lady arrived at the church early in order to arrange her wedding gown. After thirty minutes, she became concerned when her fiancé did not show up. By the time the wedding was to begin, her lover still had not arrived at the church. The next morning, his body was found lying in a boat in the middle of Lake Fort Phantom Hill. He was dressed in his tuxedo, and on his face was an expression of horror. The medical examiner was unable to determine the cause of death. Today the bride's spirit walks the shores of the lake, looking for her fiancé's killer. Her thirst for vengeance is reflected in her dark eyes.

The third variant appeared in print in the 1980s. A beautiful young woman was told by her lover to meet him by the shore of the lake after nightfall. Carrying a lantern, she wandered through the darkness, looking for their appointed meeting place. Her boyfriend arrived a few minutes later. She could tell by the fire in his eyes that he was angry. Without even greeting her, the young man began accusing her of being unfaithful. After ranting and raving for a couple minutes, he grabbed the girl by her hair and dragged her to the lake. He held her head underwater until she stopped struggling. Her ghost walks around the lake to this day in search of the man who murdered her.

Witnesses have described the Lady of the Lake as wearing a white dress and carrying a lantern. She is usually enveloped in a blue or red mist. People who have seen her have experienced nausea, dizziness, and a drastic drop in temperature. Between May and June 1996, members of the Southwest Ghost Hunters Association conducted an extensive investigation of the lake to see if they could verify any of the phenomena reported by eyewitnesses of the Lady in White. One day, the group noticed a girl walking alone along the north side of the lake. The temperature sensors the group had set up on the perimeter indicated that the temperature in the area had dropped from 70 to 32 degrees. The temperature drop coincided with the reported cold spots. At the same time, the cameras ceased working. Afterward, the group checked out the batteries and discovered that they were still fully charged.

There have been many sightings of the Lady of the Lake over the years. Many of those who witnessed the apparition have been young people who drove out to one of the lake's secluded spots to make out. The romantic elements embedded in the various versions of the ghost story have also made Lake Fort Phantom Hill an appropriate place for romantic interludes.

Marfa Lights

Marfa

Marfa was founded in the early 1880s. In the beginning, the little town was nothing more than a railroad and water stop. The town grew in the 1920s and achieved importance as the site of the Midland Army Air Field during World War II. It was also used as the training ground for the U.S. Army's chemical mortar battalions. Today Marfa attracts thousands of tourists annually from all over the nation. People come here to walk through the town square, gaze at the art hanging in the various galleries—and perhaps catch a glimpse of the Marfa Lights.

The phenomenon known as the Marfa Lights was first reported by a young cowboy named Robert Reed Ellison, who said that he was driving cattle through Paisano Pass in 1883 when he observed flickering lights in the hills. At the time, he assumed that the lights were the campfires of a band of Apache Indians. Afterward, Ellison learned that other witnesses who had also seen the lights had arrived at the same conclusion, but they were unable to find any evidence of campfires in the area. In the summer of 1919, cowboys herding cattle over the plains spotted similar lights, but they could not find any evidence of campfires either. Military personnel stationed at Midland Army Air

Field also observed the Marfa Lights. The first published report of the Marfa Lights appeared in *Coronet* magazine in an article written by Paul Moran, titled "The Mystery of the Texas Ghost Light."

Today the lights continue to be sighted, flitting around the hills of Marfa. They have been described as red, orange, yellow, and white glowing balls, about the size of soccer balls or basketballs, that float around at shoulder height. They are usually seen in clusters of two or more that appear and disappear. The movement of the glowing balls is erratic. As a rule, sightings of the Marfa Lights are reported ten to twenty times annually.

A number of theories have been offered to explain the Marfa Lights. The most popular scientific theory holds that the lights are a mirage created by the interaction between warm and cold layers of air, which bend light so that it is seen from a distance. Another scientific explanation is that the lights are created by the expansion and contraction of quartz crystals, which are converted into voltage in a phenomenon called the piezoelectric effect. Some people believe that the lights are simply the headlights of cars, but this theory does not take into account the sightings that predated the invention of the automobile. Others attribute the lights to the spirits of Apache Indians, who were living in the region long before the arrival of the white man.

The citizens of Marfa not only have learned to live with the eerie lights, but they seem to enjoy the phenomenon. The town holds the Mystery Lights Festival every Labor Day weekend. And the Texas Department of Transportation has even made it easier for visitors to view the lights by creating parking areas at the best vantage points.

The Gage Hotel

Marathon

In 1878, an entrepreneur from Vermont named Alfred Gage arrived in Marathon to take advantage of the newly settled region's wide-open business opportunities. He and his brothers started out as cowhands and eventually formed the Alpine Cattle Company south of Marathon. By the 1920s, he had amassed a fortune through banking and ranching. Later that decade, he had a luxury hotel built that was also to serve as his headquarters. When the hotel opened its doors, it attracted miners and ranchers from miles around. Unfortunately, Gage did not live long enough to bask in the glory of his new hotel. He died only a year after work on the hotel was completed. Fifty years later, the hotel was purchased by J. P. and Mary Jon Bryan. Over the next twenty years, the Bryans spent thousands of dollars renovating the hotel in order to restore its 1920s grandeur. J. P. furnished the hotel with relics from a friend's collection, including the head of a white buffalo that now hangs in the White Buffalo Bar. Today the Gage Hotel hosts many special events, such as weddings, receptions, and conferences. It is also said to host several ghosts.

In *Phantoms of the Plains*, Docia Schultz Williams writes of the various entities that seem to have been awakened while the old hotel was being remodeled. In the early 1990s, a young man who worked as a dishwasher and handyman had an eerie experience. Late one evening, he was down in the basement when he felt a hand on his shoulder. When he turned around, he saw a man who looked exactly like the imposing figure in a portrait of Alfred Gage. The apparition stared at the terrified young man for a few seconds before saying, "I do not want you in my hotel any longer." The young man was shaken to the core, but he was determined to keep his job at the hotel. He decided he would simply avoid going down in the basement. One night, however, circumstances forced the young man to return to the basement. When he did, he was filled with such an overwhelming feeling of dread that he bolted from the hotel and never returned.

Guests have also reported encountering spirits in the old hotel. Many visitors said they heard music playing in Room 10. So far, though, no one has recognized the tune. Some people heard the disembodied voice of a woman reading poetry. Several guests were awakened in the middle of the night by feeling someone tapping them on the arm.

The ghostly apparition of a woman also has been seen in the hotel. In the mid-1990s, a man staying in Room 25 told the desk clerks that he saw the misty figure of a woman in her thirties standing by his bed. A few weeks later, a maintenance man standing by one of the soda machines was approached by a woman in her thirties wearing a white blouse and blue skirt. The woman walked right past him in the direction of the courtyard and then slowly dissipated.

With its period furnishings and architectural features, the Gage Hotel transports visitors to a bygone era. One might say that the spirits haunting the hotel produce the same effect, albeit in a more terrifying way.

Fort Leaton

Presidio

Fort Leaton is a one-acre fortified compound that sits on a cliff overlooking the Rio Grande. It is located on the site of the Spanish Mission del Apostol Santiago, established in 1683. The mission was converted into El Fortín de San José in 1773, but the building was completely abandoned by 1810. Twenty years later, Juan Bustillos turned the old mission and fort into his home. In 1848, a scalp hunter and trader named Ben Leaton purchased El Fortín from Bustillos and made it his home, trading post, and personal fort. He expanded the existing fort into a forty-room compound that he called Fort Leaton. Leaton lived in his fort with a woman to whom he was not married, named Juana Padrasa, and their three children.

Leaton's primary source of income was the Indian scalps he collected and sold for the Mexican states of Sonora and Chihuahua, although he is also reported to have sold rifles and ammunition to renegade Indians. Some of his Hispanic neighbors accused him of occasionally substituting the black-haired scalps of Mexicans for Indian scalps. Leaton had not been in business very long before he was accused by the Mexican government of inciting the Apaches and Comanches to raid Mexican settlements. Legend has it, however, that Leaton was so charismatic that he talked the Mexican soldiers into leaving him alone.

Ben Leaton's dark side revealed itself most dramatically after a peace council held at Fort Leaton with neighboring tribes around 1850. Leaton was shocked to discover that the tribes had stolen all his horses and mules the night before, but he resisted the impulse to seek retribution immediately. About a year later, he invited the same Indians back to the fort for more talks. Before the talks began, however, he asked the Indians to file into a small room, where they would all have dinner together. As the story goes, midway through the meal, Leaton excused himself from the table. He then moved a cannon in front of the doorway and fired a load of canister shot into the room. Those Indians who were not ripped apart by the canister shot were gunned down by armed men, who fired on anyone who managed to stagger out of the death room. Understandably, the local Indians gave Fort Leaton a wide berth following the massacre.

After Ben Leaton died in 1851 of yellow fever, Juana married a customs agent named Edward Hall, who eventually became deeply in debt to one of Leaton's scalp-hunting companions named John Burgess. Hall was murdered by two assassins hired by Burgess, who then moved into Fort Leaton with his family. Burgess remained in the hacienda until 1877, when he was gunned down by Bill Leaton, Ben's son, as retribution for his stepfather's death. Members of the Burgess family continued to live in Fort Leaton until 1926, when the last Burgess left the hacienda for good. Homeless families occupied the old fort for the next decade. Then in the mid-1930s, Fort Leaton was partially restored as part of a government project. About thirty years later, the state purchased Fort Leaton and the five surrounding acres, and the partially restored fort became a state historic site.

Ghostly activity has been reported at the fort ever since it was acquired by the state. According to author Dave Goodwin, two park employees were assigned the task of cleaning out a deep pit that treasure hunters had dug years before while searching for Ben Leaton's buried gold; Leaton had supposedly acquired the gold from selling guns and ammunition to hostile Indians. They had not been working for very long before they felt as if something were trying to pull them into the pit. The two men dropped their tools and fled in terror. Soon after the park opened, other employees began talking about apparitions they had seen in the fort. One of these specters was identified as the ghost of Edward Hall, as he was seen in the room where Hall was gunned down. Some park personnel have sighted the ghost of an old woman, possibly either Juana Hall or Mrs. Burgess, sitting in a rocking chair in the kitchen. The third ghost, which manifests outside Fort

Leaton, is said to be the spirit of a cowboy who was riding on the plains when he was caught in a thunderstorm. As the story goes, a bolt of lightning streaked across the sky, causing his horse to rear up, and the cowboy tumbled from the saddle and became entangled in the reins. The panic-stricken horse then bolted across the plains, dragging its rider behind him. The next morning, after the storm subsided, the cowboy's companions found his decapitated corpse stuck between a boulder and a large tree branch. Their friend's head was found three hundred feet from its body. To this day, during severe thunderstorms, the unfortunate cowboy's headless spirit has been seen galloping around the fort on a white horse.

Today visitors to Fort Leaton can take a trip back in time by following tour guides through the park and viewing the exhibits on natural history and local archaeology. On weekends, docents bring the past alive by offering guided tours in period dress. Dancers perform traditional Indian and Hispanic dances during special events. One never knows, however, when the resident spirits will make an appearance.

Upstairs at the Mansion

Terlingua

Terlingua is an old mining town located in Brewster County, not far from the Rio Grande. The town came into existence not long after a prospector named Jack Dawson discovered and produced mercury from deposits of cinnabar in 1888. Before long, thousands of miners had come to Brewster County in search of mercury, also known as quicksilver. One of the mining camps operating in the area soon acquired the name Terlingua, as well as a post office. In 1910, the post office was moved to another mining camp, and the name Terlingua was transferred from the old town to the new one. Three years later, Terlingua also had telephone service, a doctor, and a commissary. A public school was finally built in 1930. The local mining company filed for bankruptcy in 1942, however, and in just a few years, most of the citizens of Terlingua had moved away. In the 1960s and 1970s, tourists visited Terlingua to see the ghost town it had become. However, by 2000, a number of people were living in the town once again.

Today a few small businesses line the streets of Terlingua, including a restored theater, a restaurant, and a few shops. The most prominent building in town is the old Perry Mansion, built in 1909 on top of a hill by mining company owner Howard Perry. Perry had intended for his wife, who had remained in Maine while he established his mining business, to move into the house with him. But when she arrived on the train, the story goes, she was so disappointed by the western-style, two-story house her husband had built for her that the next morning she boarded another train and returned home. In 1912, Perry built an addition onto his house, which became the most imposing structure in the region. Perry made extended visits to Maine but could not persuade his wife to return to Texas with him. Soon rumors spread around the little town that Perry was entertaining his wife's friends whose acquaintance he had made in Maine. The women traveled all the way to Texas to see him, likely enticed by Perry's fortune. In 1944, two years after his company declared bankruptcy, Perry, now in his eighties, was on a train headed for Florida when he suffered a heart attack and died.

The Perry Mansion stood abandoned for several decades. During that time, those people brave enough to walk through the spooky old house claimed to have seen the apparition of a woman wandering from room to room on the second floor. In *Phantom of the Plains*, Docia Schultz Williams wrote that locals believe that the ghost could be one of three women. She might be a servant girl who is still afraid of incurring the wrath of Howard Perry by leaving the house. Or she might be the spirit of one of the women who had trysts with the wealthiest man in the region inside his mansion. But a few people speculate that it is the ghost of Mrs. Perry, who has been condemned to remain in the old house forever as punishment for deserting her husband.

Like Terlingua itself, the old mansion has recently gotten a new lease on life. It has been opened to guests as a hotel that exemplifies the spirit of the old ghost town, called Upstairs at the Mansion. While sitting on the porch and taking in a breathtaking view of the Chisos Mountains, visitors can enjoy a cold beverage in the evening while listening to the locals tell tales, some of which are about the ghostly lady who has never left the Perry Mansion.

The Anson Light

Anson

The little town of Anson is located eighteen miles southeast of Hamlin. Originally known as Texas City, the town was renamed in 1882 in honor of Anson James, the last president of the Republic of Texas. The little town of approximately 3,000 people is the county seat of Jones County. Although Anson is known regionally as a center for cotton farming, it is best known as the home of the Texas Cowboys' Christmas Ball. Anson is also the place to go for anyone interested in ghost lights.

At least three stories are told to explain the presence of Anson's eerie, flickering light, which is usually sighted around Mount Hope Cemetery. In one version, a woman who lived in the area in the 1930s walked down the dirt road one cold winter's night in search of her little boy, who had wandered off. Holding her lantern, she carefully made her way over the uneven, frozen ground as she called his name. She never found her lost child, so her ghost still roams the area with lantern in hand. In a variant of the story, the mother lived with her older son, who worked for the railroad. When he arrived home by train, he signaled her by flashing his lantern three times; the man's ghost is said to continue the routine. A third version of the legend has it that the woman sent her three sons to the store one night to buy supplies. She instructed them to take a lantern with them and flash it three times if they got in trouble. She would be watching for their signal and run to their aid if they needed help. One night, her sons were struck and killed by a train on their way home. Their spirits are still trying to signal their mother to come to their aid. Some locals also believe that the light is the spirit of a child whose playful spirit leaves Mount Hope Cemetery and frolics around the tombstones late at light.

The Anson Light is said to resemble the flickering light of a lantern. Mount Hope Cemetery offers the best vantage point for viewing the Anson Light, which usually appears at a nearby crossroads. The cemetery is about half a mile down a dirt road off Highway 180. People say that the light appears if you flash your headlights three times, as in the legends. If you drive toward the light and get close to the cemetery, the light vanishes.

On August 5, 2000, members of the Southwest Ghost Hunters Association conducted a formal investigation of the Anson Light. They drove down the dirt road and turned off their engine. The light did not appear until they flashed their headlights three times. After a few seconds, a feeble, orange-colored light began floating down the road in their direction. Before vanishing about two hundred yards from the investigators, the light changed to a blue hue.

Some have sought a rational explanation for the Anson Light and suggest that it is created by the headlights of cars traveling on Highway 227, with the flickering effect caused by the foliage of tree limbs blowing in the wind. Not surprisingly, though, paranormal investigators and teenagers looking for a thrill prefer to believe it is caused by ghosts.

Fort Concho

San Angelo

Fort Concho was established in 1867 as a replacement for Fort Chadbourne, at the junction of the Goodnight Trail, the Butterfield stage route, and the road to San Antonio, to protect wagon trains, stagecoaches, settlements, and the U.S. mail. The buildings were constructed by private German contractors from Fredericksburg, who supported the sandstone walls with pecan beams and rafters. By 1870, Fort Concho included a powder magazine, two barracks, a commissary and quartermaster storehouse, and a hospital. By the time the fort was decommissioned, it consisted of forty buildings. The best known of all the commanders of Fort Concho was Col. Ranald Slidell Mackenzie, whose troopers, known as "Mackenzie's Raiders," led several attacks against the Indians from Fort Concho, including a battle with the Comanches at Palo Duro Canyon in the Texas Panhandle in 1874. Fort Concho also served as the regimental headquarters of Col. Benjamin H. Grierson, commander of the 10th Cavalry, better known as the "Buffalo Soldiers," from 1875 until 1882.

Following the arrival of the railroad in West Texas in the late nineteenth century, military protection from frontier bastions like Fort Concho became increasingly unnecessary, and Fort Concho was deactivated in 1889. Fort Concho and the forty acres on which it is located soon passed into private ownership. However, with the help of private donations, Fort Concho was deeded to the city of San Angelo in 1935. The old fort was designated a national historic landmark in 1961. Today the park includes most of the original fort, twenty-three main structures, museums—and, some say, a number of ghosts.

Several buildings are said to be haunted by the spirits of the fort's former occupants. One of these specters is the ghost of Colonel Grierson's twelve-year-old daughter, Edith, who died of typhoid fever in Officers' Quarter 1 on September 9, 1878. Her apparition has been seen in the house where she died on a number of occasions. As a rule, she is playing jacks at the time of the sighting, and the little ghost usually greets her visitors with a shy smile. Her appearances are signaled by a drastic drop in temperature.

Col. Ranald Mackenzie's spirit seems reluctant to abandon his post. His ghost has been sighted inside his house at the center of Officers' Row. Mackenzie is said to have chosen this house because it afforded him a clear view of the entire fort. A female employee of Fort Concho had a very unpleasant encounter with the colonel's ghost. She was walking through his house one day when an invisible force pushed her against a wall. Afterward, she recalled feeling very cold as she made contact with the entity. She also heard the cracking of knuckles during the incident. The young woman was convinced that she had met Mackenzie's ghost when she recalled that the colonel was known to have been a knuckle-cracker when he was alive.

Staff members who work in the Fort Concho Museum in the old barracks have seen the full-bodied apparition of a ghost sergeant. One day, a guard who was sitting in a chair felt someone leaning against the back of her chair. She told the person to stop it, and then turned around to find that no one was near her chair. Other people have seen lights flickering off and on in the museum. The heavy, disembodied footsteps of a large person have also been heard inside the museum.

Some staff members believe that the most haunted part of Fort Concho is Building 7, which was built of limestone in 1877 for unmarried officers. It is one of several buildings that were rented out as private residences after the fort was abandoned. While the building stood vacant, a man's corpse was found in Building 7 in the 1890s. His identity has never been determined, but some people believe that he was a "wolfer," a trapper who collected the bounties on wolves as well as on badgers and coyotes. Legend has it that he was killed when he trapped in another wolfer's territory. Other people believe he was a sheepherder who was shot by a rancher for trespassing on his property. After the old officers' quarters was rented out, even more stories about the haunted building began surfacing. Some people said that a small light could be seen flickering in one of the windows. Other people reported hearing strange noises inside the house. In *Phantoms of the Plains*, Docia Schultz Williams included an interview with Carlos Trevino, who lived in Building 7 in the 1960s, when he was a little boy. Trevino recalled standing on the balcony early one morning when he noticed someone walking close to the balcony door. At first Trevino thought it was his father. After the figure walked back through the balcony door, Trevino went to his father's bedroom and found him fast asleep.

The best-known "ghost" at Fort Concho was not even dead at the time of his sighting. A black soldier remembered today only as Private Ellis was searching for Comanches on the prairie in the blistering heat when he became dizzy and confused. His fellow soldiers recognized the symptoms of sunstroke, so they took him back to Fort Concho. After his friends escorted him to the hospital, Ellis tried to stand on his own, but he fell to the floor. Ellis did not respond to any kind of stimulation, so the doctor assumed that he was dead and ordered his body removed to the "Dead House," which served as a morgue. That night, his friends came by with a jug of whiskey. The men sat around the "cooling board," a board on which a corpse was laid during preparation for burial, and began drinking farewell toasts to their departed friend. Around midnight, the men heard a deep moan come from Ellis's body. At first they assumed that they were imagining things. When they heard a second moan, the men jumped through the window and ran off into the night. When Ellis awoke to find himself lying on the cooling board, he jumped up and followed his friends through the window. An orderly who was awakened by the noise walked around the back of the hospital and found Ellis lying on the ground under the window. He picked him up and helped him back into the hospital.

Ellis made a full recovery, but his friends never let him forget the time he spent in the Dead House. For the rest of his life, the private was called "Dead Ellis" by his friends. Ellis still is not completely dead. Like the other ghosts who haunt Fort Concho, he is kept alive by the stories the docents tell as they lead visitors through the old fort.

Bibliography

Books and Articles

Abernethy, Francis Edward. *Tales from the Big Thicket*. Denton: University of North Texas Press, 2002.

Abbott, Olyve Hallmark. *A Ghost in the Guest Room: Haunted Texas Inns, B & B's, and Hotels*. Dallas: Atriad Press, 2007.

———. *Ghosts in the Graveyard: Texas Cemetery Tales*. Lanham, MD: Republic of Texas Press, 2002.

Baker, T. Lindsay. *More Ghost Towns of Texas*. Norman: University of Oklahoma Press, 2005.

Belanger. Jeff. *Encyclopedia of Haunted Places*. Pompton Plains, NJ: New Page Books, 2011.

Broome, Fiona. *The Ghosts of Austin: Who They Are and Where to Find Them*. Atglen, PA: Schiffer, 2007.

Brown, Alan. *Haunted Texas*. Mechanicsburg, PA: Stackpole Books, 2008.

Chariton, Wallace O. *Exploring the Alamo Legends*. Lanham, MD: Republic of Texas Press, 1992.

Chariton, Wallace O., Charlie Eckhardt, and Kevin R. Young. *Unsolved Texas Mysteries*. Lanham, MD: Republic of Texas Press, 1991.

Christensen, Jo-Anne. *Ghost Stories of Texas*. Edmonton, AB: Lone Pine Publishing, 2001.

Clark, Anne. "The Ghost of White Rock." *Backwoods to Border* 18 (1943): 143–147.

Dobie, J. Frank. *Legends of Texas. Volume II: Pirates Gold and Other Tales*. Gretna, LA: Pelican, 1924.

Hauck, Dennis William. *Haunted Places: The National Directory*. New York: Penguin, 2002.

Howard, Stephen. *The Alamo*. Florence, Italy: Casa Eietrice Bonechi Press, n.d.

Laine, Tanner. "The Special Charm of 'Stampede Mesa'." *Lubbock Avalanche-Journal*. 16 March 2000.

Moran, Paul. "The Mystery of the Texas Ghost Light." *Coronet*. July 1957: 149–167.

Righi, Brian. *Ghosts of Fort Worth: Investigating Cowtown's Most Haunted Locations*. Atglen, PA: Schiffer, 2008.

Rogers, Mary. "Coffee Shop Talk." *Fort Worth Star-Telegram*. 21 August 1991.

Stephens, A. Ray. "D. A. Orviss: Texas Merchant." *The Southwestern Historical Quarterly* 65, No. 1 (July 1961): 32–46.

Stevens, Liz. "The Lady of Log Cabin Village . . . and Other Spirited Locales from Cowtown's Crypt." *Fort Worth Star-Telegram*. 31 October 2004: 1G.

Syers, Ed. *Ghost Stories of Texas*. Waco, TX: Texian Press, 1981.

Taylor, Troy. *Ghost Hunter's Handbook*. Alton, IL: Whitechapel Press, 1999.

Tolbert, Frank X. *Neiman-Marcus, Texas: The Story of a Proud Texas Store*. New York: Holt, 2011.

Weems, John Edward. *A Weekend in September*. Corpus Christi: Texas A&M University Press, 1980.

Whitington, Mitchel. *Ghosts of North Texas*. Lanham, MD: Republic of Texas Press, 2003.

Williams, Ben, Jean Williams, and John Bruce Shoemaker. *The Black Hope Horror*. New York: William Morrow and Company, 1991.

Williams, Docia Schultz. *Ghosts along the Texas Coast*. Lanham, MD: Republic of Texas Press, 1995.

———. *Phantoms of the Plains: Tales of West Texas Ghosts*. Plano: Republic of Texas Press, 1996.

Williams, Scott. *Haunted Texas: A Travel Guide*. Guilford, CT: The Globe Pequot Press, 2007.

Wlodarski, Robert. *Spirits of the Alamo: A History of the Mission and its Hauntings*. Boulder, CO: Taylor Trade Publishing Company, 1999.

Wlodarski, Robert, and Anne Powell. *A Texas Guide to Haunted Restaurants, Taverns and Inns*. Plano: Republic of Texas Press, 2001.

Online Sources

"About Us." *The Driskill*. Retrieved 19 April 2011. www.driskillhotel.com/about-texas-hotel.php.

Allen, Donna. "The Crying White Lady of Marshall, Texas." *Examiner.com*, February 4, 2010. Retrieved 29 September 2011. www.examiner.com/ghost-hunting-in-dallas/the-crying-white-lady-of-marshall-texas.

———. "The Haunted Hotel Lawrence in Downtown Dallas." *Examiner.com*, December 10, 2009. Retrieved 18 October 2010. www.examiner.com/ghost-hunting-in-dallas/the-haunted-hotel-lawrence-downtown-dallas.

Anders, Helen. "Ghost Tour Hits Austin's Downtown Haunts." *Austin-American Statesman*, October 28, 2007. Retrieved 3 June 2011. www.austin360.com/news/content/recreation/guides/visit/ghosttour.html.

———. "In Search of the Ghosts of Goliad." *Austin-American Statesman*, October 29, 2010. Retrieved 22 July 2001. http://www.statesman.com/life/travel/in-search-of-the-ghosts-of-goliad-1006456.html.

Anderson, H. Allen. "Fort Phantom Hill," *Handbook of Texas Online*. Published by the Texas State Historical Association. Retrieved February 28, 2012. http://www.tshaonline.org/handbook/online/articles/qbf39.

"Are We Haunted?" *Galveston Historical Foundation*. Retrieved 29 June 2011. www.galvestonhistory.org/ghosts_at_Ashton_Villa.asp.

"The Arnulfo L. Oliveira Memorial Library." *The Ghosts of Fort Brown*. Retrieved 14 September 2007. http://utb.edu/ghostsoffortbrown/page_06b_Library.htm.

"Ashton Villa." *Halloween's Unseen*. Retrieved 29 June 2011. http://halloweensunseen.com/HalloweenHauntedHouses6.html.

"Ashton Villa Mansion." *Hauntedhouses.com*. Retrieved 29 June 2011. www.hauntedhouses.com/states.com/states/tx/ashton_villa_mansion.cfm.

"Austin's Inn at Pearl Street: About Us." *Inn at Pearl Street*. Retrieved 21 August 2010. www.innpearl.com/articles.htm.

"The Baker Hotel." *Castle of Spirits*. Retrieved 9 November 2010. www.castleofspirits.com/stories04/bakerhotel.html.

"Ballinger, Texas Ghost Sightings." *Ghosts of America*. Retrieved 14 January 2011. www.ghostsofamerica.com/7/Texas_Ballinger_ghost_sightings.html.

"Battleship Texas State Historic Site." *Citysearch*. Retrieved 29 September 2007. http://houston.citysearch.com/profile/11355429/la_porte_tx/battleship_texas_state_historic_site.html.

Bethel, Brian. "The Ghost of the McDow Hole." *Texnews.com*. Retrieved 13 September 2007. http://www.texnews.com/news/ghost103196.html.

Blaschka, Shawn. "Case Review—The Menger Hotel—San Antonio, Texas." *Pat-Wausau.org*. Retrieved 17 June 2011. http://www.pat-wausau.org/cases/menger%20hotel.html.

Block, W. T. "The Legend of the Headless Yankee Cannoneer of Sabine Pass." *TexasEscapes*. Retrieved 9 January 2011. http://www.texasescapes.com/WTBlock/Legend-of-the-Headless-Yankee-Cannoneer-of-Sabine-Pass.htm.

Bonnin, Julie. "The Driskill Hotel: History on Sixth Street." *Helloaustin.com*. Retrieved 19 April 2011. http://www.helloaustin.com/travel/the_driskill_hotel_history_on_sixth_street/204435/.

Bowman, Bob. "The Ghost Road in Hardin County." *TexasEscapes*. Retrieved 15 December 2010. http://www.texasescapes.com/BobBowman/Ghost-Road-in-Hardin-County.htm.

"Bragg Road — The Ghost Road of Hardin County." *Texas Big Thicket Directory*. Retrieved 15 December 2010. www.bigthicketdirectory.com/ghostroad.html.

Branning, Debe. "Arizona Ghost Hunter Travels: Spirited Spaghetti Warehouse in Houston TX." *Examiner.com*, March 4, 2009. Retrieved 16 July 2011. http://www.examiner.com/arizona-haunted-sites-in-phoenix/arizona-ghost-hunter-travels-spirited-spaghetti-warehouse-houston-tx.

Brezosky, Lynn. "Some Say UT–Brownsville Haunted by Fort Ghosts." *Houston Chronicle*, October 30, 2004. Retrieved 3 December 2010. www.chron.com/disp/story.mpl/metropolitan/2873669.html.

Broome, Fiona. "Houston's Spaghetti Warehouse—Scary Guy's Portrait." *Hollowhill.com*, March 20, 2008. Retrieved 17 July 2011. http://hollowhill .com/houston-spaghetti-1.

Bryant, Deb. "What Everyone Should Know about Haunted Places in Austin, TX." *Yahoo! Voices*, August 29, 2006. Retrieved 24 June 2011. http://voices .yahoo.com/what-everyone-know-haunted-places-in-68264.html.

"Burlesque Haunts: Dallas." *Pincurlmag.com*. Retrieved 3 October 2010. http://pincurlmag.com/tag/haunted-texas.

"Butchering at the Gunter Hotel." *thefolklorist.com*. Retrieved 7 January 2011. www.thefolklorist.com/horror/gunter.htm.

"The Catfish Plantation." *Ghostinmysuitcase.com*. Retrieved 12 December 2010. www.ghostinmysuitcase.com/places/catfish/index.htm.

"Catfish Plantation Restaurant." *Strangeusa.com*. Retrieved 12 December 2010. www.strangeusa.com/ViewLocation.aspx?locationid=9996.

Choron, James L. "Dawn at the Alamo." *TexasEscapes*. Retrieved 24 September 2007. www.texasescapes.com/Paranormal/Alamo-Ghost.htm.

———. "Hanging Tree: The Haunted Hanging Tree of Shelby County's Square." *TexasExcapes*. Retrieved 27 August 2007. www.texasescapes .com/Paranormal/Hanging-Tree-Center-Texas.htm.

"Commissary/Guardhouse." *The Ghosts of Fort Brown*. Retrieved 14 September 2007. http://blue.utb.edu/ghostsoffortbrown/page_05 _Guardhouse.htm.

"Concordia Cemetery Ghost Tours." *El Paso Convention and Visitors Bureau*. Retrieved 9 December 2010. http://visitelpaso.com/visitors/to_do /11-tour-companies/sections/65-tour-operators-guides/places/747 -concordia-cemetery-ghost-tours.

Cox, Mike. "Dead Ellis." *TexasEscapes*. Retrieved 11 January 2011. www .texasescapes.com/MikeCoxTexasTales/260-Dead-Ellis.htm.

———. "Dead Man's Hole." *TexasEscapes*. Retrieved 10 January 2011. www.texasescapes.com/MikeCoxTexasTales/Dead-Mans-Hole.htm.

———. "Ghost in No. 7: Fort Concho." *TexasEscapes*. Retrieved 11 January 2011. www.texasescapes.com/MikeCoxTexasTales/Ghost-in-No7.htm.

———. "The Haunting of the Old Travis County Jail." *TexasEscapes*. Retrieved 10 January 2011. http://www.texasescapes.com/MikeCoxTexasTales /Haunting-of-Old-Travis-County-Jail.htm.

———. "Jake's Bridge." *TexasEscapes*. Retrieved March 5, 2012. http:// www.texasescapes.com/MikeCoxTexasTales/221-Jake-the-Bridge-Ghost -of-Williamson-County.htm.

———. "La Posada." *TexasEscapes*. Retrieved 9 December 2010. www.texasescapes.com/MikeCoxTexasTales/La-Posada-Hotel-Laredo -Texas.htm.

———. "Lechuza." *TexasEscapes*. Retrieved 4 January 2011. http://www .texasescapes.com/MikeCoxTexasTales/156Lechuza.htm.

———. "Thirsty." *TexasEscapes*. Retrieved 11 January 2011. http://www .texasescapes.com/MikeCoxTexasTales/Thirsty.htm.

"Cynthia and George Mitchell." *Mitchell Historic Properties*. Retrieved 15 July 2011. http://pressroom.mitchellhistoricproperties.com/pr/mhp/mhprs /cynthia-and-george-mitchell.aspx.

Davis, Shirley. "Ghost Hunting at the Galvez." *Quad City Times*, February 22, 2008. Retrieved 2 July 2011. http://qctimes.com/travel/article_d0b483c6 -8b1d-5d95-851a-e0888d1671e4.html.

"Dead Man's Hole," *Handbook of Texas Online*. Published by the Texas State Historical Association. Retrieved February 28, 2012. http://www .tshaonline.org/handbook/online/articles/rpd03.

Diaz, Debra Barron. "The Plaza Theater . . . Here to Stay!?" *Borderlands*. Retrieved 20 July 2011. http://start.epcc.edu/nwlibrary/borderlands/ 12_the_plaza_theater.htm.

"Early History of Presidio la Bahia." *Presidio la Bahia*. Retrieved 22 July 2011. www.presidiolabahia.org/early_history.htm.

Eckhardt, C. F. "O. Henry and the Shoal Creek Treasure." *TexasEscapes*. Retrieved 23 September 2011. www.texasescapes.com/CFEckhardt/ O-Henry-and-the-Shoal-Creek-Treasure.htm.

———. "Seguin's Headless Ghost: The Ghost on Milam Street." *TexasEscapes*. Retrieved 4 January 2011. www.texasescapes.com/Ghosts/Seguins -Headless-Ghost.htm.

———. "Stampede Mesa." *TexasEscapes*. Retrieved 2 January 2011. www.texasescapes.com/CFEckhardt/Stampede-Mesa.htm.

"1859 Ashton Villa." *Galveston Historical Foundation*. Retrieved 29 June 2011. www.galvestonhistory.org/1859_ashton_villa.asp.

"1871 Thomas Jefferson League Building." *StoppingPoints.com*. Retrieved 15 July 2011. http://www.stoppingpoints.com/texas/sights.cgi?marker =1871+Thomas+Jefferson+League+Building&cnty=galveston.

"El Paso's Boot Hill." *Concordia Cemetery*. Retrieved 9 December 2010. www.concordiacemetery.org/about.html.

"Enchanted Rock State Natural Area." *Texas Parks and Wildlife*. Retrieved 15 December 2010. www.tpwd.state.tx.us/spdest/findadest/parks/ enchanted_rock/.

"Fact or Faked: Paranormal Files: Blazing Horizon/Rollover." *Internet Movie Database*. Retrieved 21 February 2011. www.imdb.com/title/tt1696298/.

"Fayette County Courthouse and Jail." *Waymarking.com*. Retrieved 22 January 2011. http://www.waymarking.com/waymarks/WM9M55_Fayette _County_Courthouse_and_Jail_La_Grange_TX.

"Fort Clark." *Haunted Texas*. Retrieved 15 January 2011. http://www .hauntedtexas.com/index.php?option=com_content&view=article&id= 32:fort-clark&catid=14:west&Itemid=36.

"Fort Clark and the Rio Grande Frontier." *Texas Beyond History*. Retrieved 15 January 2011. www.texasbeyondhistory.net/forts/clark/index.html.

"Fort Clark Springs 'Living History Today.'" *Fort Clark Springs*. Retrieved 15 January 2011. http://www.fortclark.com.

"Fort Concho National Historic Site." *TexasEscapes*. Retrieved 10 January 2011. www.texasescapes.com/TRIPS/Fort-Concho-Texas.htm.

"Fort Phantom Hill, Texas." *TexasEscapes*. Retrieved 5 January 2011. http:// www.texasescapes.com/TexasTowns/Fort-Phantom-Hill-Texas.htm.

Francisco, Amy. "Haunted Baker Hotel Looms over Mineral Wells, Texas." *Yahoo! Voices*. Retrieved 6 November 2010. http://voices.yahoo.com/ haunted-baker-hotel-looms-over-mineral-wells-texas-100317.html.

"'Fred,' the Ghost at Buffalo Billiards." *Austin Ghost Tours*. Retrieved 9 February 2011. http://www.austinghosttours.com/index.php?option=com _content&view=article&id=32:qfredq-the-ghost-at-buffalo-billiards& catid=9:austin&Itemid=13.

"Gage History." *Gage Hotel*. Retrieved 7 September 2010. www.gagehotel .com/history.html.

"Gage Hotel: Owner Profile." *Gage Hotel*. Retrieved 7 September 2010. www.gagehotel.com/owner_Profile.html.

"The Galloping Ghosts of the Gage Hotel." *Texas Less Traveled*. Retrieved 7 September 2010. http://texaslesstraveled.com/gage.htm.

"Galveston, Texas Ghost Sightings." *Ghosts of America*. Retrieved 12 July 2011. http://www.ghostsofamerica.com/7/Texas_Galveston_ghost _sightings.html.

"The Galvez." *Haunted Galveston*. Retrieved 2 July 2011. www.galvestonghost .com/galvez.html.

Gerson, Emily Starbuck. "Austin Ghosthunters Take on the Driskill Hotel." *About.com*, October 30, 2009. Retrieved 19 April 2011. http:// austin.about.com/b/2009/10/30/austin-ghosthunters-take-on-the -driskill-hotel.htm.

"Ghost Hunt of the Baker Hotel." *Southwest Ghost Hunters Association*. Retrieved 9 November 2010. www.sgha.net/baker/baker.html.

"Ghost Hunt of Buie Park." *Southwest Ghost Hunters Association*. Retrieved 2 October 2010. www.sgha.net/tx/stamford/buie.html.

"Ghost Hunt of Crazy Man's Tower." *Southwest Ghost Hunters Association*. Retrieved 2 October 2007. www.sgha.net/tx/dallas/crazymans.html.

"Ghost Hunt of Lake Fort Phantom hill." *Southwest Ghost Hunters Association*. Retrieved 2 October 2007. www.sgha.net/tx/abilene/ ftphantominvest1.html.

"Ghost Hunt at The Old Fort Brown." *Ghosts-UK*. Retrieved 3 December 2010. http://ghosts-uk.net/modules/news/article.php?storyid=639.

"Ghost Hunt of Snuffer's Restaurant." *Southwest Ghost Hunters Association*. Retrieved 10 December 2010. www.sgha.net/tx/dallas/snuffers.html.

"Ghost Hunt of White Rock Lake." *Southwest Ghost Hunters Association*. Retrieved 17 December 2010. www.sgha.net/tx/dallas/white_rock.html.

"Ghosts of Old Waverly and the Old Waverly Cemetery: An East Texas Tale of Two Hills." *TexasEscapes*. Retrieved 10 January 2011. www .texasescapes.com/EastTexasTowns/Old-Waverly-Texas.htm.

"Ghosts of the Grove." *The Grove—Jefferson, TX*. Retrieved 23 August 2010. www.thegrove-jefferson.com/ghosts/index.htm.

"Ghosts of the Von Minden Hotel." *Exquisitely Bored in Nacogdoches*, October 31, 2006. Retrieved 21 December 2010. http:// exquisitelyboredinnacogdoches.blogspot.com/2006/10/ghosts-of-von -minden-hotel.html.

"Ghost story: The spirit that haunts Schulenburg, Texas." *Texas on the Potomac*. Retrieved 21 December 2010. http://blog.chron.com/ txpotomac/2009/10/ghost-story-the-spirit-that-haunts-schulenburg -texas/.

"Ghost Towns: Terlingua Texas and the 248 Settlement." *Zimbio.com*. Retrieved 20 January 2011. http://artistforlandscapes.wordpress.com/2008/06/13/ghost-towns-terlingua-texas-and-the-248-settlement/.

"The Goliad Massacre."*Presidio La Bahia*. Retrieved 22 July 2011. www.presidiolabahia.org/massacre.htm.

"Goliad, TX Presidio La Bahia" *Ghuru Group*. Retrieved 22 July 2011. http://ghurugroup.blogspot.com/2008/01/goliad-tx-presidio-la-bahia-100807.html.

Goodwin, David. "Fort Concho: San Angelo, Texas." *Military Ghosts*. Retrieved 15 January 2011. www.militaryghosts.com/concho.html.

———. "Fort Leaton: Presidio, Texas." *Military Ghosts*. Retrieved 15 January 2011. www.militaryghosts.com/leaton.html.

———. "Ghosts of the Alamo." *Military Ghosts*. Retrieved 24 September 2007. www.militaryghosts.com/alamo.html.

Goolsby, Dana. "Demons Rd in Huntsville and Martha Chapel Cemetery." *Texas Escapes Online Magazine*. http://www.texasescapes.com/DanaGoolsby/Demons-Road-in-Huntsville.htm.

"Gorgas Hall Administration Building." *The Ghosts of Fort Brown*. Retrieved 14 September 2007. http://blue.utb.edu/jagarcia/page_09_GorgasHall.htm.

"Granbury Opera House — Granbury, Texas." *Ghostsandstories.com*. Retrieved 20 June 2011. www.ghostandstories.com/granbury-opera-house-granbury-texas.html.

Gray, Ki. "Mount Bonnell — Austin History, Legends and Views in One Spot." *Ezine Articles*. Retrieved 9 February 2011. http://ezinearticles.com/?Mount-Bonnell—-Austin-History,-Legends-and-Views-in-One-Spot&id=2563518.

"The 'Hairy Man' of Round Rock." *Texas Cryptid Hunter*, October 3, 2009. Retrieved 4 January 2011. http://texascryptidhunter.blogspot.com/2009/10/hairy-man-of-round-rock.html.

Hashimoto, Raoul. "San Antonio's Overworked Ghost Children." *Texas-Escapes*. Retrieved 21 February 2011. http://www.texasescapes.com/FEATURES/Texas_Favorite_ghost_stories/San_Antonio%27s_ghost_children.htm.

Haughton, Brian. "Feral Children: The Wolf Girl of Devil's River." *Mysteriouspeople.com*. Retrieved 19 December 2010. www.mysteriouspeople.com/Wolf_Girl.htm.

"The Haunted Driskill Hotel in Austin, Texas." *Hauntedplacestogo.com*. Retrieved 19 April 2011. www.haunted-places-to-go.com/driskill-hotel.html.

"Haunted Places and Storys of El Paso!" *City-Data.com*. Retrieved 8 December 2010. www.city-data.com/forum/el-paso/207564-haunted-places-storys-el-paso.html.

"The Haunting of the Adolphus Hotel." *Adolphushotelghost.com*. Retrieved 18 October 2010. www.adolphushotelghost.com/.

Hayes, Joe. "La Llorona — A Hispanic Legend." *Literacynet.org*. Retrieved 26 September 2007. www.literacynet.org/lp/hperspectives/llorona.html.

Hazel, Michael V. "Old City Park," *Handbook of Texas Online.* Published by the Texas State Historical Association. Retrieved March 2, 2012. http://www.tshaonline.org/handbook/online/articles/ggo01.

"Hell's Gate" *Strangeusa.com.* Retrieved 3 July 2011. www.strangeusa .com/Viewlocation.aspx?id=9398.

"Historic Hotel." *La Posada Hotel.* Retrieved 9 December 2010. http:// laposada.com/historic-hotel/.

"Historic Rogers Hotel." *Historic Rogers Hotel.* Retrieved 9 November 2011. http://www.rogershotelwaxahachie.com/index.php?option=com _content&view=article&id=45%3Athe-historic-rogers-hotel-waxahachie -texas&catid=34%3Arogers-hotel-waxahachie-texas&Itemid=54.

"Historic Timeline of the Grove Property." *The Grove—Jefferson, TX.* Retrieved 23 August 2010. www.thegrove-jefferson.com/timeline/ index.htm.

"History of the Faust Hotel." *Faust Hotel & Brewing Co.* Retrieved 11 October 2011. www.fausthotel.com/history-of-the-faust-hotel.html.

"History & Growth." *Texas Wesleyan University.* Retrieved 13 October 2011. www.txwes.edu/info/history.aspx.

"History of the Inn." *Prince Solms Inn Bed & Breakfast.* Retrieved 3 October 2010. www.princesolmsinn.com/History.php.

"History of Loretto Academy." *Loretto Academy.* Retrieved 3 December 2010. www.loretto.org/Loretto%20Academy/history.html.

"History of Marlin, Texas." *Marlin, Texas.* Retrieved 2 January 2011. http://www.marlintexas.com/marlin-history/.

"History: Neill Cochran House Museum."*Neill-Cochran House Museum.* Retrieved 27 June 2011. www.nchmuseum.org/history.

"History of Our Hotel." *Hotel Galvez & Spa.* Retrieved 2 July 2011. www.wyndham.com/hotels/GLSHG/history/main.wnt.

"History: Rugged Beauty of Fort Phantom Hill is Rich in History."*Fort Phantom Hill.* Retrieved 5 January 2011. www.fortphantom.org/history.html.

"The History of the Sons of Herman Hall." *Sons of Hermann.* Retrieved 3 October 2010. www.sonsofhermann.com/sohh_hall_history.htm.

Holmes, Michael. "Mystery still surrounds last woman executed in Texas." *Abilene (Texas) Reporter-News.* Retrieved 10 November 2011. http:// www.texnews.com/1998/texas/last0126.html.

Hopkins, Bob. "The Ghosts of the Baker Hotel." *TexasEscapes.* Retrieved 6 November 2010. http://www.texasescapes.com/TexasPanhandleTowns/ MineralWellsTexas/BakerHotelGhosts.htm.

"The Hotel Cemetery."*The Ghosts of Fort Brown.* Retrieved 14 September 2007. http://blue.utb.edu/ghostsoffortbrown/page_02_Cemetery.htm.

"Hotel Lawrence." *Hotelplanner.com.* Retrieved 18 October 2010. http:// www.hotelplanner.com/Hotels/6119/Reservations-Hotel-Lawrence -Dallas-302-South-Houston-75202.

"Hotel Lawrence Dallas." *Dallas.com.* Retrieved 18 October 2010. www.dallas.com/hotel-lawrence/.

"The Jail at La Grange." *TexasEscapes.* Retrieved 22 January 2011. www .texasescapes.com/Jails/LaGrange-Texas-Fayette-County-Jail2.htm.

"Jake's Bridge." *Austin Ghost Tours*. Retrieved 3 January 2011. http://www
.austinghosttours.com/index.php?option=com_content&view=article
&id=17:jakes-bridge&catid=9:austin&Itemid=18.

"Jake's Bridge." *Hauntedtexas.com*, December 6, 2010. http://hauntedtexas
.com/index.php?option=com_content&view=article&id=33:jakes-bridge
&catid=11:central&Itemid=33.

Jakle, Jeanne. "S.A.'s 'ghost tracks' legend thoroughly tested on Syfy." *San
Antonio Express-News*, August 12, 2010. Retrieved 24 February 2011.
http://blog.mysanantonio.com/jakle06/2010/08/s-a-s-ghost-tracks
-legend-thoroughly-tested-on-syfy/.

"The Jefferson Hotel." *Ghostinmysuitccase.com*. Retrieved 26 August 2010.
http://ghostinmysuitcase.com/places/jeffhotel/index.htm.

"The Jett Building — Fort Worth, TX." *Waymarking.com*. Retrieved 12
December 2010. www.waymarking.com/waymarks/WM2YXC_The_Jett
_Builidng_Fort_Worth_TX.

"Josiah Wilbarger." *Austin Ghost Tours*. Retrieved 8 June 2011. http://www.
austinghosttours.com/index.php?option=com_content&view=article&
id=20:josiah-wilbarger&catid=9:austin&Itemid=18.

Kelly, Martin. "Battle of Sabine Pass II." *About.com American History*.
Retrieved 10 January 2011. http://americanhistory.about.com/od/
civilwarbattles/p/cwbattle_sabi2.htm.

King, Gwen. "The Legend Lives On: Visit the Hairy Man Festival 2010."
Round Rock (Texas) Leader. Retrieved 4 January 2011. http://rrleader
.com/main.asp?SectionID=3&SubSectionID=3&ArticleID=25543&TM=
61947.8.

Knell, Bill. "The Ghost Children of San Antonio." *Ghost Haunts*. Retrieved 21
February 2011. www.ghosthaunts.com/san_antonio_ghosts.html.

Kohout, Martin Donell, "Enchanted Rock Legends." *Handbook of Texas
Online*. Published by the Texas State Historical Association. Retrieved
February 28, 2012. http://www.tshaonline.org/handbook/online/
articles/lxe01.

Krenek, Harry. "The Scalping of Josiah Wilbarger." *South Texas Traveler*.
Retrieved 8 June 1, 2011. http://www.southtexastraveler.com/index
.php/south-texas-history-mainmenu-30/41-frontier-tales/38-the
-scalping-of-josiah-wilbarger.html.

"The Lady of White Rock Lake." *Thefolklorist.com*. Retrieved 17 December
2010. www.thefolklorist.com/horror/lakegirl.htm.

"The Lady of White Rock Lake." *Ghostinmysuitcase.com*. Retrieved 17
December 2010. www.ghostinmysuitcase.com/places/whitrock/index
.htm.

"La Lomita Texas." *TexasEscapes*. Retrieved 13 November 2010.
www.texasescapes.com/SouthTexasTowns/La-Lomita.htm.

"Lechuza, La Lechusa, Harpies." *Ghostvillage.com*. Retrieved 4 January 2011.
www.ghostvillage.com/ghostcommunity/index.php?showtopic=22977.

"Lechuza: Legend, Myth, or Real?" *Topix.com*. Retrieved 4 January 2011.
www.topix.com/forum/city/santa-rosa-tx/TIGFISDG9NEH38MME.

Leffler, John. "History of Eastland County." *Community Site of Eastland Texas*. Retrieved 17 August 2007. www.eastlandvisitor.com/eastlandCountyHistory.html.

"The Legend of Hairy Man Road." *TexasTripper.com*. Retrieved 4 January 2011. www.texastripper.com/round-rock/hairy-man.html.

Lehman, Tony. "Rescuing the Original Fort Brown." *Brownsville Talk*, December 1, 2005. Retrieved 14 September 2006. http://brownsvilletx.blogspot.com/2005/12/rescuing-original-fort-bro_113346370280173933.html.

LeLeux, Penny. "Jefferson, a spirited history." *The County Record* (Bridge City, Texas), July 30, 2009. Retrieved 12 November 2010. http://therecordlive.com/article/Hometown_News/People_and_Places/Jefferson_a_spirited_history/53872.

"Liendo Plantation — October 2010." *Aggieland Ghost Hunters*. Retrieved 16 December 2010. http://aggielandgh.com/liendo-plantation.

Loeser, Marilyn. "Ghost Hunting in Jefferson, Texas." *Travellady Magazine*. Retrieved 23 August 2010. www.travellady.com/Issues/June08/5101Ghost.htm.

"Loretto Academy." *Strangeusa.com*. Retrieved 3 December 2010. www.strangeusa.com/ViewLocation.aspx?locationid=9578.

Macleod, Marlee. "Charles Whitman: The Texas Tower Sniper." *trutv*. Retrieved 8 November 2011. www.trutv.com/library/crime/notorious_murders/mass/whitman/index_1.html.

"The Marshall Ranch and Eanes School Ghost Stories." *Austin Star*. Retrieved 9 February 2011. www.austinstar.com/hauntedhouse/.

Martina. "Ghosts of the Alamo — Haunted San Antonio, Texas." *Yahoo! Voices*, September 11, 2007. Retrieved 24 September 2007. http://voices.yahoo.com/ghosts-alamo-haunted-san-antonio-texas-531303.html?cat=10.

Matsumoto, Amy. "Hauntings & History at the Tremont House." *The Islander*. Retrieved 12 July 2011. http://theislandermagazine.com/?p=2665.

McAuliffe, Shane. "Ghost Hunt Reveals Haunting Experience at Liendo Plantation." *KBTX.com*, October 31, 2010. Retrieved 16 December 2010. http://www.kbtx.com/home/headlines/Ghost_Hunt_Reveals_Hunting_Experience_at_Liendo_Planatation_106411648.html.

McDonald, Archie P. "The Battle of Sabine Pass." *TexasEscapes*, May 27, 2001. Retrieved 9 January 2011. http://www.texasescapes.com/DEPARTMENTS/Guest_Columnists/East_Texas_all_things_historical/BattleOfSabinePassAMD501.htm.

"McDow Hole." *Austin Ghost Tours*. Retrieved 3 July 2011. http://www.austinghosttours.com/index.php?option=com_content&view=article&id=25:mcdow-hole&catid=10:texas&Itemid=17.

Mendez, Sunshine. "El Paso's Plaza Theatre is haunted according to El Pasoans." *Examiner.com*, July 29, 2010. Retrieved 20 July 2011. http://www.examiner.com/haunted-places-in-el-paso/el-paso-s-plaza-theatre-is-haunted-according-to-el-pasoans.

"Millermore Mansion in Dallas." *City-data.com*. Retrieved 5 October 2010. http://www.city-data.com/articles/Millermore-Mansion-in-Dallas .html.

"Mills Cemetery." *Ghostinmysuitcase.com*. Retrieved 16 August 2007. www.ghostinmysuitcase.com/places/mills/index.htm.

Montgomery, Murray. "Bailey's Light: A Brazoria County Ghost Tale." *Texas-Escapes.com*. Retrieved 2 March 2012. http://www.texasescapes.com/ DEPARTMENTS/Guest_Columnists/Times_past/Bailey%27s_light.htm.

Moran, Rick. "Catfish Plantation History."*Catfish Plantation Restaurant*. Retrieved 12 December 2010. www.catfishplantation.com/history1.html.

———. "Faust's Ghost: Haunted Hotel in Texas." *Real Travel Adventures*. Retrieved 11 October 2011. http://www.realtraveladventures.com/ favoritefinds/faust_s_ghost__haunted_hotel_in_texas.htm.

"More Info on Lechuza (Creepy Black Bird)." *Unexplained-Mysteries.com*. Retrieved 4 January 2011. www.unexplained-mysteries.com/forum/ index.php?showtopic=46786.

"Most Haunted Place in America: Von Minden Hotel." *Most Haunted Places in America*, September 2, 2009. Retrieved 19 December 2010. www.ghosteyes.com/paranormal-activity-von-minden-hotel.

"Mount Bonnell Austin." *Video City Guide*. Retrieved 9 February 2011. Austin City Guide. Retrieved 9 February 2011. http://www.videocityguide .com/austin/listings/mount-bonnell-austin

Nyholm, Christine Bude. "Haunted Driskill Hotel in Austin TX." *Yahoo! Voices*. Retrieved 19 April 2011. http://voices.yahoo.com/haunted -driskill-hotel-austin-tx-594240.html?cat=37.

"Old City Park Investigation 11/1/07." *Credible Paranormal Investigations*. Retrieved 5 October 2010. www.credibleparanormal.com/id14.html.

"Old Fayette County Jail." *La Grange Area Chamber of Commerce*. Retrieved 2 January 2011. www.lagrangetourism.com/History/History-Jailhouse .html.

"The Old Morgue." *The Ghosts of Fort Brown*. Retrieved 14 September 2007. http://blue.utb.edu/ghostoffortbrown/page_03_OldMorgue.htm.

"Old Waverly, Texas." *TexasEscapes*. Retrieved 10 January 2011. www.texasescapes.com/EastTexasTowns/Old-Waverly-Texas-1.htm.

"The Orviss Burial Vault, Calvert, TX." *TFC Paranormal Research Team*. Retrieved 19 December 2010. www.freakuency.org/investigations.htm.

"Orviss Vault — November 2008." *Aggieland Ghost Hunters*. Retrieved 30 December 2010. http://aggielandgh.com/?tag-orvissvault.

Paul, Lee. "La Llorona." *The Old West*. Retrieved 26 September 2007. www.theoutlaws.com/ghosts3.htm.

———. "The Legend of Josiah Wilbarger." *The Old West*. Retrieved 8 June 2011. www.theoutlaws.com/people4.htm.

Pena, Rodolfo, Jr. "The Lady in Black" *Folklore of the Rio Grande Valley*. Retrieved 16 December 2010. http://www.sanbenitohistory.com/ projects/READING%20DEPT/LopezPena/the_lady_in_black.html.

"The Perfumed Lady at the Excelsior House hotel in Jefferson, Texas." *Ghostinmysuitcase.com*. Retrieved 5 September 2010. www .ghostinmysuitcase.com//places/excelsior/index.htm.

Peschke, Alan. "The Legend of the Lechuza." *Tripod.com*. Retrieved 4 January 2011. http://alandp0.tripod.com/owls/lechuza.txt.

"Peters Bros. Hats: Our History." *Peters Brothers Hats*. Retrieved 23 September 2011. http://www.pbhats.com/private/HISTORY/Default.htm.

Pingenot, Ben E. "Fort Clark," *Handbook of Texas Online*. Published by the Texas State Historical Association. Retrieved February 28, 2012. http://www.tshaonline.org/handbook/online/articles/qbf10.

"Prince Solms Inn Bed and Breakfast: The Ghost of the Prince Solms Inn." *Prince Solms Inn Bed and Breakfast*. Retrieved 3 October 2010. www.princesolmsinn.com/ghosthistory.php.

"Prince Solms Inn Bed and Breakfast: The History of the Inn." *Prince Solms Inn Bed and Breakfast*. Retrieved 3 October 2010. www.princesolmsinn.com/History.php.

Reinhold, Robert. "Galveston: A 19th-Century Island City." *New York Times*, October 31, 1982. Retrieved 15 July 2011. www.nytimes.com/1982/10/31/travel/galveston-a-19th-century-island-city.html.

Reynolds, Jennifer. "Crew Restores Iron Façade." *Galveston Daily News*. Retrieved 15 July 2011. http://galvestondailynews.com/photo/225970.

Rimmer, Terri. "Ghost Legend of Jamba Juice's Jett Building." *Yahoo! Voices*, October 11, 2007. Retrieved 5 November 2011. http://voices.yahoo.com/ghost-legend-jamba-juices-jett-building-600221.html.

Roberts, Tim. "Fort Leaton." *Texas Beyond History*. Retrieved 15 January 2011. www.texasbeyondhistory.net/trans-p/images/he2.html.

"The Rogers Hotel." *Texasfirsthand.com*. Retrieved 9 November 2011. www.texasfirsthand.com/index.php/haunted-places/65-the-rogers-hotel-waxahachie.

Ross, Loretta. "Echoes: Ghost Riders in the Sky." *Unexplained Mysteries Discussion Forums*. Retrieved 3 January 2011. www.unexplained-mysteries.com/forum/index.php?showtopic=62235.

Roy, Adam. "Enchanted Rock, Texas." *Travelsinparadise.com*. Retrieved 15 December 2010. www.travelsinparadise.com/travelarticle/enchanted-rock-texas.html.

Rudine, Ken. "Using Dead Reckoning to Follow Seguin's Headless Walker." *TexasEscapes*. Retrieved 4 January 2011. http://www.texasescapes.com/KenRudine/In-Search-of-Seguins-Headless-Ghost.htm.

"Saint Olaf Cemetery at the Rock Church." *Mustangtexas.com*. Retrieved 5 January 2011. http://old.mustangtexas.com/St_Olaf_Cemetery.htm.

"San Antonio: A Supernatural Stop." *TexasTripper.com*. Retrieved 5 September 2010. www.texastripper.com/san-antonio/art-haunted-san-antonio.html.

"San Antonio, Texas — Ghostly Gravity Hill." *Roadsideamerica.com*. Retrieved 21 February 2011. www.roadsideamerica.com/tip/1298.

"San Bernard River." *Handbook of Texas Online*. Published by the Texas State Historical Association. Retrieved February 28, 2012. http://www.tshaonline.org/handbook/online/articles/rns07.

"Scenic White Rock Lake Park." *An Unofficial Guide to Scenic White Rock Lake Park*. Retrieved 17 December 2010. www.watermelon-kid.com/places/wrl/lore/ghost.htm.

Schlosser, S. E. "Ghost Handprints: A Texas Ghost Story." *Americanfolk-lore.net*. Retrieved 21 February 2011. http://americanfolklore.net/folklore/2010/07/ghost_handprints.html.

Shade, Heather. "Ghostly Nun of Loretto Tower." *Lost Destinations*. Retrieved 22 July 2011. http://www.lostdestinations.com/loretto.htm.

Smith, Julia Cauble. "Fort Leaton." *Handbook of Texas Online*. Published by the Texas State Historical Association. Retrieved February 28, 2012. http://www.tshaonline.org/handbook/online/articles/uef10.

"Snuffer's Restaurant." *Ghostinmysuitcase.com*. Retrieved 10 December 2010. www.ghostinmysuitcase.com/places/snuffer/index.htm.

"Snuffer's Restaurant—Dallas, Texas." *Ghosts and Golf*, March 25, 2009. Retrieved 10 December 2010. http://ghostandgolf.com/?p=71.

"Snuffer's Restaurant & Bar: History." *Snuffer's*. Retrieved 10 December 2010. www.snuffers.com/history.aspx.

"Spaghetti Warehouse Is Considered Haunted?" *Houstonarchitecture.com*. Retrieved 16 July 2011. http://www.houstonarchitecture.com/haif/topic/586-spaghetti-warehouse-is-considered-haunted/.

"The Spanish Governor's Palace." *Michael Bourne's Book of Thoth*. Retrieved 5 September 2010. www.book-of-thoth.com/article1832.html.

"Spanish Governor's Palace in San Antonio." *City-data.com*. Retrieved 5 September 2010. www.city-data.com/articles/Spanish-Governors-Palace-in-San-Antonio.html.

Spence, Sydney. "Mount Bonnell—A Hiker's Dream." *Wryte Stuff*. Retrieved 9 February 2011. http://sydney-spence.wrytestuff.com/swa571760-Mount-Bonnell-A-Hikers-Dream-Austin-Tx.htm.

Stahl, Robert. "The Haunted Bar at the Stoneleigh Hotel." *Examiner.com*, October 31, 2009. Retrieved 28 September 2011. http://www.examiner.com/bartender-in-dallas/the-haunted-bar-at-the-stoneleigh-hotel.

"Stampede Mesa." *Austin Ghost Tours*. Retrieved 3 January 2011. http://www.austinghosttours.com/index.php?option=com_content&view=article&id=66:stampede-mesa&catid=10:texas&Itemid=17.

Stefko, Jill. "Ghosts of Haunted Fort Concho." *Paranormal @ Suite 101.com*. Retrieved 10 January 2011. http://jill-stefko.suite101.com/ghosts-of-haunted-fort-concho-a204665.

"Stephen F. Austin University-Griffith Hall." *Twilight Paranormal Society*. http://twilightparanormalsociety.com.

"Strange Happenings at the Jefferson Hotel." *Ghostvillage.com*. Retrieved 26 August 2010. www.ghostvillage.com/encounters/2006/05082006.shtml.

Stucco, Johnny. "Baker Hotel: Mineral Wells, Texas." *TexasEscapes*. Retrieved 6 November 2010. http://www.texasescapes.com/TexasPanhandleTowns/MineralWellsTexas/BakerHotelGhosts.htm.

———. "The Jail at La Grange." *TexasEscapes*. Retrieved 22 January 2011. www.texasescapes.com/Jails/LaGrange-Texas-Fayette-County-Jail.htm.

Sullivan, James. "Austin's Driskill Hotel Ghost Haunts Concrete Blonde Singer Twisted Tales." *Spinner*, March 11, 2011. Retrieved 19 April 2011. www.spinner.com/2011/03/11/driskill-hotel-haunted/.

"Summary of Jake's Bridge." *Central Texas Ghost Trackers*. Retrieved 3 January 2011. http://www.centexghost.org/html/williamson005.html.

"Summary of the Metz Elementary School Legend." *Central Texas Ghost Trackers*. Retrieved 13 December 2010. http://www.centexghost.org/html/travis022.html.

"Texas Ghost Tracks: Do Spirits Haunt the Tracks in Texas?" *Paranormal Zone X*. Retrieved 21 February 2011. http://sites.google.com/site/paranormalzonex/evidence/ghost-ghosts-haunted-082.

"Thistle Hill Ft. Worth." *Your Ghost Stories*, September 12, 2007. Retrieved 6 November 2010. www.yourghoststories.com/real-ghost-story.php?story=1930.

Thykeson, Laura. "Discovery Channel Investigates Reports of Ghost in Granbury Opera House." *HubPages*. http://laurathykeson.hubpages.com.

Tipping, Joy. "Haunted Dallas: Resident ghosts make their presence known." *Dallas Morning News*, November 1, 2010. Retrieved 10 December 2010. http://www.dallasnews.com/entertainment/headlines/20101029-Haunted-Dallas-Resident-ghosts-make-7549.ece.

"The Top Most Haunted Locations in Jefferson, Texas." *Haunted America Tours*. Retrieved 12 November 2010. www.hauntedamericatours.com/ghosts/JeffersonTexas.php.

"The Tremont." *Haunted Galveston*. Retrieved 17 July 2011. www.galvestonghost.com/tremont.html.

Troesser, John. "The Cozy Theater." *TexasEscapes*. Retrieved 19 December 2010. http://www.texasescapes.com/FEATURES/Schulenberg%27s_Haunted_Von_Minden_Hotel/Von-Minden-Hotel-2-Cozy-Theater-Ghosts.htm.

———. "Schulenburg's Heartbreak Hotel: The Uninvited at the Von Minden." *TexasEscapes*. Retrieved 23 December 2010. http://www.texasescapes.com/FEATURES/Schulenberg%27s_Haunted_Von_Minden_Hotel/Von_minden_hotel_I_haunted.htm.

———. "Woman Hollering Creek." *TexasEscapes*. Retrieved 26 September 2007. http://www.texasescapes.com/TexasFolklore/WomanHolleringCreek/WomanHolleringCreek.htm.

Tucker, Shelly Kneupper. "Ghost Hunt at The Driskill Hotel. Part 2." *This Eclectic Life*, August 12 2009. Retrieved 29 April, 2011. http://thiseclecticlife.com/2009/08/12/ghost-hunt-at-the-driskill-hotel-part-2/.

———. "Ghost Hunting at the Saint Anthony Hotel. Part One." *This Eclectic Life*. http://thiseclecticlife.com/2010/11/ghost-hunting-at-the-saint-anthony-hotel-part-one.

Turner, Allan. "Sounds of Ghost's Violin Fill Ideson Library's Hall." *Houston Chronicle*, October 31, 2006. Retrieved 17 July 2011. http://www.chron.com/disp/story.mpl/metropolitan/4298763.html.

Unger, Casey. "The Children Left." *Freakuency.org*. Retrieved 30 December 2010. http://www.freakuency.org/stories/caseythechildrenleft.htm.

"Upstairs at the Mansion — Terlingua, Texas." *Odd Inns and Uncommodations*. Retrieved 20 January 2011. http://www.oddinns.com/index.php/pages/UpstairsMansion.html.

Van Ostrand, Maggie. "The Hairy Man of Round Rock." *TexasEscapes*. Retrieved 4 January 2011. www.texasescapes.com/MaggieVanOstrand/Hairy-Man-of-Round-Rock.htm.

"Von Minden Hotel." *Halloween-Headlines*. Retrieved 21 December 2011. www.halloween-headlines.com/haunted/hotel_vonmindenTX.htm.

Warm, Luke. "Love in the Time of Diphtheria, *or* Art and Science on the Brazos." *TexasEscapes*. Retrieved 16 December 2010. http://www.texas-escapes.com/Ghosts/Love-in-the-Time-of-Diphtheria.htm.

"The Weinert House Bed and Breakfast." *Weinert House Bed and Breakfast & Special Events*. Retrieved 7 September 2010. www.weinerthouseseguin.com/aboutus.html.

Weiser, Kathy. "Ghost Children upon San Antonio's Railroad Tracks." *Legends of America*. Retrieved 21 February 2011. www.legendsofamerica.com/tx-ghostlychildren.html.

———. "Ghosts of the Alamo." *Legends of America*. Retrieved 24 September 2007. http://www.legendsofamerica.com/tx-alamoghosts.html.

———. "Ghosts of Fort Phantom Hill." *Legends of America*. Retrieved 2 October 2007. www.legendsofamerica.com/ tx-FortPhantom.html.

———. "Haunted Gunter Hotel in San Antonio." *Legends of America*. Retrieved 5 October 2010. www.legendsofamerica.com/tx-gunterhotel.html.

———. "Haunted Menger Hotel in San Antonio." *Legends of America*. Retrieved 29 September 2007. www.legendsofamerica.com/TX-MengerHotel.html.

———. "History and Hauntings of Fort Brown." *Legends of America*. Retrieved 3 December 2010. www.legendsofamerica.com/tx-fortbrown.html.

"Welcome to Buffalo Billiards." *Buffalo Billiards*. Retrieved 9 February 2011. www.buffalobilliards.com/austin/.

"White Oak Manor: Jefferson Texas." *I See Ghosts*. Retrieved 23 August 2010. www.iseeghosts.com/whiteoakmanor.htm.

"Wilbarger." *Haunted Texas*, December 6, 2010. Retrieved 8 June 2011. http://hauntedtexas.com/index.php?option=com_content&view=article&id=18:wilbarger&catid=7:austin&Itemid=6.

"Wink Texas Ghostly Tales Continue." *Cheap Tricks and Costly Truths*, June 2, 2009. Retrieved 16 December 2010. http://jamminmole.blogspot.com/2009/06/wink-texas-ghostly-tales-continue.html.

Yarbrough, Shannan. "Haunted Jails and Jail Museums in Texas." *TexasEscapes*. 22 January 2011. http://www.texasescapes.com/FEATURES/Texas-Haunted-Jails-n-Jail-Museums.htm.

About the Author

*A*lan Brown is a professor of English at the University of West Alabama in Livingston. Brown has written extensively about the folklore and the ghost stories of the South. He is the author of *Haunted Texas*, *Haunted Georgia*, *Haunted Kentucky*, *Haunted South Carolina*, and *Haunted Tennessee*. When he is not teaching or writing, Brown gives ghost tours of the city of Livingston and UWA's campus.